5:41

Stories from the Joplin Tornado

RANDY TURNER

JOHN HACKER

COVER DESIGN BY DAVID HOOVER

INTERIOR DESIGN BY NINA ENGLISH

DEDICATION

Dedicated to those whose lives were changed on May 22, 2011.

CONTENTS

INTRODUCTION

"IF THERE WERE 50,000 PEOPLE IN THE CITY MAY 22, THERE ARE 50,000 STORIES, ALL CENTERING AROUND WHAT HAPPENED AT 5:41... THIS BOOK WILL SERVE AS A REPRESENTATIVE SAMPLING OF AN EVENING JOPLIN WILL NEVER FORGET."

- RANDY TURNER

T ragedy brings people together.

I saw evidence of that right in front of me as I walked along the checkout lines a the Seventh Street Wal-Mart in Joplin looking for one of those blue hand baskets so I didn't have to push an unwieldy cart around the store.

I saw two of my former students, a brother and sister, sitting on a

bench, apparently waiting for other family members to finish shopping. The older one had just finished her first year in college. When she was in my eighth grade English class, she was a gifted writer with a way of translating her feelings and fears into poetry. From Facebook conversations with the girl's younger sister,

another former student of mine, I knew that her family had been hit particularly hard by the May 22 tornado that hit this city.

The girl had her arm around her younger brother in a manner that could only be described as protective.

She spotted me approaching and shouted, "Mr. Turner!" drawing the attention of those in the checkout lanes directly behind us.

For the next 20 minutes, I heard a harrowing story of how her family had been right in the middle of the most destructive tornado to ever hit our city. She was home alone at 5:41 p.m. She was the only member of her family who did not get hit by the tornado.

The family was rushing home to be with her when torrential rain began, accompanied by hail. Her father pulled over and they ran into the AT&T building, which proved to be no protection when the tornado hit.

Her mother and her sister were badly injured and had to be taken by helicopter to a Springfield hospital. Thankfully, both survived, though they have a long road ahead of them.

After our conversation ended, I finally found a hand basket and began shopping. As I walked through the aisles, I saw more people who were stopped and talking than I had ever seen in a Wal-Mart store before.

I caught bits and pieces of the various conversations. Not one of them failed to include at least some mention of the tornado. For the first few weeks after May 22, the tornado was the only topic of conversation here.

I changed the way I approached conversation and I am sure others did, too. When I ran into friends, acquaintances, and former students, after the initial greeting, I always asked if they had been hit by the tornado. The last thing I wanted to do was start up some silly chatter with people who may have lost someone or who had been displaced.

After I asked, nearly every time the question was greeted with a story. It also changed the way we talked about where we lived. When I was asked the tornado question, I always replied, "No, I was lucky. I was about three blocks from where the tornado hit."

I quickly realized that I was not the only one to take that approach. I cannot count the number of people who told me how many blocks they were away from the tornado.

I wish everyone could have had that answer. Sadly, many of my conversations were with people who had lost their homes and all of their possessions. Some were staying with relatives. Some had been lucky enough to locate scarce rental property. Some feared they would never again live in the city limits of Joplin.

Every one of the people I talked to had a story about the Joplin Tornado. And every one of them will remember that time, 5:41, forever.

I heard the tornado stories while going about my everyday routine. For my co-author, John Hacker, it was part of his job. John, the editor of *The Carthage Press*, was in Joplin less than a half hour after the tornado. Though he has a well-earned reputation as one of the best reporters in Missouri, and is a skilled interviewer, he discovered what many reporters who have covered the aftermath of a tragedy have long found to be true- people want to talk.

As John walked through the heart of the devastation that evening, he heard many stories, some of which are included in this volume.

When we decided to write this book, it did not take long to come up with a title. As we wrote our stories and had others sent to us for inclusion in the book, for some reason I thought about the tag line in *Naked City*, a black-and-white television series from the early '60s, about police work in New York City. Each episode ended with the narrator saying, "There are eight million stories in the *Naked City* - this was one of them."

When the series ended after a four-year run, there were still more than seven million stories waiting to be told.

This collection of stories from the Joplin Tornado is far from comprehensive. If there were 50,000 people in the city May 22, there are 50,000 stories, all centering on what happened at 5:41. We hope the few dozen stories and photographs in this book will serve as a representative sampling of an evening Joplin will never forget.

SURVIVING

"IT WAS A SCENE THAT IF IT WERE PLAYING ON THE SCREENS AT NORTHPARK CINEMA MIGHT BE PRAISED BY CRITICS AS A WELL-REALIZED VERSION OF NUCLEAR ARMAGEDDON."

- JOHN HACKER

Moments after a category EF-5 tornado turned the heart of Joplin's residential district into a post-apocalyptic wasteland, bloodied, wet and tired survivors began to emerge from the wreckage and take stock of a new reality.

Larry Thomas, who somehow managed to emerge uninjured from the rubble that was once the Missouri Place Apartments, did not take the time to consider the enormity of what had just happened His first instincts were to help others.

"I came down to see if my professor's family is all right," he said, as he walked along an unrecognizable Wisconsin Avenue near the remnants of the Peace Lutheran Church. "They went to the graduation so they might still be over there."

As he walked, Thomas told his story. "I opened my bedroom window and looked in this direction and heard the freight train coming.

5

I was in the hallway and we've got glass doors on both ends and it just busted the windows out. The wind shoved me into a vacant apartment."

It wasn't just property that felt the wrath of the tornado. "There's some fatalities back there. I suspect that the woman across the hall from me stayed in her apartment thinking she was going to be safe…and it's gone, too."

Larry Thomas looked around him, taking in the destruction that was evident as far as his eye could see. To the left of him, crumpled buildings, once full of life, now ripped apart. Tall trees felled in seconds by 200 mile per hour winds. People dazed and bloodied, wandering up and down the street, searching for any evidence that life would ever be the same again.

It was a scene that if it were playing on the screens at Northpark Cinema might be praised by critics as a well-realized version of nuclear Armageddon.

This was no movie, however. This was Joplin's reality.

Thomas continued his story, as he took in the damage. It helped to talk. "I lived in Missouri Place apartments and they're gone. So is the Summerset apartments; they're gone. I've lost a lot of property in there," he paused, "but I came out of it - let me see. Do I have any scrapes? I have mud on me. I'm alive."

The words continued to come, a stream of consciousness. "My desktop and laptop are gone and I'm due to start school in two weeks at Pitt State. I have one summer class and this fall I have my practicum and then I've got my bachelor's degree. I don't have transportation to get there now; it's trashed.

"I was in the hallway when it first assaulted the building and it forced the door open into a vacant apartment and I got into the kitchen, which is a narrow little place, and I hunkered down.

"I survived two hurricanes in Honolulu," Thomas continued, "Hurricane Eva in 1982 and Iniki in 1992. Then I came over here and they had hurricane season; they had their third one. One thing about a hurricane, you can watch them coming for days."

And that spelled the difference between the hurricanes and the tornado.

"You can see where the tree line starts to the north and to the south and that's how wide this bugger was. It just came through here relentlessly. I think there are maybe two elderly people in my building that didn't get out of here. The old man who lives right below me. I didn't see him and his unit is wide open; the whole face of it is blown off.

"My professor's home is gone."

Now Larry Thomas found himself in a familiar position. "I'm the vice chair of the homeless coalition for Jasper and Newton counties. I know how to survive homelessness. I've been homeless six times.

◆

Entire families walked helplessly along the street, including Holly Fleming and her children.

"This is unreal," she said. "I wasn't home; my kids were and they hid in the bathroom. If you look at our house, that the only thing standing."

"I was hugging the toilet," one child said.

Another child, pointing to what was left of the home at Montana Place and Wisconsin, added, "You see that big old pile of stuff over there? We were right in underneath that. We jumped in there but just before it hit.

The tub was the only thing left of the home.

• ✦ •

All over the neighborhood south of 20th Street and east of the shattered Joplin High School, victims became rescuers as they struggled to deal with the loss of homes and loved ones.

Several people took crowbars and their bare hands, anything they could find to rip into a small white Toyota on the side of Wisconsin Avenue and pull two older women out of it.

Though all were invested in the rescue operation, one man, covered with blood and with a swollen face, helped in any way he could, desperation evident in his face.

When the tornado hit, he had been in that car. His wife and his mother were still trapped inside.

The three were headed home, trying to beat the storm, but they didn't make it.

"I got hit in the face by a two-by-four, or that's what it felt like," he said. "I lifted my head up for a second when the wind started pushing the car and something hit me.

"I was in the back seat of the car. I don't know how I got out. I can't do anything because if I do anything, I'll start bleeding again." He held up his bloody hand.

"We were driving down here; we were out on Rangeline and came down 20th. We turned here on Wisconsin, but we didn't make it. We live in the 2900 block of Wisconsin."

With the doors jammed, the man's wife and his 82-year-old mother were trapped, both covered in blood from cuts and scrapes. Debris covered the Toyota; some had come through the windows and pummeled the three occupants.

As the rescue operation took place, shouts could be heard from people asking for help at the nearby Mormon church on Indiana. People were trapped in the flattened building.

• ✦ •

"I just went through the storm," Edward Allen, a resident at 2308 Illinois, said. "You know you look out the window and the storm's a-coming. The last I saw on the TV, it was going off and on, and they said you take cover. If you can still hear us, take cover. So I ran in the bathroom and all I had in there was one of those mats, the big fuzzy one, and I put it over my head. There are some two-bys fell right there beside me.

"I knew it was a tornado and it was a-coming, and I was just wondering when it was going to stop.

"The bathroom was kind of in the middle of the house; that's what they recommend. It did work because these other places and my place are just gone. After it hit, the top of my bathroom was gone. I

went to another room because it began to hail real bad, so I got in the other bathroom and other closet and that area still had kind of a cover over it, so I got in there."

Allen said he had called his son, who lives near Duenweg, and he was coming to pick him up.

"I've never been through anything like this. My garage blew down, too. The west wall came in on the east side and all that is laying on my car.

"I look up and say, 'God, I'm thankful I'm still alive.' That's what you can do."

Fortunately, he said, he did not have to worry about any other loved ones being caught in the tornado. "I don't have any loved ones in Joplin. My son lives in Duenweg and my daughter lives in western Kansas."

·✦·

The early evening air was filled with the sounds of shouting coming from all directions.

A woman ran from a home on 24th Street, screaming. "I need to find help." Her 10-month-old baby was still in the rubble of her home.

Ron and Ellen Smith and their dogs, Buddy and Buffy, survived the tornado, thankful they were alive, but left with nothing else but their lives.

"It destroyed everything," Smith said. "Most of the people I know around here have already gotten out."

Mrs. Smith began their story. "There was a big roar. We were in the dining room and the TV went out and I heard the roar toward the west and there was some kind of banging all of a sudden. We grabbed the dogs and headed to the bathroom."

"I was sitting in the dining room watching TV thinking, 'Oh, it's just another damn storm,'" Smith said. "She came in and said, 'Did you hear that roar?' and I started to hear it. We barely made it to the bathroom in the hall with the dogs.

"See that fireplace wall and big brick wall; that was all that saved us. All of our upstairs, all of our house is gone. She's in the bathroom crying and crying and I said, 'Why are you crying? The four of us are okay, to hell with our house.

"When I was a kid in southwest Oklahoma, I used to sit on my mother's front porch and watch tornadoes go by. But they were in the distance."

10

Ellen said, "We got our dogs from Carl Junction after the 2003 tornado. I've never heard of anything like this.

"That's my bedroom downstairs. We crawled out of there and it looks like the places on TV from Alabama. You never expect this."

"We may end up having to spend the night right here in this truck," Ron said. "They're not going to get any of these side streets open. It'll take forever.

"We've got a storm shelter, but it's buried; no one would have ever known we were in it. I lost my job a few months ago and we had to cancel the insurance on the house last month. I couldn't afford it; it was $400 a month. We've got probably a good $40,000 to $60,000 worth of furniture in there and it's all ruined."

Moments later, about the only bright spot of the evening came for the Smiths when their daughter Joanna and granddaughter Hannah arrived, ending a frantic search.

"We called and called and called," Joanna said. "We had to park down by the school to get up here. The whole area is gone. It was a half a mile away from us. We live behind the mall.

"We didn't hear about this until 30 minutes after, and they said the Joplin school is gone. We had to get over here, we had to. I didn't care how long it took us. It took us an hour to get here from the mall. We went down one road and had to turn around, down another road and they said it was blocked. The closer I got here, the more damage you could see.

"We're getting the hell out of here. We've got to get out of here." She turned to her parents, "Now where are you going to stay? You all are going to have to come to my place now."

As the reunited family hugged, just down the street, the search continued for others with the fear that when the loved ones were found, they would no longer be among the living.

45 SECONDS THAT CHANGED EVERYTHING

"THE SKY WAS THE MOST OMINOUS THING I HAD EVER SEEN IN MY LIFE..."

BY KELLY MADDY

It started much like any other Sunday. Getting up around 9ish, mowing a few lawns, and Adriel bustling around the house cleaning up before we started our work week. It is always our day to get the house looking good for the week so it doesn't stress us out through the busy days when we don't have time to mess with it.

Later on, it would all seem so funny. Washing the dishes, putting clothes away, storing my lawn mower nice and snug by my garage with weed-eater. We had no idea this would all be for naught.

3:40 p.m. - I was finishing my last lawn and started heading back on East 32nd toward my house on 20th and Kentucky. I was watching the development of a supercell storm on my phone's radar application near Parsons, Kansas, and starting to take notice.

Through the years I have been very interested in meteorology, plotting storm tracks by making my own maps and jumping up and down from the roof of my childhood home to make sure I caught all the "Local on the 8's" via the Weather Channel. I knew the May 22nd storm was going to most likely produce a tornado; I just didn't realize the scale of what was about to happen.

That was a bad idea.

The shear was strong and it was a towering, independent cumulonimbus cloud that would be relatively easy to navigate around the south side ... so I thought. I sent my wife Adriel a text message asking her if she wanted to go chase the storm and try to catch a glimpse of some rotation.

4:30 p.m. - After putting up my lawn equipment, we went in our Ford Focus down Seventh Street and then to Stateline Road. We stopped at the gas station near the Stateline Road and Seventh Street intersection, got a tea to drink and then gauged where to go next.

I was observing the storm was still on an East-Northeast track, bringing the southern portion of the cell, in my estimates to cross around Stone's Corner (Main Street and Airport Drive intersection north of Joplin). We dipped around the Galena area for a moment through some country roads and observed the transpiring rotation on the southern flank of the storm.

The rotation looked robust and we were experiencing dime size hail at the time.

4:55 p.m. - We got out of that area and took Stateline Road to SE 110 in Kansas all the way up to Fir Road and started heading toward Stone's Corner. We pulled into Snak-Atak and waited with our vehicle watching the storm come in.

I don't know how to explain it, but I *knew* something wasn't right.

It had nothing to do with the storm data, reports on the radio, etc. I just somehow knew this wasn't like other storms. Not sure if it was the purple and black, bubbling mammatus clouds, or the obvious shift in the winds, but I tried to remain calm because I didn't want to worry Adriel.

Things that didn't have much scientific meaning started racing through my brain and veins and I became very nervous. I noticed the body of the storm is a lot farther south, not the earlier east-northeastern trek I had envisioned. So I took myself about a half-mile south hoping to get out of the bulk of precipitation and back to a good vantage point for the southern end of the storm.

14

5:11 p.m. - The first sirens sounded with spotters indicating a strengthening rotation via Doppler radar just west of Joplin. We are now at the Community Bank and Trust on North Main Street (across from Black Cat Fireworks) under their ATM roof to avoid precipitation and the sky was the most ominous thing I had ever seen in my life.

Little did I know it would be trumped merely 35 minutes from that moment. Thinking we needed to get out of the way and back to the house, we started in that direction. Driving down Main and onto Murphy Boulevard, we pulled behind the Landreth Park stage. It was about 5:35 and the air had dried up considerably but the darkness had begun to wrap the city. I should have noticed the rear flank of the storm pulling in all the precipitation, but I didn't. I saw what appeared to be a large area of precipitation and thought I should just get inside and somewhere safe if something were to happen, still thinking it wouldn't.

5:41 p.m. - The second sirens sounded and I knew this was what appeared to be a last ditch effort to warn of what was most likely a tornado on the ground near Joplin.

I could no longer contain how nervous and panicked I was to my wife. We accelerated quickly, racing across Joplin going down Pennsylvania Avenue all the way from Fourth Street. I am going as fast as I can when I start to notice something far out of the ordinary. I look ahead near the chain-link, surrounded playground and I see a misty, gray edge-defined area of rain that is swirling. I continue to advance about half a block to about two houses before Orient Express on 20th Street. I throw the car in park and just wait on the side of the street.

As I look to my left, I notice there is much more than rain in these clouds as the first large branch stuck our vehicle and more are in the air about to rain down with other debris. Then it all starts.

5:50 p.m. - Trees, fences, utility poles, anything moderately exposed and sticking vertical out of the ground started to break and be blown around. As the strength of the winds grow I look and not only see debris and branches out of my driver side window, I start to see sections of roofs and houses hundreds of feet in the air.

I will never forget the imagery as it is burned into my brain as sure as anything I can ever recall. Then our windows start going ... both driver side windows first. I push Adriel into the floorboard of the front seat and lean over her to shield her from anything that might fly in while trying to protect the back of my neck and head. I hold her tight and we exchange "I love you's" over and over again. It was all I could say that offered any sense. I couldn't describe the storm, yell obscenities, or breathe like I was panicked. I could only say, and in turn receive, the only thing that made sense at the time ... to exchange the very simple phrase "I love you".

We continued to yell this to each other as the storm lifted my driver side up in the air, buffeting the underbelly of the vehicle with the most unsettling force I have ever felt in my life. The car was only probably up on the passenger side wheels for 15-20 seconds, but it seemed like an eternity as I am sure many have said. It was like 1,000 golf clubs beating apart the vehicle and trying to toss it at the same time.

A large piece of debris came and shattered the back glass and I wondered, "Will it ever end?" It finally did but the rain kept coming down.

6:05 p.m. - Shocked, the radio still blaring, "Take cover Joplin!" we lifted our heads to see what had happened. My wife says, sobbing, "Kelly our house...Kyle's house....where is our roof? There isn't a garage."

Kyle, my brother, lived right next to us. His house was severely damaged as well. He and his fiancé Kelsi were inside with their animals as far as we knew. We had to get to them to make sure they were okay along with our neighbors.

My roof was crashing into Kyle and Kelsi's house and car. The car was still running and I attempted to pull onto 20th, but my path is blocked by debris, trees and power lines. I reverse and manage to make it to 19th and over a block to my street of Kentucky Avenue. Again, it was blocked with power lines but these were up off the ground enough for us to sneak under. It wasn't a great idea, but we had to.

I ran with Adriel hand in hand across 20th Street as fast as I could to my brother's house. Their home was caved in and none of the doors are able to open, so we kicked ourselves in to find them and their animals okay, but very disoriented and stunned.

We still had standing walls at our house so we collected all animals and our thoughts for a brief moment and charted a plan of action. I was going to check on neighbors while Kyle stayed with the

animals and girls.

6:15 p.m. - My block. War zone.

Walking down Kentucky Avenue that night was the most heartbreaking and gut-wrenching thing I have ever experienced. While battered and bruised, making my way through the block, my neighbors appeared to be all safe.

At the end of our block was another story. I don't want to elaborate on any of that, as these people were brothers, sisters, sons, daughters, wives and husbands of my neighbors. I will say a little bit of me changed that day with what I had seen. Some people deal well with trauma, but I am not one of those. I nearly became physically ill on the curb and had to go back to check on my family.

Before I did, a house fire broke out in the 2100 block of Kentucky Avenue and people were walking the streets with severe injuries, carrying what they could, heading to somewhere, but I don't think anyone really knew where we all were going.

Just about that time a large Great Dane dog came running up on our property. He looked really familiar. It belongs to my brother's friend, Nick Dagget, who lived behind Dillon's grocery store. Seeing that dog alone made our hearts drop.

Kyle could barely contain the thoughts of what might have happened to his best friend and we all kept him as calm as we could, promising we were going to put the dog up and head toward Nick's house.

My family across town made their way to our house by this time and we saw them running across 20th toward us. We got the car out of the street and into the parking lot of Brandon's Gun Shop on 20th and start to head the only way we can, west on 20th. We filled up the car, not knowing how long traffic out of town would be stuck. We then circled around and made it to Interstate 44 so that we could come into Joplin off Rangeline and get to Nick's house that way.

We approached Nick's house from 26th and Connecticut and found a route there unobstructed after trying multiple streets. When we reached his neighborhood and I looked toward the west, I soon realized what had taken place. Like the path of my lawn mower on a grassy overgrown lot I had pushed hours before, I could see a clear path all the way to St. John's hospital. A path that is still viewable all the way from the former Wal-Mart to this day. Bare of trees, structures, etc.

This was a war zone. We searched frantically for Nick in the rubble of his house; nothing indicated he was there. His cell phone and a small amount of blood were in the tub, but no Nick. We couldn't do anything else as dark was approaching and we were without flashlights and rescue crews hadn't made it to this area yet. We reassured Kyle that he probably made it out, like his dog, but was at a local hospital with modest injuries. Thankfully, that is exactly what happened and we received information later that night that Nick was okay.

We made it back to my brother's house in Webb City and attempted to sleep, but as for me, and I am sure the others in the basement, I didn't get a wink of sleep. It would stay that way for about a week.

After May 22nd - Starting that night and continuing to this day, my friends, people I never met, and more took to the streets to do what we could. We loaded trucks and sharpened chainsaw blades to offer help and rescue, doing what we could.

Everyone is still doing what they are able, but it is no surprise that we will need help for years to come. Our city has been bent, but not broken and in turn has become a more solidified community that can rise from a storm like this and impatiently ask, "What is next? What can I do? How can I help?"

Hearing those questions and them in turn being answered by groups of regular people is the most heartwarming thing I have ever seen. Through cleanup I was approached by churches, local businesses, people from all of the country...putting their hand on our backs and asking, "Can I do anything? Are you ok?" etc. while handing us food, supplies, tetanus shots, and tools to aid the cleanup effort.

A month of this has impacted my life and motivated me to live for others, not just in times of tragedy, but throughout the rest of my life. None of us are going to have all the answers about how to deal with this or other hard situations in life, but I came away knowing it does get better and that the astounding momentum of the human spirit is something a horrible EF5 tornado can't stop. Life isn't over; it is just different after the 45 seconds that changed everything.

ARMAGEDDON AT THE HOSPITAL

"AS I WORKED, SURROUNDED BY DEVASTATION AND SUFFERING, I REALIZED I WAS NOT ALONE."

One of the memories of the tornado was provided by Dr. Kevin Kitka, an emergency room doctor at St. John's Regional Medical Center, and is shared courtesy of Mercy Medical.

My name is Dr. Kevin Kikta, and I was one of two emergency room doctors who were on duty at St. John's Regional Medical Center in Joplin on Sunday, May 22, 2011.

You never know that it will be the most important day of your life until the day is over. The day started like any other day for me: waking up, eating, going to the gym, showering, and going to my 4:00 p.m. ER shift. As I drove to the hospital I mentally prepared for my shift as I always do, but nothing could ever have prepared me for what was going to happen on this shift. Things were normal for the first hour and a half. At approximately 5:30 pm we received a warning that a tornado had been spotted. Although I work in Joplin and went to medical school

in Oklahoma, I lived in New Jersey, and I have never seen or been in a tornado. I learned that a "code gray" was being called. We were to start bringing patients to safer spots within the ED and hospital.

At 5:42 p.m. a security guard yelled to everyone, "Take cover! We are about to get hit by a tornado!" I ran with a pregnant RN, Shilo

Cook, while others scattered to various places, to the only place that I was familiar with in the hospital without windows, a small doctor's office in the ED. Together, Shilo and I tremored and huddled under a desk. We heard a loud horrifying sound like a large locomotive ripping through the hospital. The whole hospital shook and vibrated as we heard glass shattering, light bulbs popping, walls collapsing, people screaming, the ceiling caving in above us, and water pipes breaking, showering water down on everything. We suffered this in complete darkness, unaware of anyone else's status, worried, scared. We could feel a tight pressure in our heads as the tornado annihilated the hospital and the surrounding area. The whole process took about 45 seconds, but seemed like eternity. The hospital had just taken a direct hit from a category EF5 tornado.

Then it was over. Just 45 seconds. 45 long seconds. We looked at each other, terrified, and thanked God that we were alive. We didn't know, but hoped that it was safe enough to go back out to the ED, find the rest of the staff and patients, and assess our losses.

Like a bomb went off. That's the only way that I can describe what we saw next. Patients were coming into the ED in droves. It was absolute, utter chaos. They were limping, bleeding, crying, terrified, with debris and glass sticking out of them, just thankful to be alive. The floor was covered with about 3 inches of water; there was no power, not even backup generators, rendering it completely dark and eerie in the ED. The frightening aroma of methane gas leaking from the broken gas lines permeated the air; we knew, but did not dare mention aloud, what that meant. I redoubled my pace.

We had to use flashlights to direct ourselves to the crying and wounded. Where did all the flashlights come from? I'll never know, but immediately, and thankfully, my years of training in emergency procedures kicked in. There was no power, but our mental generators were up and running, and on high test adrenaline. We had no cell phone service in the first hour, so we were not even able to call for help and backup in the ED. I remember a patient in his early 20's gasping for breath, telling me that he was going to die. After a quick exam, I removed the large shard of glass from his back, made the clinical diagnosis of a pneumothorax (collapsed lung) and gathered supplies from wherever I could locate them to insert a thoracostomy tube in him. He was a trooper; I'll never forget his courage. He allowed me to do this without any local anesthetic since none could be found. With his life threatening injuries I knew he was running out of time, and it had to be done. Quickly. Imagine my relief when I heard a big rush of air, and breath sounds again; fortunately, I was able to get him transported out.

I immediately moved on to the next patient, an asthmatic in status asthmaticus. We didn't even have the option of trying a nebulizer treatment or steroids, but I was able to get him intubated using a flashlight that I held in my mouth. A small child of approximately 3-4 years of age was crying; he had a large avulsion of skin to his neck and spine. The gaping wound revealed his cervical spine and upper thoracic spine bones. I could actually count his vertebrae with my fingers. This was a child, his whole life ahead of him, suffering life threatening wounds in front of me, his eyes pleading me to help him. We could not find any pediatric C collars in the darkness, and water from the shattered main pipes was once again showering down upon all of us. Fortunately, we were able to get him immobilized with towels, and start an IV with fluids and pain meds before shipping him out. We felt paralyzed and helpless ourselves. I didn't even know a lot of the RN's I was working with. They were from departments scattered all over the hospital. It didn't matter. We worked as a team, determined to save lives. There were no specialists available -- my orthopedist was trapped in the operating room. We were it, and we knew we had to get patients out of the hospital as quickly as possible. As we were shuffling them out, the fire department showed up and helped us to evacuate. Together we worked furiously, motivated by the knowledge and fear that the methane leaks to cause the hospital could blow up at any minute.

Things were no better outside of the emergency department. I saw a man crushed under a large SUV, still alive, begging for help; another one was dead, impaled by a street sign through his chest. Wounded people were walking, staggering, all over, dazed and shocked. All around us was chaos, reminding me of scenes in a war movie, or newsreels from bombings in Baghdad. Except this was right in front of me and it had happened in just 45 seconds. My own car was blown away. Gone. Seemingly evaporated. We searched within a half mile radius later that night, but never found the car, only the littered, crumpled remains of former cars. And a John Deere tractor that had blown in from miles away.

Tragedy has a way of revealing human goodness. As I worked, surrounded by devastation and suffering, I realized I was not alone. The people of the community of Joplin were absolutely incredible. Within minutes of the horrific event, local residents showed up in pickups and sport utility vehicles, all offering to help transport the wounded to other facilities, including Freeman, the trauma center literally across the street. Ironically, it had sustained only minimal damage and was functioning (although I'm sure overwhelmed). I carried on, grateful for the help of the community.

Within hours I estimated that over 100 EMS units showed up from various towns, counties and four different states. Considering the circumstances, their response time was miraculous. Roads were blocked with downed utility lines, smashed up cars in piles, and they still made it through.

We continued to carry patients out of the hospital on anything that we could find: sheets, stretchers, broken doors, mattresses, wheelchairs—anything that could be used as a transport mechanism.

As I finished up what I could do at St John's, I walked with two RN's, Shilo Cook and Julie Vandorn, to a makeshift MASH center that was being set up miles away at Memorial Hall. We walked where flourishing neighborhoods once stood, astonished to see only the disastrous remains of flattened homes, body parts, and dead people everywhere. I saw a small dog just whimpering in circles over his master who was dead, unaware that his master would not ever play with him again. At one point we tended to a young woman who just stood crying over her dead mother who was crushed by her own home. The young woman covered her mother up with a blanket and then asked all of us, "What should I do?" We had no answer for her, but silence and tears.

By this time news crews and photographers were starting to swarm around, and we were able to get a ride to Memorial Hall from another RN. The chaos was slightly more controlled at Memorial Hall. I was relieved to see many of my colleagues, doctors from every specialty, helping out. It was amazing to be able to see life again. It was also amazing to see how fast workers mobilized to set up this MASH unit under the circumstances. Supplies, food, drink, generators, exam tables, all were there—except pharmaceutical pain meds. I sutured multiple lacerations, and splinted many fractures, including some open with bone exposed, and then intubated another patient with severe COPD, slightly better controlled conditions this time, but still less than optimal.

But we really needed pain meds. I managed to go back to the St John's with another physician, pharmacist, and a sheriff's officer. Luckily, security let us in to a highly guarded pharmacy to bring back a garbage bucket sized supply of pain meds.

At about midnight I walked around the parking lot of St. John's with local law enforcement officers looking for anyone who might be alive or trapped in crushed cars. They spray-painted "X"s on the fortunate vehicles that had been searched without finding anyone inside. The unfortunate vehicles wore "X's" and sprayed-on numerals, indicating the number of dead inside, crushed in their cars, cars which now resembled flattened recycled aluminum cans the tornado had crumpled in her iron hands, an EF5 tornado, one of the worst in history, whipping through this quiet town with demonic strength. I continued back to Memorial Hall into the early morning hours until my ER colleagues told me it was time for me to go home. I was completely exhausted. I had seen enough of my first tornado.

How can one describe these indescribable scenes of destruction? The next day I saw news coverage of this horrible, deadly tornado. It was excellent coverage, and Mike Bettes from the Weather Channel did a great job, but there is nothing that pictures and video can depict compared to seeing it in person. That video will play forever in my mind.

I would like to express my sincerest gratitude to everyone involved in helping during this nightmarish disaster. My fellow doctors, RN's, techs, and all of the staff from St. John's. I have worked at St John's for approximately 2 years, and I have always been proud to say that I was a physician at St John's in Joplin, Missouri. The smart, selfless and immediate response of the professionals and the community during this catastrophe proves to me that St John's and the surrounding community are special. I am beyond proud.

To the members of this community, the health care workers from states away, and especially Freeman Medical Center, I commend everyone on unselfishly coming together and giving 110% the way that you all did, even in your own time of need. St John's Regional Medical Center is gone, but her spirit and goodness lives on in each of you.

EMS, you should be proud of yourselves. You were all excellent, and did a great job despite incredible difficulties and against all odds.

For all of the injured who I treated, although I do not remember your names (nor would I expect you to remember mine) I will never forget your faces. I'm glad that I was able to make a difference and help in the best way that I knew how, and hopefully give some of you a chance at rebuilding your lives again. For those whom I was not able to get to or treat, I apologize wholeheartedly.

Last, but not least, thank you, and God bless you, Mercy/St John's for providing incredible care in good times and even more so, in times of the unthinkable, and for all the training that enabled us to be a team and treat the people and save lives.

Death, Destruction Hit Joplin, Missouri

"As I write these words, slightly more than 14 hours have passed since the city of Joplin was changed forever."

(This essay, written by Randy Turner, first appeared in the May 23, 2011, *Huffington Post*.)

Each year, my eighth graders at Joplin East Middle School look forward to their first official visit to Joplin High School.

They have heard the horror stories about the school, how they, as freshmen the next year, will need to stay clear of the seniors who have worked their way up to the top of the food chain.

They speak in hushed whispers of Eagle Alley, a near mythical hallway that one almost needs a guide to navigate.

That first trip, which was scheduled for Wednesday, will never happen.

Eagle Alley is a thing of the past. After the devastating killer tornado that ripped through the heart of my city Sunday night, Joplin High School, the place where so many of my former students have learned the skills they need to succeed in life, the place where

they made friends, created memories, and prepared for their passage into adulthood exists only in memory.

As I write this, at least 89 people are reported dead and hundreds injured as a result of the first major tornado to hit Joplin in four decades.

Those of us who were fortunate enough not to be in the path of the storm (it hit approximately a quarter of a mile from the apartment complex where I live) waited in the center of a darkened city, praying that loved ones had somehow managed to remain safe in what reporters were describing as a scene from a war zone.

With nearly all power gone in this city of 50,000, the night sky was still illuminated by jagged streaks of lightning in the distance and by the lights from emergency vehicles as they passed every few seconds.

When morning arrived, we were greeted by a sun that seemed almost foreign in light of what had happened.

And now the waiting begins. Every few moments I scan through Facebook postings, heartened by messages that indicate my students and former students are alive. So far, none have been listed among the casualties through word of mouth, but it may be only a matter of time. Officials have yet to release any of the names of those who were killed.

The Joplin School District has canceled classes for today and they may well be finished for the school year, which had another nine days to go. Three of our school buildings are gone forever and the middle school where I teach no longer has a roof.

Many of my former students received their high school diplomas Sunday afternoon during graduation ceremonies at Missouri Southern State University, commemorating their achievements over the past four years at Joplin High School. Now that ceremony, which should have been a memorable milestone in their young lives, will always be tainted by tragedy. As I write these words, slightly more than 14 hours have passed since the city of Joplin was changed forever.

The welcoming sunshine of just an hour ago has vanished, replaced by darkening clouds and the steady, insistent rumbling of thunder.

And now we wait.

NIGHTMARE AT FREEMAN

"SOME OF 'US' WERE MEANT TO BE THERE TO BE STRONG IN THE FACE OF DEVASTATION WHERE HOPE COULD NOT BE SEEN. ALL OF 'US' WERE SCARED TO DEATH BUT DIDN'T SHOW IT..."

BY KRISTEN HUKE

I was at Freeman Hospital in Joplin visiting my sister who had given birth to my newest nephew in the early morning hours of May 22nd. I found myself in the middle of things in the ER late that same day. I've tried talking about it, but can't put into words what I saw that night. It's so hard, even this doesn't do what happened justice, but it is a bit of what I saw, and hope none of those people have to suffer through anything like it again.

We had just gotten back to Freeman from a late lunch at Freddy's and a quick trip to Joann's Fabrics on Rangeline. We were sitting in my sister's room, when nurses asked us to go to the birthing center's waiting room because a tornado warning had been issued. My sister, baby and husband were told to get into the bathroom inside their hospital room and wait it out.

From Freeman's first floor waiting room, we could hear rain, thunder, hail, etc. But once we lost TV reception then power, we had no idea what had gone on just a few blocks away.

My mother, father and I emerged from the cafeteria to see if things were okay and slowly ventured up a spiral staircase to see a little debris in the parking lot, but not a lot else. The trees, cars, and doctor's offices to the east looked just fine. Within minutes - it was not. A frantic nurse came running into the hospital and downstairs almost falling with every step - soaking wet. We soon found out she had gotten caught in the storm, was in a ditch, and a stranger picked her up and brought her to the hospital. She was hysterical. That set the tone for the evening to come.

The first car pulled up and actually parked out in the parking lot. It had 4x4 posts and lumber sticking out its front grill - broken windows - and looked like it had been shot up with a machine gun. Six people emerged from the car with various injuries and cuts all over. After they were in the hospital, I walked out to the car and couldn't believe they were able to drive it anywhere. Not wanting to be in anyone's way or gawk, I went back inside.

Nurses starting coming from departments with extra wheelchairs, beds, and cots, anything they had. But there was a large metal door that had separated the ER and tower from the rest of the hospital, and they were unable to get supplies through. The only way was a hallway in the tower, so a bunch of us started hand-carrying cots through to the ER.

Out front, things started picking up and soon the front entrance of the hospital was lined with cars in various states of destruction, unloading victims of a terrible storm ... some not even knowing who drove them there. Loads of people piled into vehicles just to get somewhere safe because their homes were gone. Truckloads with

people unable to sit up lying on found doors and lumber just to get there. Several of "us" jumped in to help, not knowing what was to come and how long we would be needed. Three security guards were trying to direct traffic when they saw that they had to just get the people into the hospital. We were told to put on plastic gloves if we were willing to help. The injured were all in various states of shock, shaking, bleeding, not able to answer simple questions. They would just stare at you, unable to believe what had just happened to them. We were unable to believe what had happened to them because for us to

28

look to the north, Freeman blocked our view of the destruction just beyond our reach. Just on the other side of 32nd Street, we had no idea what they'd been through - just that they needed help.

A truck with a man and his wife in the back pulled up. He was talking a mile a minute. He did not know the driver; they had been picked up somewhere around the Stained Glass Theater. They were so thankful for the driver; he said they were standing and getting hit by hail when he pulled up to help. He kept saying, "It's gone... it's all just gone! We'll never have anything there again... It's just GONE!" He had a large cut in the back of his head and could barely stand, but was more worried about his wife and refused help. Almost falling, he finally agreed to sit in a wheelchair and I pushed him into the ER behind his wife as she lay on a gurney. I kept telling him I would push him as far as I could, but they might try to stop me once we got back to the swinging doors. I'd do whatever it took to make sure they stayed together, but didn't know if I could keep my promise. Luckily, a nurse ran up to us, and I told her over and over... "You have to keep them together... that's his wife!" I never saw them again.

I saw so many things that will stick in my mind forever. Strangers helping strangers, neighbors helping neighbors. A beautiful elderly lady who was dug out of her house by her neighbors and couldn't move from her La-Z-Boy ... so they lifted her, chair and all, into the back of their truck and drove her to the hospital. Once there, we had no more gurneys, so they once again lifted her and her chair and I made a path for them to get her into the ER waiting room. She sat there for hours - I brought in another beautiful woman about the same age and sat them by each other. I kept checking on them and getting them water, and as hurt as they both were, they were more worried about others than they were themselves.

Before I left that night, I went back to see how they were and they had both been taken somewhere. But the old green broken La-Z-Boy remained. I was happy to see it empty, but worried and hoped wherever she was, she was okay.

Another young man I helped in the door was immediately given a cup of water. He drank it in one gulp and asked for more. I made three trips to the only water fountain I knew of in the tower hallway. Each time I came back with a full cup, he would ask for more. He was so thankful, I was so glad I could help.

Whole families came from blocks away just walking down the streets to the hospital, needing refuge from the storm. Homes and all forms of transportation gone, scared to death, children traumatized, mothers crying, fathers trying to be strong for their families.

An SUV zipped in and everyone getting out looked okay, but then opened the back of the car to expose a young man who was not. His grandmother was screaming for help. We were doing all we could. The older woman's daughter and her young daughter were frantically calling for us to help him. Three generations of women begging for help. While the men were unloading the boy, I looked the young girl square in the eye and as calm as I could told her it would be okay, that "the nurses are doing all they can, and screaming for help is not going to help" her grandmother, it would only make her more upset.

I sincerely thought her grandmother might have a heart attack on the spot. My guess was the little girl was 9 or 10, and I think something clicked with her. Her attention went from complete distress over the hurt young man to soothing her panic-stricken grandmother. That little girl sat with her grandmother the rest of the evening and took care of her. I consider that little girl a hero.

Later, I ran into her mother outside and told her how proud I was of her young daughter. She thanked me and assumed I was a nurse. I apologized to her and told her I was just an artist who decided to do what I could and pitch in. She shook her head and thanked me again.

We quickly ran out of wheelchairs, and instead used conference room rolling chairs to unload victims that were too shaky and hurt to walk. Several of us made trips to the heart wing of the hospital to rob their linen closets of blankets, sheets, towels, whatever they could spare. People were pouring in the doors soaking wet with what clothes they had left, no shoes - shredded, torn, covered in glass and dirt. If nothing else, at least we could try to cover them and give them some decency.

A family I sat next to just an hour before the storm was helping find and hand out blankets - they were from Las Vegas here to visit their newest family member - a baby in the neonatal intensive care unit, but seeing the need started helping without any hesitation.

On my second trip for blankets, I helped a beautiful young lady and her newborn twins that had been born that morning at St. John's

via Caesarean section. I told them to avoid the ER and head straight to the birthing unit. Unfortunately, that was down a set of stairs, a spiral staircase at that. She said it was no trouble - she had just walked herself down 6 flights of stairs at St. John's with her husband and twins to get to Freeman ... one more set of stairs was not going to stop her. The babies were wrapped in so many blankets they looked like white balls.

When we ran out of gurneys, we resorted to getting people out of the backs of trucks still laying on the door or other debris and sitting them on sawhorses till they could be moved inside.

Doctors and nurses started arriving in shorts and t-shirts, some in scrubs, some pulling suitcases behind them, knowing they would be there for awhile. Eyes wide as they approached - unable to believe what task was before them. A truck of supplies came from Lamar - and I showed them where to get a large rack to put the supplies on to get them into the building. The rack once held blankets and sheets, but they were all gone.

It was particularly hard to see the patients from Greenbriar Nursing Home. They were so scared. One elderly woman was on a board in the back of a truck waiting her turn to get carried inside, I stood by the truck and tried to talk to her, not knowing where she had come from. I'm not sure if she "couldn't" talk back or was so scared and in shock she was unable. I held her hand till they took her in. She was shaking, wide-eyed, cold. Dirt and debris covered her face, ears, hair, and was jammed under her fingernails. Someone had written on her forehead "3".

Once in a room just inside the hospital doors, I made sure she was okay, and replaced her head as it was slightly off the side of a dirty decorative couch pillow. She looked me in the eye and smiled, and in the background another lady in the room was yelling "AMEN", over and over.

There was blood on the pillars, walls and floor. I pulled a used towel from a mountain of dirty linens, and with my foot mopped up a line of blood that ran from the scrub store to the waterfall, then there were too many people to maneuver around and I didn't want trip anyone. I saw a man with a huge blue cart for the linens and told him where the biggest piles were.

The traffic out front started slowing down, but I soon realized that was not a good thing ... there was a reason they were not in a hurry. The truck was asked to pull around back and if he could possibly leave his truck there for awhile till they could get to the "DOA", a temporary holding area for those who couldn't be saved in the back. I guess it was another version of a temporary morgue. That was the hardest to see.

Helicopters buzzed overhead, waiting their turn to scoop up a victim from Freeman and transport to another hospital. A helicopter with a searchlight scanned over St. John's looking for more wounded. A line of school buses and ambulances to carry people to other hospitals was strung out in the parking lot to 32nd Street.

Packed in the ER waiting room, down the hallway, past the water fountain to the gift shop, people everywhere were pacing back and forth. Scared, wondering where their loved ones were. A young man in the foyer was in agony and disbelief. He'd just lost his two young children.

And there we were - not nurses or doctors - ordinary people, doing our best. Some of "us" were meant to be there to run for supplies for the nurses. Some of "us" were meant to be there to hold a hand. Some of "us" were meant to be there to carry people who couldn't walk. Some of "us" were meant to be there to sit with others and pray. Some of "us" were meant to be there to be strong in the face of devastation where hope could not be seen. All of "us" were scared to death - but didn't show it.

I stayed till 2 a.m. Eight hours had gone by, but it felt more like 10 minutes. Mentally and physically exhausted, I got in my car and started to leave the parking lot. I stopped one last time to look back and try to process what had just happened. All I saw was the lights of Freeman - like a beacon in a sea of black nothingness. Blinking strobe lights from school buses and a line of frantic flashes from tops of ambulances. I drove myself home, probably not the best idea.

As I merged onto I-44, I quickly realized I was the only car on the interstate, aside from an occasional ambulance. I almost didn't notice I was at the Rangeline exit; it was pitch dark - black. One police car light was all that lit up Rangeline to the north or south. I didn't see the devastation ... I think God was protecting me from what I was about to realize when I finally got home to Carthage and turned on a TV. I simply couldn't believe my eyes. I didn't realize how close we were to being in serious danger. I regret leaving the hospital - I should have stayed.

It's been nine days now, but I constantly relive it like it was yesterday. Seeing the mauled faces of people I may never see again. I'm not scared of it, if anything it has made me stronger, and made me realize life's so precious. "Don't sweat the small stuff" is an UNDERstatement. I have so much to be thankful for. We all do.

I don't write this to say what "I" did. I just happened to be there. I write this to help people understand what the nurses and doctors at Freeman did, and the challenges they faced in a very dire situation. I did what we could to help them, so they could help everyone else who was hurt. People flocked to Freeman because they knew there would be help and possibly a bit of hope, refuge from the forces of nature like we've never seen.

Freeman is an amazing facility. But I will never walk through those doors again without thinking and seeing what went on there the evening of May 22, 2011. The day my nephew Gunner Madden Choate was born to my sister, Jennifer, a Freeman post-operative nurse. The day that changed my life forever.

To the people whose lives were touched by this event: may your path be blessed with happiness and love.

THE FIRE CHIEF WAS A HERO

"I HAVE A RESPONSIBILITY HERE..."
- MITCH RANDLES,
JOPLIN FIRE CHIEF

BY JOHN HACKER

He lost his home, and most of his belongings, but once Joplin Fire Chief Mitch Randles knew his family was safe on May 22, he knew what he had to do.

City Manager Mark Rohr said he met Randles on Main Street immediately after the EF5 tornado tore up Joplin.

"I could get as far as J-town then I parked my car and went three blocks, and found him at a Mexican restaurant on Main Street," Rohr said days after the tornado. "As I made my way there, I was shocked at what I saw. There were two deceased individuals right there in a vehicle where I met him. While I was on my way to meet him (Randles), he was pulling people out of a basement."

Then the pair drove to survey the damage when they were flagged down near the Joplin High School and helped pull people from a church east of the railroad tracks on 20th Street.

"We went by the high school and across the railroad tracks near the high school someone flagged us down at a church that had collapsed," Rohr

said. "He and I went over and there were deceased individuals in the church. We were working with different people who were there, I believe they were church members, lifting debris and moving people out of the way that couldn't benefit from help and pulling people out of the wreckage.

"The fire chief was a hero," Rohr said. "I was very impressed with him and continue to be impressed with him."

In the days immediately after the storm, Randles said he and his family lived at his office at the fire station at 303 East Third Street while Randles directed the around-the-clock effort to find victims of the tornado.

"My family spent the first three days after the tornado with me in the office," Randles said on May 26. "Two kids, a wife and two wiener dogs, it got kind of crowded, but I've got my family in with my sister now."

Hundreds of volunteer and professional rescuers converged on Joplin from across the country. Randles' job was to coordinate their efforts while trying his best to keep them from being hurt.

He said the help was desperately needed in the days immediately after the tornado.

"We're a department of 80 people, it would be a challenge for us to take care of one block of this," Randles said "We're literally talking about miles of this and there is no way my department could deal with it. We're just not physically capable, it wouldn't be possible for any department, solo, to handle something like this."

Randles said he had to put the thoughts of what to do about his home in the back of his mind while dealing with the rescue effort.

He said his wife and children took care of assessing the damage at their home for the first week or so after the tornado while he led his battered fire department in the effort to save lives.

"Of course I haven't seen my home, I don't even know what I'm dealing with," Randles said four days after the tornado hit. "I've been told, my wife has been out there, my son has been out there, that the home is destroyed. My wife, she's a trooper. She's out doing the things that I need to be doing, but I have a responsibility here."

DEATH AT THE
FULL GOSPEL CHURCH

"I REMEMBER THINKING THAT I KNEW I DIDN'T WANT TO LIVE IF SHE DIDN'T LIVE..."
- LATINA PUEBLA

BY RANDY TURNER

It was an awful rumbling, the loudest thing I had ever heard," Latina Puebla said after surviving the tornado that ripped through the Full Gospel Church on South Michigan in Joplin at 5:41 p.m. Sunday, May 22, 2011, just a few moments before evening services were scheduled to begin - the tornado that took their life of her daughter Natalia and sister, Sandra Thomas.

Natalia had always been in a hurry during her short life, her mother said. She had mastered the alphabet at 18 months, mastered the piano, and was already sharing her love of music by teaching others to play.

Only 17, she had already completed her first year at

Ozark Christian College, where she recorded a 4.0 grade point average.

The brunette, bespectacled Natalia had wisdom far beyond her years and had already created a bucket list. Topping that list was one wish. "I want to be someone that people can look up to," she wrote.

Her mother believes that Natalia could see something awaiting her. Natalia had written a prayer in her journal for Joplin, Latina told the Jasper County Citizen. It read, "God, you said you would spare the city if only 10 righteous men were found. Lord, please spare Joplin!"

The family arrived well before church services were scheduled. About 30 had gathered in the nursery. Children were singing "Praise You in This Storm," when the tornado sirens sounded.

"Get in the middle of the church," someone shouted.

Then the roof collapsed.

"I couldn't breathe," Latina said. At first, she could hear Natalia praying and speaking in tongues. "She was in direct communication with the Lord she was about to see."

Latina could hear her sister screaming because a portion of the roof had fallen on her. The sound grew weaker with the passing of each moment. She no longer heard her daughter's voice.

"I remember thinking that I knew I didn't want to live if she didn't live," Latina said. "I said, 'God, if you've taken my daughter, take me, too,' but God had other plans."

Natalia and Sandra and two others, Moises Carmona and his daughter Arriy, died in the church that evening.

Moises Carmona, a native of Mexico, had worked hard to earn American citizenship, and to take care of his family. His daughter was only a few feet away from him when their bodies were found.

"The ones who got under the pews didn't have a scratch on them," John Myers, pastor of the church for the past quarter of a century, told the Tulsa World, choking up with tears, "but the others...we lost four."

The last Facebook post of Natalia Puebla shows she was ready for whatever happened.

"No guilt in life, no fear of death-this is the power of Christ in me. From life's first cry till final breath, Jesus commands my destiny. No power of hell, no scheme of man, could ever pluck me from His hand. Till He returns or calls me home, here in the power of Christ I live."

GOD IS WITH ME

"AS I WORKED, SURROUNDED BY DEVASTATION AND SUFFERING, I REALIZED I WAS NOT ALONE."

BY MELISSA RAINEY-CAMPBELL

It all started on Sunday, May 22nd, the evening that changed lots of lives forever throughout the city of Joplin, Missouri.

An F-5 tornado ripped through the central part of my hometown. It destroyed almost everything in its path. Everywhere you turn there is some kind of destruction. So many homes, businesses, churches, and schools destroyed. Three-fourths of my family lost their homes that evening. All I can remember is the terrible noise ripping my house apart as my family and I huddled together praying in the bathroom, debris flying, glass breaking and scattering, the roof lifting off the back of our home. I prayed for protection for my family and those around me.

After it all settled, the back of my house and roof were gone, our car heavily damaged. Comforting my children crying and shaken with fear, I began to make my way to find my Dad across the street. The destruction was overwhelming; it was like nothing I'd ever seen in my life. My husband cautioned carefulness due to debris, downed trees, downed power lines, massive gas leaks, and it was still raining and lightning.

I could finally see my dad making his way out of the debris of my childhood home. My heart felt a small bit of relief. Than I looked up behind where he lived and could see all the way to Rangeline Road. There was nothing but rubble. All I could think of was my brother John and his family. There was still that strange kind of quiet – shock, I guess.

Our cell phone reception was not working very well. You could not get out, but you could text. Soon we started hearing sirens everywhere trying to get to the injured. We turned to see the high school was on fire. Neighbors were in shock, there was nothing left of our neighborhood to the north of us.

My husband had received word that our employer, MERCY St. John's hospital, had been heavily damaged. I then thought of my mom who was there working on the fourth floor oncology unit. My heart sank because they were saying there were injuries. I began to pray for my mom and my co-workers at St John's, as I was receiving news that my brother and his family were safe, but their home was totally gone.

My husband was called to work and little did I know that I would not see him for more than 24 hours. My children and I were taken to the safety of my in-laws' home. My husband kept checking in with me to give status updates of trying to find my mom. My heart was heavy and I cried and prayed for her safety. I finally received the long-awaited text that she had been located.

She was banged up, but had been working to save lives of the patients on her floor. She had to hold on the foot of a patient bed to avoid being sucked out of a window of the hospital. Her hands were so bruised from holding on to that bed. She got her patient to safety and began helping with carrying others to safety down the stairs. The next couple days were a blur going back into town, seeing the devastation and going through the rubble of what used to be our home. It was very difficult, but God was there with me on my emotional rollercoaster.

Seeing people help people, the compassion and generosity has been amazing. MERCY has been good to us. Brad is working like a crazy man and I am working from our temporary home. My husband's cousin suffered the loss of her daughter on Saturday, June 4, due to injuries from the tornado. We are continuing to hold her up in prayer during this difficult time. My grandmother (mom's mother) passed away Saturday evening, June 11. My mom and her siblings really need lots of prayer. I will miss my grandma. Now she is watching over me. She was a very special lady and I loved her so much.

Now my poor baby girl, Abigail, has chicken pox from head to toe. I'm doing all I can to keep her comfortable in this heat. I thank the Lord for my wonderful in-laws who have been here with us every step of the way. Their unconditional love and support have been amazing! I am so blessed to have such wonderful people in my life.

I know God will not give me more than I can handle. I know he has a plan for Brad and me. I will continue to praise Him in the storm. For those of you who might read this, please keep us in your prayers. We do know God has a plan for us.

BACK TO THE COUNTRY FOR ME

"I'M NOT ASHAMED TO SAY I SAT DOWN ON WHAT WAS LEFT OF MY FOUNDATION AND CRIED."

BY GARY HARRALL

It was just a typical Sunday afternoon, if you know what I mean. I was dreading the next day because it starts another work week.

I was watching TV when I heard people yelling outside. I stepped out on the front porch and heard what sounded like a freight train. It was loud and getting louder.

I ran through the house and into the basement. The lights went out and I heard the house collapse behind me in the basement. I saw the door into my basement rip off the hinges like it was nothing.

When I came out of the basement my first words were, "Oh my God!" The devastation was amazing. And I'm not ashamed to say I sat down on what was left of my foundation and cried.

I walked to my grandma's house over on Indiana Street. I lived at 2315 Kentucky Street.

My place of work, Vitran Express, got destroyed, too. All of our trucks, trailers and freight - destroyed.

I'm moving back to the country where I belong. I can't stand it in town.

LAELA'S STORY

"I BELIEVE THE HEALING PROCESS HAS BEGUN. JOPLIN WILL HEAL, JOPLIN WILL MOVE ON."
- LAELA ZAIDI

BY KAYLEA HUTSON

The devastation in Joplin is overwhelming, but the words of local clergy and President Barack Obama left one Joplin High School student with hope that her community will recover.

Laela Zaidi, 15, now a sophomore at the ruined Joplin High School, not only lost her school when the F5 tornado blew through Joplin, but also her home and three homes of family members.

She also knew several students who died as a result of the twister.

Yet, after hearing the President and others speak during Sunday's memorial service, Zaidi is confident Joplin will not only recover, but also be better than ever.

"There was hope in the air," Zaidi said. "We have a very resilient community. I left wanting to go hug my world, and help – volunteer doing anything I could for the community."

Having the President speak at the service, she believed, gave community members the push to know that Joplin will survive.

"It was a huge morale booster to have our own President standing there, saying the community will rebuild," Zaidi said. "I believe the healing process has begun.

"Joplin will heal, Joplin will move on."

Zaidi, who is Muslim, said she especially appreciated the words of the Rev. Aaron Brown, of Saint Paul's United Methodist Church, when he said death never wins in the end.

She agreed, adding that one way to honor those who lost their lives in the storm is to celebrate their legacy.

That statement was especially poignant for Zaidi, as she mourns the loss of a high school friend, Will Norton.

"We've all heard his story and are horrified by it, and are all grieving deeply," she said, "but the fact that death doesn't win – I believe there is life after this.

"Will was such a humble guy. We can live, and in doing so, honor him."

Zaidi believes the entire service, whether viewed in person or viewed on TV, touched everyone who experienced it.

"It's sad that it took a tragedy to get him [President Obama]

Official White House Photo by Peter Souza

here," Zaidi said. "I feel honored that he was here... He gave us a push. He gave us hope."

LOOKING TOWARD THE FUTURE

When the tornado struck, Zaidi was at a friend's house. Her mother, Vaidi Saba, was at home, taking shelter with several family members, while her father, Dr. Navid Zaidi, was at work at St. John's Regional Medical Center.

Because Zaidi and her extended family lived in the same area of Joplin, she not only lost her home, but also the homes of two aunts and her grandmother.

In all, more than 20 members of her family found themselves directly impacted in one way or another by the tornado. At one point, many took shelter on the campus of Missouri Southern, in the Leggett & Platt Center.

"I thank God that we are all okay and all alive," Zaidi said. "A house is a house, you can rebuild it, but you can't rebuild a person."

"My dad said the community will have to start from scratch. [But] I have so much faith, probably even more faith than in my whole life. Things are going to get better."

EVERYDAY HEROES

In his address, President Obama talked about how everyday heroes made a difference in the immediate hours after the tornado struck.

Zaidi agrees. She is quite proud of how her father, a pulmonary and internal medicine physician with St. John's, has responded during the crisis – providing medical care at the Missouri Southern shelter even as he found himself finding shelter.

"He truly is a hero," she said, "He doesn't realize the good he's done for the community." Not only would Navid Zaidi walk around the shelter, talking to people and caring for them, but she said he made sure the patients knew where he was sleeping, so they could seek him out in the night if something went wrong.

RETURNING TO NORMAL

A week after the storm, as the healing process begins; Zaidi finds herself looking for signs of normality.

"Everyone is appreciating the little things in life at this point," she said. "When the Starbucks re-opened, it was one piece of my life that was back to normal. I could go [there] with my friends."

The other piece of normality may not come, until she is able to see friends on a regular basis. When that happens, "I'll be the happiest person in the world," she said, adding that she's sure the new high school will be "one of the best schools around" when it is rebuilt.

SARCOXIE SOLDIER SAVES LIVES AT WAL-MART

"I'M NOT GOING TO TELL YOU I WASN'T SCARED, I WAS SCARED TO DEATH ... I DID WHAT I HAD TO DO."

- SPECIALIST JEFFREY PRICE

BY JOHN HACKER

National Guard Specialist Jeffrey Price doesn't consider himself a hero, but his actions on May 22 earned him special recognition on May 26 from Major General Steve Danner, adjutant general of the Missouri National Guard.

Price, 22, of Sarcoxie, a member of the 294 Engineer Co., based in Carthage, worked at the 15th Street Walmart on May 22, when, "it got real noisy from the wind and the rain."

"Then I saw the beams on the roof start pulling off the concrete so we went to the actual inside because we were in the back," Price said. "We were standing back there where all the associates were and the beams started moving. Then the panels in the ceiling started moving and then the only way I can describe it is a pop can. It was like a pop can crushing and the next thing I know, I look up and all I can see is sky."

Everyone hit the ground and held

on for dear life as the roof was ripped from the store and shelves started crashing down around them.

Price is a small man and initially his supervisor and another manager jumped on him to protect him.

"He said he thought it was funny because he thought I was a kid. I'm a small guy, so he was trying to protect a kid so he jumped on me," Price said. "When it got done, me and my supervisor got up, he was the one I was most concerned about because the last time I saw him, he was standing up.

"That's when I started hearing all the sounds and I kept hollering for him. Finally I heard his voice and found out he was okay."

Price said everyone tried to find anything to protect themselves from pelting hail that fell in the minutes immediately after the tornado hit. Then, Price, his supervisor, who is an ex-Marine, and the others started looking for a way out of the store.

That's when Price's small stature paid dividends.

"The back wall had caved in and it had a gap underneath it and we had tried to see if we could go out that gap, but we decided if we moved anything there it might fall," Price said. "The inner roof had come down so we decided I was the only one light enough to walk on that roof so it wouldn't hurt anyone, so I climbed up there and helped people up. My supervisor was helping lift them up and I was escorting them across the roof and helping them over."

Price said he considers himself lucky because all he lost in the storm was a motorcycle while others, including his supervisor, lost everything. He doesn't consider himself a hero.

"My boss at work said in his eyes I'm a hero. I don't believe that," Price said. "I'm not going to tell you I wasn't scared, I was scared to death, but in the same sense, I was seeing people who were just standing there, in shock, and I was trying to get them to get out. I did what I had to do."

A Survivor's Story

"In those surreal moments, you could see siren lights everywhere, but so many people were walking down the streets absolutely silent..."

By Rhonda Hatfield

As we left a few minutes early from Joel's Joplin High graduation ceremony at Missouri Southern State University, we hurried to our cars so that we wouldn't get rained on. Aunt Vicky rode with another aunt and uncle, Jackie and Vickie, to race back to my house so she could put the top up on her convertible. I rode with my mom, Diana, and step-dad, Chuck, and Tavis rode with my dad, Harlan.

As we got home, we noticed that Aunt Vicky's car top was up. My husband Brent and son Travis were out on the patio because Brent was cooking hot dogs and hamburgers. I went into the house and started getting the fixings out for the burgers. Aunt Vicky started cutting up tomatoes and onions. I put the sugar paste graduation cap onto Joel's cake, took a picture and was off on another errand.

Joel, the guest of honor, showed up. Dad and Tavis had already made it back. Joel opened one of his cards and then the sirens blared. We turned to watch the TV and were told that there was a funnel cloud between Joplin and Galena. The gray area took up one-quarter of the screen and once I saw a transformer blow on the screen, I said "that's not a funnel cloud, that's a tornado."

We all thought it would take its normal path by going toward Carl Junction; we went back to what we were doing. A few minutes later the hail came, quarter-size and odd looking. Joel, Brent and my dad were all outside and Joel showed us a piece of the hail. The rest of us continued talking and I remember telling Jack and Vickie that if the tornado came this way it was their fault because it was following them, since they've been hit numerous times. I was joking, of course. Then we heard one of the guys come into the house screaming that it was here and I immediately yelled, "My six into my bathroom, everyone else into the guest bath!" And we ran.

Then I heard it - the large train coming our way, and I knew we were in trouble.

I got a blanket, covered Mylee up and stuck her in the bathtub. Tavis was on the left of her in the tub, Travis on the right. I hollered for Joel and I heard him yell that he was getting a mattress. I got on my knees and leaned over the tub watching my children and then it hit. I had no idea where my husband or my oldest child was. I don't remember what it sounded like after that.

Tavis screamed "I love you mommy," and I hollered back, "I love you too, Tavis. It's going to be all right." I could feel dirt and objects just pounding me. I got hit several times in the back and behind with pieces of lumber and bricks and I knew the next time I got hit that I was gone and I was at peace with that, but I just didn't want my children hurt.

The wall behind the kids starting coming down and I stuck out my arms to it and started screaming, "No," as I watched it fall further and further onto my kids. I was just thinking, "Please God, not my babies!" and then silence.

It was gone and I leaned up, asked Tavis if he was okay, then Travis pulled the cover off of Mylee to check her. Travis had just gotten hit in the head by a part of the wall. No one noticed any minor injuries on themselves; you couldn't even feel them at this point. All were okay, but I didn't know where Joel was, so I screamed for him. He answered. He had been a couple of feet from me lodged between the toilet and vanity. Brent had been behind me. He had gotten into the bathroom after the roof had already been ripped off.

After I figured out that all my kids and husband were safe, we quickly noticed that the rest of our family members were all buried under debris and walls. We saw an arm of one and that was it. We pulled my Aunt Vicky out first, followed by my mom, Jackie, who was in serious pain, then Chuck. Vickie and my dad were buried deep. While others were trying to get them out, I was trying to find shelter for mom, Mylee, Tavis and Travis to get under to protect them from the rain.

Mom was shaking terribly and I knew Mylee was cold as well. A minivan had landed just up the street from us and the back had popped open so I put them in there so they could get warmed up. It was so quiet out.

In those surreal moments, you could see siren lights everywhere, but so many people were walking down the streets just absolutely silent. I went back to help with my family members. Kevin, Tavis's dad, arrived shortly and took Tavis with him so they could go find their other family members.

As people passed by I asked if they could help but anyone that was in that area were searching for their own family members and I understood that. An EMT worker came down through our area; she checked Uncle Jackie out and said it wasn't life threatening so she continued on. Shawn, Saundra and Walter Emarthla showed up too. Shawn stayed behind and the others went back to Miami. Joel was all over the neighborhood helping, and then he came to me and told me he found our neighbor lady that lived behind us dead in the backyard.

I hollered for dad but heard nothing, but the others were telling me he had been talking to them from under the rubble. I had thought they were lying to me to keep me from panicking. I walked mom and Mylee up to 24th and Main so they could sit in the ambulance and warm up and then I returned to my home to help find my family members. My aunt and dad had been pulled out safely, thanks to a construction worker who knew just what pieces of a wall to pull up so that the wreckage wouldn't then collapse again on my dad.

As soon as I arrived back at the house I hollered for my dad and someone told me he was out and okay but I didn't believe it until I saw my dad walk around some debris. I just remember hugging my dad and breaking down. We were all alive.

We searched for something to put Uncle Jackie on because he was in such severe pain. We finally found one of our doors that was very sturdy and placed him on it. We loaded him in the back of a stranger's pickup, Vickie with him and then off to the hospital they went. Joel and Brent went to several surrounding houses to help others.

Travis's family showed up to check on him, but he had already headed toward their house to check on them. Uncle Tom showed up. Chuck, Vicky, Tom and I went up to where I left mom and Mylee but they were no longer there.

Somehow I told them to go on and that I would keep looking. I went back down by the house looking for anybody that I knew and went back up to Walgreen's where I met up with Brent and Shawn. We went to Memorial Hall, then to one of the schools looking for mom and Mylee.

A volunteer drove us all over town helping us to find our family. Finally I asked that they take us to my grandma's and there Mylee was, asleep on the couch. That was after 10 p.m., nearly five hours after the tornado hit. Mom had gone back out with Tom and Vicky. My brother David's kids were there as well. He had gone to find dad since he didn't realize he had been pulled out. Rowdy, my dad's stepson, came and picked dad up and took him home. Shawn had gotten picked up and went back to Miami.

Finally, we knew we were all accounted for.

Then the search was on to find out where Uncle Jackie was taken and that search ended about 3 a.m. when we found out that he had been taken to Rogers, Arkansas, with non-life threatening injuries.

In the aftermath, our family was left battered and bruised, but alive. Uncle Jackie was released from the hospital the next day with several broken and fractured ribs, Aunt Vicky had a sprained ankle, Mom had crushed arm bones, Aunt Vickie hurt her back, Joel cut his head, Tavis had glass lodged in his back, my Dad fractured a rib, Chuck scratched his arms up badly, Travis had a sore head, Mylee had a tiny little scratch on her foot and I scratched up my arm and was left with a sore butt and back.

Our home on Grand Avenue was destroyed. Seven of our vehicles were destroyed and one was found a block away, demolished in someone's yard. Tragically, we lost many of our neighbors and Joel lost one of his very best friends, Caley Lantz Hare. He was 16. He was no doubt the biggest lost we suffered. Lantz was on his way to our house for the party that night.

This retelling of the worst night of our lives is dedicated to my heroes - H. Joel King, who refused to stand by and wait for help to save his family members and surrounding neighbors, and Tavis Beaver, who was willing to give his young life to protect his little sister and to the one we lost, "Lantz Pantz."

MCCUNE-BROOKS HOSPITAL DEALS WITH DISASTER

"THE FIRST WAVE OF THE INJURED THAT CAME, THEY KIND OF HAD THAT 100-MILE STARE THAT REMINDED ME OF WHAT YOU MIGHT SEE IN A DOCUMENTARY ON A WAR."
- DR. ROBERT ARNCE

BY JOHN HACKER

When the deadliest tornado to hit the nation in more than 50 years took out half the medical infrastructure in southwest Missouri, McCune-Brooks Regional Hospital in Carthage suddenly found itself the largest fully operational hospital in the region.

The injuries the doctors, nurses and staff at McCune-Brooks treated in the hours after 5:41 p.m. on May 22 were horrible — and they kept coming — but the staff was up to the task, treating more than 300 injured people in the 24 hours after the tornado.

"After it was all said and done, I was very proud of how this hospital stepped up," said Dr. Robert Arnce, an emergency room doctor who was on duty when the tornado hit Joplin. "The staff functioned above and beyond their normal capabilities, just rose to the occasion. Their training came to the fore in this disaster."

A DOCTOR'S PERSPECTIVE

Arnce and the rest of the McCune-Brooks emergency room staff were working their way through a relatively routine spring day that Sunday when the skies turned dark.

Severe thunderstorm and tornado warnings are part of that routine in May in Southwest Missouri and at first this didn't seem any different.

"We had heard that there was bad weather coming and of course that's not uncommon," Arnce said in an interview on June 1. "We had heard that there was a tornado cell or supercell approaching Joplin from the west, then we heard it had touched down and it had hit parts of Joplin."

That's when routine went out the window.

"Not too much longer after that, we heard it had hit St. John's," Arnce said. "The EMS community is pretty quick to get everybody up to date and we realized that St. John's was incapacitated and a lot of the injuries would be coming here so we activated the emergency disaster plan and got tremendous response with that. A lot of people had seen it on television about the time the pages went out so nearly 100 percent of our medical staff responded and we had multiple doctors down here waiting on patients."

Within minutes, the first patients made their way to the McCune-Brooks emergency room. It was the beginning of a night that would stretch the imagination and present challenges that Arnce had never encountered in his career as an emergency physician.

"The first wave of the injured that came, they kind of had that 100-mile stare that reminded me of what you might see in a documentary on a war," Arnce said. "We had a lot of people who brought their loved ones over here in private vehicles that were without windows, some without doors, just demolished. Some even had dead family members in the cars with them. They didn't know what to do with them so they would show up and there might be one in a family with minor injuries, one with major injuries and another family member dead.

"Some people even apologized for bringing their dead family member over here, they just said they didn't know what to do with them. We told them, you don't have to apologize, we'll take care of them. I've never seen anything like it."

The injuries were similar to what a doctor might see in a combat zone, with sticks, rocks and other debris whipped around so fast it acted like bullets. The injuries were severe and graphic.

"We saw a lot of serious injuries in that first wave, traumatic injuries to the eyes. A lot of people were hit by flying debris and had ruptured globes with objects impaled in their eyes," the doctor said. "They had pieces of limbs cut off, crush injuries, open fractures, a lot of lacerations, a lot of bad internal injuries. A lot of the people we've seen have been injured in ways that I've never seen before. A lot of them had penetrating trauma injuries like you normally think of with people who were shot with a gun."

Arnce said, as the night of May 22 and May 23 progressed, he could track the progress of the rescue workers by asking patients where they came from.

"I could tell where the rescuers were because we kept getting people from those areas," he said. "As they headed down Range Line, we'd get people and we'd ask, where are you from and they'd say 'I'm from the AT&T store', "I'm from Academy Sports', then 'I was across the street at Taco Bell.' We could track the progress by where the people were coming from as they dug people out."

He said staffers at McCune-Brooks were performing jobs they didn't normally do to help out.

"You had family practice docs, internal medicine docs, OB docs, all down here, out of their element, but pitching in," Arnce said.

Pam Barlet, public relations officer with the hospital, said administrators and front office workers came in and worked to help the medical staff keep treating patients through the night.

"Our patient accounts manager, her staff and volunteers did $600 worth of laundry at Uptown Laundromat because we ran out of linens," Barlet said. "We needed clean blankets, warm blankets, cloths, gowns and other things for all these patients."

Arnce said the top administration was on hand all night and granted emergency privileges to doctors who came from Springfield and Branson to help.

He said those volunteers brought more than just themselves.

"It was interesting, we never ran out of stuff," Arnce said." We'd get low; literally, we got low on stuff to sew people up with, about that time in would come a group of docs from Skaggs in Branson with two cases of suture material, or in would come four doctors and a bunch of nurses from Cox with material we needed.

"It was amazing. The response was amazing, multiple doctors from multiple disciplines, even multiple cities who came in. The administration was in here and granted them emergency privileges to help and they just dived right in."

A NURSE'S PERSPECTIVE

Linda Carnes, the head emergency room nurse at McCune-Brooks, was not working on May 22. She was attending a birthday party for her grandson at a home east of Carthage when the clouds started moving in.

"We saw the storm coming in and we were looking at it and all of a sudden we saw this debris flying through the air, pieces of plywood and shingles and we were like, 'where is this coming from?'" Carnes said. "We heard the tornado sirens go off, and then the hail, I mean large hail and in the back of my mind I knew something bad was going on and I knew I probably needed to get to the hospital, but I needed to make sure it was safe for me to travel first."

Carnes ran home, changed into scrubs and arrived at the hospital about 7 p.m. to find that the disaster plan had been implemented and patients had started arriving.

"When I got to work, I was so surprised that, first of all, the entire ER was set up for a disaster, there were hallway beds, there were hallway chairs, clipboards were there, everything was labeled, charts were there," she said. "The staff did a miraculous job of setting the ER up, they did wonderful."

Triage, the prioritizing of patients by the kinds of care they needed, took place at first at the emergency room lobby, but that was quickly overwhelmed, so a second triage center was set up in the main lobby where medical people saw patients who needed treatment, but didn't need to stay at the hospital.

Barlet said among the patients that came to McCune-Brooks were 23 pregnant women who came to the hospital for evaluation because they had been scratched and bruised in the tornado and were concerned about their babies.

Carnes said most patients came straight from where they were rescued in Joplin to McCune-Brooks.

"Most of the people I personally took care of knew St. John's

was gone, knew Freeman was going to be overwhelmed and so they left their homes, dug themselves out of the rubble of their homes and came straight to McCune-Brooks because they knew they would not get seen over there," Carnes said. "Of course we welcomed them with open arms and did what we could for them."

Barlet said 22 local doctors responded to the hospital's pages for help.

"We got them here, and then when we opened up the other area, we decided to split the doctors up," Carnes said. "When we did triage, we said they have a laceration that needs to be sutured, we sent them to the outpatient lobby because we had doctors over there who were strictly suturing up wounds and taking care of x-rays.

"We kept the more serious in the ER lobby, the ones we thought might need to go to surgery or had the deeper lacerations that took multiple layers to close or may need to go to surgery to get cleaned out. We had some amputations and some compound fractures, the ones with bones sticking through the skin, that we kept on this side and saw and took care of."

Barlet and Carnes both said the tornado victims were calm and patient as they waited for care. "My observation of being back here was that the people didn't whimper. They were so accepting of anything that you could give them," Barlet said. "They were waiting in line to be seen and they were so accepting of our situation. I would be running back and forth and there would be one guy in the hallway and he had a blanket on, but he we cold so we switched out the blanker and kept him warm and they were just like, 'thank you.' We'd ask, 'Are you doing alright?', as good as they can, and they said 'yes.'"

Barlet said McCune-Brooks staffers were starting to wear down, but the patients were still coming in around 2:30 a.m. when unexpected relief arrived.

About 2:30 in the morning, we were exhausted, and this busload of 22 professionals from Cox, who had worked all day at Cox Medical Center in Springfield," Barlet said. "Five of them were doctors and the rest were trauma nurses and techs and they showed up and said, "What do you want us to do?""

"And they brought supplies," added Carnes. "We had run out of laceration kits, they brought laceration kits.

"It was like a godsend. We were overwhelmed; we're just a little hospital, we worked in trauma and lots of blood and crap for hours and then these people showed up, ready, willing and able. It was great because they didn't bypass us and go straight to Joplin. They stopped to see if we needed anything and oh, my god, that was so great."

Barlet said volunteer doctors and nurses came from other places, including Skaggs Memorial Hospital in Branson.

"Then we had another doctor, Stephen Waller, son of David Waller here in town," Barlet said. "He heard about the tornado, got in his car and drove down from Kansas City just walked in and said 'I'm here.' He's an infectious disease doctor in Kansas City.

"Dr. Judy Parton came here and worked in our triage. We had nurses from St. John's who knew they couldn't go to their hospital so they came here to help. St. John's Springfield, Cox Springfield nursing staffs were here. Those people coming in, they just showed up and we utilized them. They checked in like everyone else and we put them to work."

One problem that concerned McCune-Brooks administrators was that they had no communication with the medical services in Joplin and no way to tell how long the emergency would last or what else McCune-Brooks could be doing to help their cohorts in the heart of the storm.

"We had no communications with Freeman and St John's because the cell phones were down," Carnes said. "Landlines were tied up because of the increased calls. At one point Bob Copeland finally texted Gary Duncan so they could talk and then not long after that, that was probably 2 a.m., finally we got a call from Freeman telling us what they were doing and we could tell them what we were doing and we were able to touch base."

Coordination among the hospitals started improving later the morning of May 23 when St. John's set up its temporary hospital at Memorial Hall in Joplin and Dr. Tia Strait, dean of the school of technology at Missouri Southern, set up a temporary hospital at the brand new health sciences building at the University.

"When St. John's set up at Memorial Hall, we were able to call them and they were able to talk to us about what we could take and what we were treating," Barlet said. "St. John's called us and said, 'we have no way to sterilize our equipment, can you sterilize our equipment?' So they sent their own tech and we sterilized all their equipment. Actually we did if for two or three days, we sterilized all of that.

"Tia Strait was in touch with us from Missouri Southern and they knew what they could send us, what we were able to take care of, and what they needed to send to Springfield. They knew Freeman was pretty well booked so they started sending patients straight to Springfield."

Barlet and Carnes said a big part of the treatment provided at McCune-Brooks was just listening to the patients tell their stories. They said taking the time to listen helped the patients cope with what had happened to them, but it had practical medical applications as well.

"It also helped because you knew the circumstances they were in so you knew better where to look for injuries," Barlet said. "Even though their legs weren't hurting, a lot of people had injured legs but that's not what they noticed."

"You checked every inch of them," Carnes said. "Their backs had cuts and scrapes, you get them undressed and you look at their backs and stomachs and you look at their legs. You actually touch them all over and ask, does this hurt and ask what hurts. We had a little three-month-old baby, I think she was okay, but she had these cuts and scrapes all over here, just like her parents. They were in a house and had to dig out from all the rubble and we did x-rays and cleaned them all up. We had a team specifically, that was all they did, was clean people up. We took some of the nurse aids and some of the non-clinical people and had them just cleaning wounds."

Arnce, Carnes and Barlet all said the loss of St. John's Regional Medical Center was a blow, professionally and emotionally, to everyone at McCune-Brooks.

"I was kind of teary about it," Arnce said on June 1. "I had worked at St. John's for 13 years and had run the ER before we formed our own company and came over here. I still have a lot of friends over there, a lot of colleagues so my concern was, just like for loved ones, did anybody get hurt or are they alive or not alive. First you locate your family then you start to think about your friends. St. John's holds a kind of special place in my heart and I have yet to go by the building. I don't even know if I want to. I want to remember it the way it was."

Barlet agreed.

"Those are our cohorts, our teammates over there, our coworkers," she said. "We have a lot of PRN people who work over here that work there too. We have a lot of staff that are full-time here that are PRN there, per diem workers there. I have family who works there and I was worried that they were working, and then the patients, it's a tower and they have, like us, lots of windows, and I'm instantly worried about the patients."

Since the tornado, McCune-Brooks has established a talent-sharing program where more than 100 St. John's employees, from doctors to cleaning staff, will work at McCune-Brooks for the next two years or so as the Carthage hospital doubles its bed capacity to help fill the gap left by the destruction of the more-than-300-bed St. John's.

Arnce said he finally drove over to Joplin and saw parts of the destroyed area about a week after the tornado.

"The other thing that went through my mind was as bad as it was, and I don't want to minimize how bad this was, but it could have been worse," Arnce said. "If it had gone a third of a mile further south than it was, it would have taken out both of those hospitals. Then what do you do? The other thing I think about is what if it has been during a weekday, all of those kids in school, there would have been people in all of those office buildings west of St. John's that are basically just gone. I don't ever want to minimize how catastrophic it was, but it could have been worse."

CODE BLACK

"...AFTER THAT, HE KEPT HIS HEAD DOWN AND WAITED FOR THE NIGHTMARE TO END."

BY RANDY TURNER

Close to 150 people were in the 15th Street Wal-Mart 5:30 p.m. Sunday, May 22, 2011. On a normal Sunday, you might have expected more, especially when you had hundreds of people who had just left the Joplin High School commencement ceremonies at Missouri Southern State University.

But this was no ordinary Sunday. The tornado sirens had already sounded, but perhaps thinking them something akin to the boy who cried wolf, many Joplin residents were used to ignoring them.

The sirens went off all of the time and nothing ever happened.

The last major tornado in the city had been in 1974, 37 years earlier. Thirty-seven years is plenty of time for a city to grow complacent. In that tornado, the fatalities had stayed in single digits, the same as when a 1971 tornado had cut a swath through the city.

So with just 11 minutes to go before the storm hit, for many of the people on Rangeline, the hub of Joplin's economy, it was business as usual.

Even as people were still walking the aisles, gathering items, managers at the Wal-Mart store were already preparing for the worst. When they received word that a funnel cloud had touched down in Galena and was heading their way, the store went into Code Black.

Wal-Mart associates began moving customers toward the Site-To-Store area in the back of the building, a procedure they had gone over time and time again during required emergency training.

Just before the storm hit, some people pulled off Rangeline, parked their cars in the Wal-Mart lot and raced into the building. One of those people, fresh from buying a riding lawn mower for his dad, was Tommy Carpenter.

"We saw that wall of storm heading at us."

The danger of that wall is that it hid the tornado funnel clouds until it was too late.

As they moved customers back, associates swapped jokes, in an effort to keep their spirits, and the spirits of their customers up.

Then the lights began flickering. For a moment they went off, and then they came back on again. Finally, it was complete darkness.

Nineteen-year-old Cameron Paul, a Wal-Mart associate, had watched as one woman angrily left the building a few minutes earlier because she was not allowed to buy groceries after the Code Black procedures began.

Paul stood by the front entrance until the winds sucked the doors off the building. He ran to the back of the building, taking any stragglers with him. As he reached the electronics department, the tornado ripped the roof off the building. He watched helplessly as a support beam fell onto a couple and their child only a few feet away from him, killing them instantly.

After that, he kept his head down and waited for the nightmare to end.

"This is where we're all going to die," he thought. As the tornado hit, another 19-year-old Wal-Mart associate, Breann Ferguson, shouted, "Get down on the floor!" aiming the warning at everyone in sight. "It sounded like someone was taking a sledgehammer and swinging it around and around and hitting everything in sight," she told a Wall Street Journal reporter.

As she finally hunkered down on the floor, she began praying for what seemed to be an eternity, but was only a few brief moments.

The Wal-Mart associates tried to keep the customers calm. That is what they have been taught to do, but that was in pretend situations. This was the real thing.

In the back of the store, customer Debbie Chaligoj's main concern was for her three-month-old grandson Grayson, who was in the store to have his picture taken. It might have been the last picture taken of the toddler had not it been for Tommy Carpenter's decision to ride out the storm at Wal-Mart.

As the storm hit, Tommy Carpenter, on his knees, covered Grayson and the car seat in which the child was sitting, keeping him from harm.

From that vantage point, he could hear screams, prayers, and people crying out in agony as they were struck by falling beams or hit by flying debris.

And then as quickly as it began, it was over. As rain poured down with no roof there to stop it, Wal-Mart associates began pulling people out of the debris. Cameron Paul, whose father was an Army medic, began grabbing first aid supplies that had been blown away from the pharmacy and treated the wounded. At first, some balked at being treated with materials that were partially covered in dirt after the storm, but Paul calmly explained that they would all have to take tetanus shots anyway. That explanation satisfied the doubters.

Debbie Chaligoj was reunited with her grandson. It wasn't until later that she learned the identity of the man who saved the child who came to be known as "the Wal-Mart baby."

As Breann Ferguson passed through the center of the store, she saw a man lying on the floor, lifeless. She said a silent prayer.

The associates began escorting people out of what was left of their workplace. As Cameron Paul guided a child through the store, trying to keep him from seeing the worst, his effort was unsuccessful. The boy said, "There's a dead guy over there."

Cameron did not know how to respond.

It took an hour to get the building evacuated. Tommy Carpenter, the hero who had saved the Wal-Mart baby, found the riding lawn mower he had come to town to get had not survived the storm; it lay crushed beneath his pickup.

That didn't seem to matter much, though, as he looked around and saw mangled cars in every direction, some of them holding the bodies of people who had decided to wait out the storm in the parking lot.

As for the lady who was upset and stormed out of the store because she was not allowed to buy groceries, Cameron Paul hoped she had not become another statistic in the worst tornado to hit the United States in six decades.

People wandered about, since most of them lost their cars to the tornado. Some like South Middle School communication arts teacher Kathy Baker and her three daughters, Breanna, Molly, and Maggie, began the long walk home.

Only an hour earlier, the family watched proudly as Breanna received her high school diploma during ceremonies at the Leggett & Platt Center on the Missouri Southern State University campus, the same campus she will attend in the fall as a college freshman.

Three days earlier, Kathy expressed her feelings about her first-born graduating. It seemed like only yesterday that she was taking

Breanna to kindergarten for the first time. "I watched her walk in the kindergarten classroom, go to the desk that had her named printed on a strip of paper and begin playing with Play-Doh."

Now that Breanne had crossed the threshold of adulthood, the horror of the last few moments, made Kathy want to hold on to her and her other daughters and never let them go.

But that would have to wait. Their car was gone and they had a long walk home.

MISSOURI SOUTHERN HEALTH SCIENCES BUILDING TESTED AFTER TORNADO

"WITHIN THE FIRST THREE HOURS, I BET I HAD 70 VOLUNTEERS .... AS THE WEEK PROGRESSED I WAS JUST UTTERLY AMAZED...."

BY JOHN HACKER

I n August 2010, Missouri Southern State University started using a facility that had been in the works for more than a decade to build, a state-of-the-art training hospital with 29 hospital beds and robotic patients to allow student nurses to train without fear of hurting a real person.

Dr. Tia Strait, dean of the school of technology at Missouri Southern, knew the potential of the building she now managed, in fact, less than a month earlier, the University and the American Red Cross signed a memorandum of understanding to use MSSU facilities in case of a disaster, turning the Health Sciences Building into a hospital was one of the options.

"We didn't develop it or design it at first to serve as an alternate treatment location, but when several people from the hospitals came through, they said, Tia, you really need to be a part of the Jasper County, Joplin Emergency Health Care Coalition," Strait said in an interview on June 2, 10 days after the deadly EF5 tornado hit Joplin.

"I started attending those meetings this fall, as well as our safety director here on campus. We signed a contract with the Red Cross to be a sheltering facility three weeks before the tornado," Strait said. "Really, we were working on this. Last Tuesday (May 24, 2011), McCune-Brooks, Freeman and St. John's representatives were going to meet with me here at the university, we were working on a Memorandum of Understanding as to how we would all work together in the event of a disaster."

Little did everyone know how soon this capability would be needed.

Strait said she was watching the news from home when a friend told her to check the Weather Channel.

She left her home in Carthage so quickly to go to Missouri Southern to start clearing the Health Sciences building for use as an emergency hospital that she missed a call from someone at Freeman Health Systems asking her to do exactly what she was already doing.

"This devastation that occurred on Sunday and we pretty much just sprang into action," Strait said. "When I saw St. John's hospital, I told my husband 'Get ready, we've got to go.' As we were driving over here I was trying to reach my department heads, not knowing who had been affected, who hadn't, and those kinds of things, so we could get things going. We started moving simulators and all that kind of stuff out of the hospital beds to prepare for any kind of patients that would come."

Strait said she started with very little, treating people and sewing up wounds with the material and drugs they had in the dental clinic, where the public can come in and have their teeth cleaned by dental students. That quickly changed.

"When we first started treating patients, the only things I had was dental sutures, dental lidocane and anything that we treated patients with in the dental world," Strait said. "But within 24 hours, I bet I had probably close to a million dollars worth of medical supplies so we could treat patients.

"It was a God thing, because God sent me the right people. I was coordinating all of this and trying to get everything put together, but within four hours I had a dispensary. I had Tim Mitchell from Family Pharmacy in Neosho, bless his heart, he was here within two hours of a telephone call and he pretty much took that and ran with it and I had that pharmacy staffed 24 hours a day with two pharmacist volunteers."

Volunteers started showing up from across the region more quickly than the patients as the community started to adjust to the reality that St. John's, one of the city's two major hospitals, was knocked out.

"It took a while because I don't think people really knew we were here," Strait said. "I think Freeman hospital knew we were here because when I went home Tuesday, I had a call from Freeman. I think they knew that we had that capability and we talked about being a treatment facility in case of disaster, but to begin with here, the halls were full of volunteers. I had to finally move them to one end of the hallway to free up the main entrance where we could intake patients. Then I would go to that room where we had all those volunteers and tell them I need you to work here, here and here. Probably the picture that McCune-Brooks saw and Freeman saw was probably a little more traumatic than what we saw.

"Within the first three hours, I bet I had 70 volunteers, doctors, nurses, anesthesiologists, orthopedists, radiology techs, respiratory therapists, paramedics," Strait added. "As the week progressed, I was just utterly amazed at the people that came from all across the country to volunteer. I had a group of physicians from Arkansas, from the medical school in Jonesboro, Arkansas; they brought up some residents and interns with them that actually stayed with me for three days. They were there 24 hours a day and slept so that, no matter what, I knew I had medical coverage. There were other doctors, Girard Medical Center sent over doctors. It just really restores your faith in people, the American spirit and how people really care for one another."

Strait said for more than a week, a building that was built to teach people how to treat patients, was used to treat the real thing, and take up the slack created by St. John's destruction.

"We have 29 beds and our simulation center is designed kind of like an ICU, and that's kind of how we used it," Strait said. "Those hospital beds function just like they do in the hospital with oxygen, the medical airs and gasses and suction, so we could do basically everything over there except surgery.

"We did not have a surgery center, but in the Justice Center, the Franklin Tech surgical tech program has their tech lab down here and I know that when this started, one of the anesthesiologists and my husband took my keys and got stuff where, if we needed to do surgery, we could have done some minor surgery. We just kind of raided their area and I knew they wouldn't care. We have a close working relationship with the Joplin School District."

Strait said while the staffs at Freeman Health Systems, McCune-Brooks Regional Hospital and St. John's Regional Medical Center, after they moved to Joplin's Memorial Hall, saw some horrific injuries, the staff at her hospital, saw those with more minor wounds.

"Most of the injuries we saw were broken bones, lacerations, people that had been battered," she said. "We would see people who had a bruise every quarter inch on their body from stuff hitting them. We saw people who really needed to be observed overnight because they had head injuries, those kinds of things.

"Then we tried to find a place for them to go when we released them, other than the shelter. If they were elderly, we tried to find a nursing home. I had one of the individuals who was helping me start calling all the long-term care facilities and assisted living facilities to see, 'do you have space?, can you take somebody?'. So we tried to find a more stable environment for everyone we saw, or to get them back with family."

Strait said the environment was very orderly and organized.

"It wasn't chaotic at all," she said. "We put the patients in a classroom, we had a couple of classrooms set up where we actually would have a doctor come in and assess the patient and determine whether it was something we could treat right there or if they needed to be kept overnight. If we needed to do sutures or set a broken bone, we sent them to the dental clinic because those dental chairs worked for that kind of situation. It was an organized chaos because we didn't know what was coming in, but we had the space to see these individuals and try to keep some semblance of confidentiality and privacy."

Twice in that first week after the tornado, Strait said she and her staff had to move patients from their beds, on the third floor of the building, to the lower floors because of tornado warnings.

Strait said she saw numerous stories and examples of heroism in the 10 days or so the clinic was open, but it was a friend and coworker and his wife who provided one of the most inspiring stories Strait saw.

She said the Dean of the School of Arts and Sciences, Richard Miller, and his wife, Cindy Miller, came to help, but it wasn't until days later she learned they could have been doing something else instead of spending their time at the University.

"Within one hour, this is the resiliency of our people, Dr. Miller and his wife were in the health science building and what they said to me was 'Tia, we're here to help, put us to work,'" Strait said. "His wife is a nurse for St. John's so I put her to work doing triage. Probably an hour and a half later, someone said 'did you know Richard and Cindy lost their house?' I had no idea. When I talk to Richard now, and his wife, I asked his wife, 'why did you come here?' She said 'I asked Richard, 'where do we go?' and he said we're going to the University because Tia will have her health sciences building up and running.'"

In the second week after the tornado, St. John's was setting up their hospital in a tent just east of their ruined building and they were still providing care from Memorial Hall. Water had been restored to full capacity at Freeman Health Systems and other hospitals were taking up the slack, so Strait was told she could shut down the clinic at Missouri Southern.

"We were blessed here at Missouri Southern that we weren't harmed by the tornado and we are all just thankful that we can give back and help in any way we can," Strait said. "I think it will make this community closer and even the towns around us, it's going to bring us all closer and I think we all feel we're neighbors and we're taking care of neighbors. I think that's all come out."

HELL'S HALF HOUR

"INSTEAD OF THE CRIES AGAINST GOD, HE HEARD CRIES OF PEOPLE LEFT BEHIND HELPING OTHERS."

BY MICHAEL R. SHARP

On the morning of Sunday, May 22, 2011, Satan rose to take stock in what he claimed as "his" portion of the world. In every town, every state, every country in the world, some part of it is claimed by him. A person, an act, anything contrary to Christ's teachings falls into Satan's house.

On this day, several conditions were brewing which would lead to a disaster of rare proportions. As he looked out into the world, he settled his sights on the community of Joplin, Missouri. At about 50,000 persons living within the city's limits, Joplin is not a particularly large or spectacular town. While Joplin lies within the "Bible Belt" portion of the United States, there are any number of persons residing there who renounce Jesus Christ as their Lord and Savior, and more whom don't lay claim to either side.

Satan saw in this city an opportunity to cause massive heartache and mayhem on this day, and in doing so, perhaps claim even more of its citizenry as his own. As the day progressed, he quietly guided some atmospheric conditions to the point where they would collide directly over Joplin. Stirring the clouds with the tip of his forked tail, he cackled with glee as he watched the cold front from the North collide with warm, moist air from the South. Then, just as they were at their most potent, he re-directed the jet stream to a point which would cause the

67

storm to rise to its most deadly heights. He then sat back, and waited, smiling an evil grin in anticipation of the pain and suffering to come.

Just to the South and East of the small town of Galena, Kansas, a funnel cloud descends. To some watching, it appears almost poetic, perhaps even magical in its destructive majesty. That curious portion of humanity called storm chasers, who have pursued the storm across the miles in anticipation of this very moment, report to the masses watching on the airwaves with anticipation and excitement as the funnel cloud kisses the earth to become an actual tornado. With a gentleness belying its power, it brushes the ground, ripping limbs, leaves, and even the very bark from trees in a careless motion.

Continuing to the East, the vortex comes in contact with a set of power lines and poles. A bright flash and lines begin to fall. Massive power poles built to withstand Mother Nature's fury are snapped in half with no more effort than a child snaps a piece of straw. As it moves farther along the predestined path of destruction, the funnel cloud meets up with its first habitation. This lasts no more than a thought, and the tornado continues on its way. More houses and possessions are torn asunder, and the tornado rises slightly to regain some power. Like a person taking in a great breath, the storm gathers up its resources, and forges forward with renewed vigor. Satan begins to laugh, as he knows he has begun a terrible catastrophe from whence he alone can reap the benefits.

As the storm approaches Joplin proper, the funnel cloud fully descends onto the ground. To this point, it has been playing as a cat plays with its prey. Delicately slapping the mouse that is Joplin around, the town now gains its full attention. Approaching 32nd and Schifferdecker, it slams to the ground with a fury rarely seen in nature. Throwing cars, trucks, and houses aside with equal disregard, it continues to the East towards what has become Satan's primary focus: the hospital named after one of Jesus' own disciples, St. John's. As it approaches this edifice built to reflect the desire to ease others' pain and suffering in this world, it ravages the landscape before it, destroying anything and everything in its path. Gathering its strength, the tornado throws trees, telephone poles, and even thrusts a wooden chair into the concrete side of the building. Windows blow outward as though a massive bomb has gone off within its halls. Patients who should be finishing their evening meals are cast from their beds onto a floor strewn with the litter of the walls and windows of this hospital. Even before those within have gained their breath, the tornado takes sight of its next target: St Mary's Catholic Church. Continuing to gather strength from Satan's stirring of the atmosphere, the tornado grows ever larger, with winds approaching 300 mph, and a footprint of almost a half-mile wide. It slams into the church, using all of its massive power to try and bring down the iconic iron cross which stands before the church. Hit repeatedly by all manner of debris, the cross flexes and strains to remain upright. For what appears to be an eternity, the storm rages around this point.

68

Finally, it moves onward, content that it has done Satan's work to destroy this building dedicated to the glory of God the Father. However, as it leaves, continuing East Northeast, it sees that, although it had hit the cross with everything Satan could manifest, the cross stood firm in its resolve, and remains standing tall and proud above the wreckage. Furious, the tornado turns its attention onto the school called Irving, and quickly reduces it to a pile of barely recognizable rubble.

The tornado now fulfills its promise, growing to almost a full mile wide, and full of a power to which mankind cannot hope to withstand. As it crosses 26th and Main Street, it sees in its path a group of neighborhoods. While it has demolished a few of these neighborhoods along its path thus far, it has not seen anything such as this to this point. Stretching for a full 3 miles West to East, and varying from ½ to a full mile wide North to South, nothing stands between this monster and these homes.

Full of its failure to destroy the cross, the storm descends on the homes, bent on reducing them to nothing more than firewood. Carelessly throwing parts of what had been homes to the left and right, it tops a modest hill, and sees before it another monument to the people of Joplin: Joplin High School. Redoubling its fury, it tears across the landscape bent on nothing less than utter annihilation. With a sound reminiscent of the most massive of trains, it flows into the modest valley which contains the school. Tearing through the middle of the building, it demolishes what had recently been hallways filled with students.

Even today, not moments before the storm began, students and families were rejoicing in the seniors graduating from their school. In times past, this was held in the high school itself, but due to the large number of family members gathering together on this day, the ceremony was moved to the local university. No one was home at the time the tornado ripped through the building and only broken brick and mortar, twisted steel and splintered wood is left behind.

Continuing on its path of destruction, the tornado rips hundred year old trees from the ground as though they are no more substantial than a single stalk of grass—stripping the living bark from them even before casting them aside in search of new victims. Nothing stands a chance at this point: not trees, not buildings, whether steel, wood, or stone. The only salvation comes to those who moved to the farthest reaches of their homes, on the East side of the houses. If they are able to withstand the initial attack of the EF5 tornado, the walls might hold up against the winds long enough to allow the destructor to move on. Not many would.

As the vortex moves eastward along 20th street, it spies a local grocery store, followed by several sets of apartments rising a modest three stories high. Looking through the storm, Satan guides the path straight into these buildings, flattening them as though they were made of straw blown apart by the wolf outside the door. Seemingly requiring no effort to accomplish this, it moves onward towards more neighborhoods and Rangeline Road. This street has, over the years, become a primary means of moving north and south in Joplin. Some say as many as 250,000 vehicles traveled it in a single day, many times the normal amount of cars and trucks within the city limit.

Angling itself so as to cause the maximum damage, the tornado bores down on Walgreens pharmacy, Home Depot, Academy Sports, and Wal-Mart #59. Beneath its attention, yet within its grasp, sits more stores: Pizza Hut; Sonic; Jiffy Lube; Wendy's; Payless Shoes; Pizza by Stout; The Big Nickel; Aldi's; and the local Pepsi Distributing Plant. Swatting these to the left and right, it continues east. Standing in its way is a tiny building, Efird's Auto.

Redoubling its efforts yet again, it bores down on this location. The owner, Dave Efird, is known to offer assistance to those who required work on their autos, but may not have the funds readily available to have the work done. This is just the type of Godliness Satan despised, as it so often ran contrary to his plans. Descending on the small building, it tears it apart. Not even the cars within the building are spared. In its wake, a 40 by 60 foot slab of concrete were all that remained. Had the vortex been able to rip that from the ground, that too would have been gone.

Deep within itself, the tornado feels something wrong. A weakening, a lessening of the winds, perhaps. Satan can only hold together these monstrous powers for so long. Looking ever eastward, he sees one last target: East Middle School. Only two years old, and heralded as big enough to be a high school itself, the school had been built at a cost of almost $25 million to the city. Gathering what strength remained, the tornado takes aim at the school. Forging into it, it gives almost all that remained in its ability. Ripping the roof off, and doing its best to level the school, it could only inflict modest damage. While the storm still had some time before it spent itself completely, the worst was

past. A short distance on, the funnel cloud begins to dissipate, torn apart at last by the very forces which spawned it.

All in all, the path of devastation covered just short of 14 miles on the ground. Another lesser tornado had attacked just south of Interstate 44, which bounded Joplin on the south side. Another small twister caused some trouble near the Northpark Mall, tossing some cars about in its effort to contribute to Satan's cause. All totaled, the storm had damaged or destroyed nine schools and the Joplin Schools Administrative Building; two fire stations; innumerable businesses and homes; numerous churches; and more lives than can be imagined. As the funnel cloud rose into the sky from whence it came, Satan eased back, rejoicing in the moment. Any second now, those below should begin decrying God. "Why did this happen to us? We don't deserve this trouble! God, why did you send this to our community?"

Waiting for the cry to come, Satan took stock of his 15 minutes of fame in Joplin. Close to 8,000 buildings had been damaged or destroyed. Virtually everyone in the surrounding area was affected, either through family ties, or homes and jobs lost. As he relished the moments following the storm, he cocked an ear to the area. He waited to hear the cries of the people remaining alive, and a sinister smile formed upon his cruel lips. Softly at first, he heard cries for help. As the sound mounted, he began to discern words. With a start, he refused to believe what he was hearing. Instead of the cries against God, he heard cries of people left behind helping others! "How could this be?" Satan thought. "I have just delivered to this town the single most destructive storm in the past 60 years! These people should be cursing God, not offering to help one another!"

But that is exactly what was happening. Instead of ripping the city apart, dividing it into sections separated by more than just streets, Joplin was closing together more quickly than he could conceive. Everywhere, people were crawling from beneath what remained of their homes and businesses to offer assistance to those unable to crawl from beneath themselves. Once above ground, those rescued became rescuers themselves, helping even more citizens out of the remnants of Joplin. It didn't matter what race, religion, or other seeming differentiation Satan had tried to create to keep those citizens apart, when they had the most reason to help only themselves, the people came together to help each other.

Howling and cursing, Satan could only helplessly watch as assistance arrived within moments from outlying towns and cities. Webb City, Carl Junction, and Galena had crews to the hardest hit portions of the city almost before the storm had moved off. As the evening wore on, more distant cities sent help. Within hours, the rubble was alive with activity, searchers digging and pulling survivors from beneath the remnants of buildings and out of the mangled wreckage of cars. While Satan's minions had their moments, such as those who looted buildings for earthly goods, and chose to step over injured to reach into jewelry counters rather than reach into the rubble for the jewels of life, for every one of those souls bound for eternal damnation, a thousand were bound for glory for assisting their fellow man.

As the days passed, stories came to light. Randy Kendrick, an Assistant Manager at Academy Sports, herded his customers and associates into the safest place in the store. He then went to the front of the store, and watched and waited. Guided by his handheld electronic device, he watched the tornado bearing down on the store. Literally seconds before the tornado hit, an associate came running to the door to gain entrance into the store as a place of safety. Randy pulled the person inside, and together they ran for the back of the store. As the tornado chased them through the store, they dove for safety with the others huddled together. As prayers went up to heaven, they clung together beneath the walls of what was Academy, but once had been Kmart's. The builders who built those walls all those years ago knew what they were doing: they withstood the fury and protected their charges. Not one was seriously injured.

Across the parking lot from Academy, Pizza Hut manager Christopher Lucas moved his patrons and co-workers into the cooler. Trying to hold the door closed was impossible, but Christopher was up to the challenge. Wrapping a bungee cord around the door handle, then around his own arm, he braced himself against the storm. Straining with all his might, he held off the tornado for as long as he could. Finally, the door gave way, and he disappeared into the maw of the storm. While the storm took him, no other person within that cooler was lost to the storm.

The father of a local resident, John Serr, was in St. John's on the fifth floor. At the moment of the tornado's impact, several nurses converged in his room, covering the man's body with their own, in order to protect him from the fury of the storm. While the tornado surged around the building, demolishing windows and walls, they selflessly covered and protected this man who was unable to do so for himself. With only minor injuries, all came through alive.

In perhaps the most courageous moment of all, Don Lansaw threw his wife Bethany into the tub, and covered her with his own body. The storm beat him about the back, but he refused to move. Perhaps God and Jesus knelt with him in that moment, murmuring words of comfort to him while tears of joy were streaming down their faces at the sacrifice this man was so willingly giving, so his loved one could survive.

Furious, Satan turned his back on Joplin. With impotent rage, he cursed whomever he could reach in order to blind himself from the ultimate failure: himself. He simply could not understand the pure love man has for one another in times of need. Perhaps, someday, we will find a way to live Jesus' example every day. Some do, and blessed are those who do. Some only realize what they can be in times of trouble.

My hope is that this day opens their eyes to what they can become. We, as Americans, need to walk the path of righteousness every single day, lending assistance to all who are in need, whether requested or not. Offer because it is the right thing to do. The Golden Rule is so very simple. "Do unto others as you would have others do unto you." If we were to do this daily, oh, what a wonderful world it would be. Just by doing it in Joplin, we have seen what a wonderful place it is.

A Graduation Day
I will never forget
"There's not a day that goes by that I don't think about that day."

By Lacy Heiskell

I was outside Missouri Southern after my graduation taking pictures with my family when it began to sprinkle and the sirens went off. Like almost everyone else in Joplin, we didn't think much of it and continued with our picture taking, then decided to leave. I was driving my Nissan Sentra and was planning to drop my mother and stepfather off at home then meet up with my boyfriend to go eat.

Sitting in the traffic of the parking lot, we felt something smash against my car. My mom asked if it was hail and we all replied that we didn't know. It happened again and we knew this time it was hail. Still, we didn't think much of it.

I started driving and began to turn onto 7th and Rangeline when the radio announced that a tornado had touched down there, so I turned my car around and headed down Duquesne. It began raining so hard that I couldn't see anything outside any of my windows and we began to panic.

I pulled over and my stepfather and I traded places. He got into the driver's seat and I climbed into the backseat (looking back, I realized we were both in such a panic that neither of us re-buckled our seatbelts). He started to drive, making his best attempt to figure out what we should do or where we could go. Finally we pulled over, unable to drive anymore. We couldn't see outside the windows.

At this point, we're on 20th and Duquesne, near the roundabout, and across the street from the gas station (yep, the one with all the videos on YouTube). My mom tried running out of the car to the building we were next to, but my stepdad quickly grabbed her and pulled her back in.

The next thing we knew, we saw what looked like a giant black wall heading toward us. The driver's side window was the first to blow out and then complete chaos hit. We all ducked down and covered our faces. I remember glass and wood hitting my body and the wind howling. Then my car began to move and I thought, "This is it, I'm going to die right now."

I had never been so sure of something in my life and in that moment all I could do was scream, cry, and pray. I started off praying, and then I began begging. I begged God to save my family and me. I later heard that the tornado only lasted about 45 seconds. This stunned me; it felt like hours. Then it was finally over.

My stepdad kept asking if I was okay, but all I could do was cry. I was in such shock and I still am. We didn't know what to do. My roof had caved in except for the last layer of metal. We attempted to drive a little but all the wheels of my car where popped except one and there was too much debris in the roads to get anywhere anyway.

We finally got out of the car and looked around us. Everything was gone, including the building my mom was trying to run to. Cars twice the size of mine were flipped, smashed or wrapped around what was left of buildings. It literally looked like someone had taken a bomb and dropped it on that area.

We began to walk and the destruction continued. We ran into a woman who was kneeling and crying, her children were in a red truck that was flipped, smashed into the ground, and had another car on top of it. There were more people walking the streets, some crying, others not saying a word.

We walked for a while and then a family was nice enough to pick us up - complete strangers who were willing to help people in need. All their windows were busted out besides the front windshield. We drove past Home Depot - gone. Wal-Mart - gone. Half of Rangeline - gone. Then a thought occurred to me: 'Is everyone safe?'

I tried countless times to reach my boyfriend, my family, friends,

somebody, anybody, but the phone calls refused to go through. We got almost to my house (I live behind Lowe's) and the family couldn't take us any further because of all the trees in our roads, so we headed home, unaware of if we had a home to go to or not.

Just then we realized my mother's

leg was cut up very bad. A neighbor of ours (who we had never met before that day) offered to help. The man was an ex-EMT and cleaned my mom's wound but told her she would definitely need stitches and should get it checked out before it got infected.

I wore my graduation robe throughout the whole ordeal and I think that's part of the reason I wasn't injured as bad, just a few minor cuts and bruises. My stepdad walked the rest of the way to our house while we waited for my mom's wound to be cleaned. The man pulled out glass, grass, and insulation from my mom's leg.

We were very fortunate to be alive and to have a home to go to. My car was destroyed, but it kept us alive and you can't put a price tag on life. I later went back to my car and found pieces of lumber, glass, insulation, dinner plates, pictures, and building blueprints inside.

There's not a day that goes by that I don't think about that day. The town I was born and raised in was destroyed in seconds. The school I had attended for the last four years was gone. You can look at pictures of Joplin but it's nothing like actually seeing it and living through it. The images still make me sick to my stomach. I have blocked out a lot of images from that day, but I will never forget May 22, 2011. I know God has a plan for me and for Joplin.

In an Instant, Everything was Gone

"We found that if you didn't laugh the only thing you could do was cry. We've done both."

By Iris Fountain

I want to begin by thanking you all for your outpouring of care and concern, your thoughts, prayers, donations, and phone calls during this very difficult time. As you know on May 22nd a devastating tornado ripped through our town. It destroyed our home along with 8,000 other homes and businesses in the Joplin community.

Our lives were going along as usual on that Sunday afternoon. Gene was on the phone with a friend. I was doing the dishes when the tornado sirens sounded. With a quick glance to the sky we knew something was terribly wrong. Philip and I took

cover in the bathroom and Gene lay on the hallway floor because there was not enough space for the three of us to fit in the small bathroom. We held hands, covered our heads with bean bags, and prayed. Within a matter of minutes everything we had collected in 36 years of marriage along with our home of 20 years was torn apart.

Angie was our stronghold throughout it all. We called her from our cell phone and only had about a minute to tell her that the tornado, that was supposed to be heading towards her house, had hit ours instead. Then due to poor cellular connections the phone went dead after less than a minute. All she knew is that we were crying and panicking saying that our house was destroyed and was caving in on us.

It took Angie and Robert three long hours to finally reach our house. The traffic was crazy! Everyone was trying to find out about their loved ones. Debris and power lines were all over the roads. At one point they had to give a group of firemen a ride in the back of their truck with their rescue gear. They were trying to find an 80-year-old lady who was trapped in her house and couldn't get out and was suffering from a puncture wound from the debris. After helping the firemen get as close as they could to the address, Angie and Robert had to park at a church and walk almost three miles to reach us because there was no possible way to drive into our neighborhood. As they walked for as far as the eye could see the houses in the neighborhood she grew up in were all but rubble, there was the sound of hissing gas from the gas leaks, and small fires were breaking out everywhere. I can only imagine the horror she and her husband felt not knowing what they were going to find when they finally reached us. After all they only had that one quick panicking,

heart-stopping, phone call.

Immediately following the tornado, after calling Angie, we looked outside and realized it wasn't only our home, but the entire neighborhood was gone. It was unreal. We were living a nightmare. We immediately went across the street to find our neighbors climbing safely out of the rubble.

Their house was more damaged than ours. They are strong Christian people and other than a small scratch on him they were safe as well. Then together we went and checked for our other neighbors, some of whom we've called neighbors for the last 21 years. Thankfully they were all safe. This in itself was a miracle! My neighbor Mary and I stood in the street, in the rain, hugging each other and crying. We kept reassuring each other saying, "These were just material items, we are okay," but tears for our homes were falling down our cheeks along with the rain that was still falling from the dark sky.

By the time Angie and Robert arrived we had gathered a few necessary things such as medication and a few other things we could find to take with us. It was growing dark very quickly. Because of the loss of light we had to leave almost immediately after they got there. I kept trying to save things and had a large pile of items in the front yard that I wanted to take. Angie told me, "Mom you can only take what you can carry. That stuff has to stay. We'll come back and get it tomorrow. It's just stuff, you're okay, that is all that matters. We can take care of the stuff tomorrow."

The five of us walked away from our home in the dark with only what we were able to carry in our arms. Robert was holding a leather bag with Philip's kidney pills and a few other small but important items. Gene had our large lab Patty on a leash. Philip is night blind so Angie and I took turns holding his arm and guiding him in the dark while trying to juggle our small dog Oscar in his kennel and my purse. That was it.

We were so tired and so much in shock, what a sight we must have been. But it wasn't only us. Everywhere you turned there were people walking their dogs and taking nothing else with them. We were all trying to find a safe way out of the neighborhood. The further we walked the flatter the houses became. There were ambulances and emergency vehicles parked along the streets. The road was filled with power lines, trees, debris and the ground was a thick layer of mud from all of the rain.

Angie and Robert let us stay at their home that night and for the rest of the week. We had no clothes so we borrowed their clothes to sleep in. Later it was a small joke about where all of our underwear ended up. We couldn't seem to find it anywhere. Was it in one of the neighbors' trees? But really it wasn't funny. It was a way for us to make light of a horrible situation. We found that if you didn't laugh the only thing left to do was cry. We've done both. We had no idea our life would change forever that day.

After we got home and realized to some extent the amount of damage that had occurred that night, we knew housing would be in short supply and high demand. The next morning Angie woke Gene up at 6 am. Together they sat down with the paper and began making calls. Many rental houses had already been taken and the list wasn't very long in the first place. The first rental house that we found available we took. We never even looked inside. This was probably one of the smartest things we could have done during this crisis. Even now almost a month later FEMA trailers are just now arriving in town. They are estimating there may be at least 900 hundred of those. Every hotel room is booked, there are no houses available to rent unless you want to drive an hour to get to work each day. We even have a tent city set up where many now homeless people have been living since Memorial Day.

It was several days before we really knew the extent of the damage. We had no time to watch television or to read the newspapers. We heard whatever they were telling us on the radio as we traveled in the car. That was really it. And that was all that was on the radio for the first two weeks. All music stopped. The radio became our city's lifeline. With phone lines no longer working and over a thousand people missing in the beginning, the radio became a place where people could call in to try to find others. So while the rest of America knew how bad our tornado had been, it wouldn't be until the next weekend that we would slow down enough to really learn the full extent.

We had family and friends who lived far away calling us and telling us all about our hometown. Celebrities from the national news along with the National Guard and even the President were all here. We missed all of it. As a matter of fact for a while even the experts didn't know the extent of the damage. At first they said it was an EF4 with 6

miles of destruction. But a few weeks later they pronounced it an EF5 with 14 miles of destruction and they announced that 151 lives had been lost.

We knew it was bad enough just trying to drive to and from Angie's house. In the daylight the next day we all drove back to "our home." After living in Joplin for so many years we couldn't even tell where we were at in our own neighborhood. The roundabout and the dead cows in the pasture told us it was time to turn. There were no other street signs or recognizable landmarks left standing. There were just miles and miles of piles of rubbish. We didn't have the heart or the stomach to watch the news and go see any more of it for ourselves than we had to. Philip told us it was an EF5 as he looked out the window during one of those first car rides. We didn't need to wait for the experts to tell us that, how could it have been anything less? We already knew that. The pictures and the videos, by the way, do it no justice. They never do. You would have to see it for yourself to fully comprehend the devastation. Even then it is incomprehensible.

We spent that second day in the pouring rain trying to save as many items as we could. This was a very difficult task because our house had no roof. We had to carry whatever we could save out to our shop and try to dry it off with wet towels because everything we had, including the towels, was already wet and covered in sheetrock and insulation. Through thunder and lightning and in three inches of water on the floor of our home we worked. We worked all day saving as much as we could, and the next, and the next. It rained most of the week. Everything was soaked. All of the wood furniture, our chairs, couches, beds. We spent three full days at the laundry mat trying to wash clothing, curtains, and bedding. Each time the clothes came out we had to wash the washer between the loads because it was full of leaves, sheet rock, and insulation. I can say we managed to save quite a bit.

You realize how quickly that material worth is nothing compared to human life and you had better have your soul right with God. It was almost like the Bible says, "God will come quickly like a thief in the night."

Do you know our bathroom is the only room still intact? Or it was until the house was demolished last week. We walked out of our home unharmed. Not even one scratch. I do believe God had his hands resting on us that night.

I also want to say it was awesome to see how fast everyone came to help on that night and the next day and the weeks to follow. People from all over the country came to help our city, thousands of them. Wow! They drove down the roads offering us gloves, tarps, warm food, watermelon, Gatorade, water bottles, Bibles. Complete strangers. One day a man walked up to Gene and asked, "Do you live here?" Gene answered "yes." This isn't an uncommon question these days. Everyone wants to know if you lived here, if you've filled out these papers, talked to these people, and gone to this place or that.

So boy was he surprised when the man handed him a hundred dollar bill and walked away.

Some days we would pull up in our driveway to find an army of complete strangers clearing our debris for us. Do you know we'll never be able to thank so many people for all of the kindness they have shown us? How can saying thank you ever be enough especially when you don't even know who all to thank? If you know my husband Gene, you know he is a man full of pride. He is not one to take handouts from anyone. But just this one time we were able to convince him that he couldn't do this all by himself. That even with Angie and Robert helping there was no way we could do all of this by ourselves. We had no choice but to accept and embrace the help.

When you go through a crisis like our family has with our community you realize so many people really do care. Thank you does not seem like much for all you have done for our family during our time of need. We don't know what will happen tomorrow. We are taking it one day at a time. We are mentally and physically exhausted. But your support and acts of kindness have given us the strength to go on and to start over again. Thank you from the bottom of our hearts. Each and every one of you has helped to make our situation a little more comforting and bearable knowing that you have offered so many gifts and prayers. Your generosity is amazing. God bless you all!

AN INCREDIBLE RIDE

"IT WAS CALM CHAOS. HUNDREDS OF WOUNDED, COVERED IN BLANKETS, SITTING IN CHAIRS, LYING ON THE FLOOR IN ROWS, BLOOD EVERYWHERE."

BY JOHN, WHO DESCRIBES HIMSELF AS "A MAINTENANCE GUY" FROM FREEMAN HOSPITAL

Okay, everybody. Here we go. What a ride it has been. I just woke up from crashing finally. I was at work at Freeman Hospital when the tornado hit. I was the only maintenance man on the evening shift. The alert sounded, said it was a warning for Carl Junction, which is 10 miles north of where we were. I started all the generators, 10 of them, just in case.

When the storm hit, we did not realize what had happened only a quarter of a mile north of us at St John's. Not until the caravans of people started coming in. St. John's took a direct hit, blew out all the windows, then had a gas leak and an explosion. The tornado was about eight blocks wide and went through Joplin west to east. It never left the ground.

We had people coming in pickups with wounded, cars with all the windows blown out, people on boards, doors, tables. We emptied four conference rooms of the rolling chairs ... about 100 ... to use as wheelchairs.

We had four triage areas going full blast, one at each entrance. People were lined up for 10 blocks or more just to get to our driveways. We had just gone through an earthquake drill last week, so every one knew where their supplies were. It was calm chaos. Hundreds of wounded, covered in blankets, sitting in chairs, lying on the floor in rows, blood everywhere.

The nurses and doctors were great. Our phones were out instantly. The cell towers were inundated, couldn't get out. We couldn't call for reinforcements. They just started showing up from everywhere. EMTs, nurses, doctors, local and even from out of town.

The few in the kitchen started making sandwiches. We brought out all the blankets we had, brought up rolling supply carts of bandages, cases of bottled water. We formed small groups of volunteers to manage traffic so the ambulances could get in and out. School buses of injured started coming in. Truckers were bringing in semi loads of injured. There were no lights in Joplin. We have a six-story tower and all you could see were blue and red lights everywhere.

I personally took the first six bodies and started a temporary morgue.

The stories people were telling were beyond belief. We had probably 10 or 12 dogs running somewhat loose in the hospital that people had brought in with them. There was smoking in the hospital on a no-smoking campus. There were cries of pain, sorrow and – yes - even joy, when people would find loved ones.

The situation in town is so much worse than you see on TV. I came home in the dark and did not know where I was because of the destruction, until I came to a roundabout in the road and realized I had gone a mile too far. I couldn't get through to Sandy on the phones and people started coming in from the area I lived in with horror stories of total destruction. The Home Depot you see on TV is just blocks from us.

Finally, another employee came in and said his mom was okay and she just lives two blocks from us. The tornado just missed my son by two blocks as well. My daughter-in-law is a therapist and has no

office building to go to anymore. Her father is a dentist who also has no office left.

Joplin will take years to rebuild. It feels kind of like the destruction of the World Trade Center. You can actually see all the way through town, end to end.

The high school is gone. A major business street, going east and west on the east of town is flat on both sides of the street for two miles, with nothing left standing. Thousands of people have lost their homes, and their possessions, and their income because their places of employment have vanished off the map.

On the other hand, THANK THE LORD, I have my home, my possessions and my job. I never had to serve in combat, but surely this has to be somewhat similar in relation of chaos. I kind of know what the Japanese must feel like after the tsunami now.

Yes, I know some of the dead in Joplin personally.

Freeman Hospital still looks kind of like it did that night. We still have stuff everywhere. The floor is still dirty because Joplin has virtually no water pressure. We barely have enough water to run our sterilizers for instruments.

Only two bathrooms work in the hospital. I don't know why they do. The water company has so many broken pipes in houses that are gone, that it can't get the pressure to come up. A large area of the roof blew off and the rain collected and ran down in between the layers of roofing and into the areas full of pipes and wires and is still dripping and, of course, the rain won't stop so we can fix the roof. We have buckets all over the halls and even have a couple of areas of rooms we can't even use because the water keeps coming out of the ceiling area. We have removed hundreds of ceiling tiles that have gotten wet and were coming down anyway.

The fire alarms keep going off all the time because the wiring system is getting wetter and wetter with all of the leaks. We have to check each alarm to make sure there is no fire and then silence it.

Please pray for us. A lot of people's lives are changed forever. Mine is. And I am all right.

THE DAY THAT CHANGED EVERYTHING

"THE NEXT THING I KNEW WE WERE ALL PRAYING ...."

BY SHANEY DELZELL

It started off as a normal Sunday. I was hanging out with my family and my best friend Maddie. We knew a storm was coming in, but we didn't know how bad it was going to be.

When the sirens went off the first time we all loaded up in the car to leave the house because we lived in a trailer. We decided to go to the 15th Street Wal-Mart. When we got there, a police officer told us to go to the back of the store, where everyone else was.

My mom, Maddie and I had met my mom's best friend's daughter, Cheyanna, at Wal-Mart. She had just gotten off work. Maddie and I had to go to the bathroom. When we got out, the police officer wouldn't let us leave that area because it was the Wal-Mart "safe spot," and they had just spotted the funnel cloud. I called my mom and had her and Cheyanna come back to me and Maddie.

About the time they got back there, my boyfriend, Kyle, text messaged me and told me there was a tornado down on Seventh and Rangeline. His dad is the battalion fire chief so he would know more than anyone at Wal-Mart. When Kyle called me, the tornado was closer to Fifteenth Street. I was on the phone with him when it hit and the last thing I said to him was "I'm getting hit! I'm getting hit!"

About that time, the police officer was telling everyone to get down and cover their heads. My group was pushed into the men's bathroom. We took shelter under the urinal. Cheyanna and I under one, Maddie and my mom under the other. I made myself as small as I could get to fit underneath the urinal. The next thing I knew we were all praying, and then the urinal busted, and the roof and walls caved in. I would probably be dead if I had not been under the urinal, because where I would have been was where everything fell. I wasn't even paying attention to the sound that the tornado was making. I was focusing on keeping myself calm.

When the tornado passed, the first thing my mom did was scream my name because no one could see me. Then this very generous man pulled Maddie out and dug me out of the rubble and pulled me on top of the roof to get out. The first thing I saw was St. John's Hospital and that it was destroyed. And the first thing that popped in my head was "Is my dad okay?!?" He stayed at the house.

When everyone that was with me was pulled out, Cheyanna was handed babies who had also been nearby with family members. When that family were dug out, we took off walking to what used to be the front of the store to try to find a way out. We were being told to pick up whatever we could find to cover our heads from the hail. When we got halfway through, I saw my dad, and I started crying tears of joy because he was still alive. He had skirted the tornado, and was dodging trees, houses, and a whole bunch of debris to get to us at Wal-Mart!

Later he said he thought he was going to die.

My mom's car was nowhere to be found. We saw Cheyanna's and it was able to be driven. It won't even start now. We got to Elaina's and her family was so nice to us. They gave us dry clothes and blankets.

We were sitting there listening to the radio about all the destruction. We sent my dad right down the road to where our house should have been. He came back to get me and my mom after Maddie was reconnected with her parents who live right next to Elaina. My dad told us our house was gone and took us home to get what we could. And still to this day (June 26th, 2011) we have no home.

THE VOICE OF JOPLIN

"IT REALLY DOESN'T FEEL LIKE WORK WHEN YOU FEEL LIKE YOU'RE DOING SOME GOOD."
- ROB MEYER,
KIX 102.5 PROGRAM DIRECTOR

BY RANDY TURNER

The story of the Joplin Tornado may have received more attention than any event in southwest Missouri history.

Unwillingly, our city found itself featured on page one of major newspapers in the United States and throughout the world. We watched as Diane Sawyer of ABC, Anderson Cooper of CNN, and reporters from every major network and regional television station found their way to a city that few of them had ever seen before it was touched by tragedy.

One of the "bigfoot" reporters had a familiarity with Joplin - Brian Williams, NBC Nightly News anchor, started his career at KOAM and had lived in the area that was wiped off the map by the tornado.

During much of the time that the networks and the reporters from Kansas City, St. Louis, Tulsa, and Springfield television stations were here, we were not seeing any of their reporting.

The storm knocked television and cable service off the air in Joplin. Some of what was being done could be viewed via the internet, but not in those hours just after the tornado. In a time when any tidbit of news was vital as Joplin residents tried to find out what was going on around them, there was no way they could wait until the next day to have the *Joplin Globe* put events into context.

The need was immediate; the need was now.

And that need was met by radio, more specifically, News Radio KZRG and the Zimmer Radio Group. Relying on Zimmer stations during weather emergencies is nothing new for those of us in the Joplin area. During a recent ice storm, when electricity was out, it was Zimmer that put all of its stations into public information mode. The same thing occurred each time the area was threatened by severe thunderstorms or was put under a tornado watch. It was that reliability that enabled Joplin residents to know where to turn when skies darkened and the winds began to pick up.

Seeing that it could be one of those days when the weather would be a major concern, KZRG News Director Josh Marsh reported to work Sunday afternoon and broadcast the first tornado warnings, for southeast Kansas, at about 4 p.m.

"That's what we usually do," Marsh said in an interview with Ignite TV. It was obvious, he added, that what was coming could be far worse than just threatening weather. "This was one of those days when you are really concerned because of just how hot and humid it was and a cold front was just passing through." The big concern, he said, is that it was going to be "a nasty situation."

And then it happened.

"I don't think anyone was prepared for what was going to happen," Marsh said. Marsh was talking with the city of Joplin's emergency director Kent Stammer "when he said there was a tornado on the ground."

As I sat in my apartment, I heard Marsh relay the information that a tornado was down at Seventh and Rangeline, only a few blocks from where I live. I went into my bedroom and hit the floor, covering myself with a blanket and pillows, not much protection from what turned out to be an EF-5 tornado.

The tornado, however, never came in my direction, missing my apartment complex by a few blocks. I continued to listen to the reporting of Marsh and his co-workers at Zimmer.

"Your mind doesn't jump to an EF-5 and you don't think it's going to go through the middle of Joplin," Marsh said in the Ignite Church interview. Soon KZRG, just like most of Joplin, was bathed in darkness. "Our generators kicked in and we kept broadcasting. We had no radar, just a microphone and a few lights on our mixing board.

"It was unreal."

As the heart of Joplin was laid bare by destruction, Marsh felt the same fate was going to befall his workplace. "We were watching huge stuff flying past the window. We thought the studio was going to be hit."

At home listening, it was amazing just how calm Marsh remained. I knew something terrible had happened to my city, but just how bad it was came when I heard the live broadcasting of a KZRG reporter who was driving through the streets after the tornado.

"It's horrible; it's horrible," he said. "The high school is gone."

I thought it was exaggeration. I prayed it was exaggeration, but as he kept providing information on apartment housing that had been blown away, on people roaming the streets after their homes had been destroyed, it became obvious that he was providing an accurate description of the horror that Joplin had become.

As Marsh sat in the nearly pitch-black studio, he worried about his wife and whether she had survived the storm. "I kept trying to help people," he said. "It was scary. I didn't know if my wife was safe. There was no way to get a message to her."

Thankfully, she was uninjured.

From the first moment the tornado struck, and for the next few weeks, KZRG and the Zimmer stations became the center of our community. It wasn't just Marsh; it was every on-air personality from each of Zimmer's six Joplin stations, including seven who lost their homes. People who normally listened to rock or country or syndicated talk shows tuned in hour after hour as up-to-date information was provided.

At times, what we heard was heartbreaking. Such was the case when a man named Frank Reynolds called to tell listeners about the search for his 16-month-old great-nephew Skyular Logsdon, a fighter who had survived a premature birth. Reynolds left a number for anyone with information to call him.

The child's body was later discovered.

But there were also tales of triumph mixed in with the sadness. According to KIX 102.5 Program Director Rob Meyer, another Zimmer employee who kept broadcasting after losing his home, "It really doesn't feel like work when you feel like you're doing some good."

And there were times when the radio station was able to relay good news to its listeners. When they were able to reunite family members, "the feeling was great," Meyer told KY3 in Springfield. "It was incredible."

And through it all, the six Zimmer stations were wall-to-wall local coverage, 24 hours a day.

"We kept on broadcasting," Marsh said. "We knew that's what we were supposed to do."

If Joplin city or school officials held a press conference, it was live on the Zimmer stations. Whenever there was an update on the number of dead or what needed to be done with debris, it was covered live.

It was not the official moments that made the coverage so riveting and made it a lifeline to Joplin residents for days after the tornado, but the conversations between on-air personalities and those same residents.

They passed on information as people tried to find out where their loved ones were. They listened to survival stories, they took the questions provided to them by listeners and posed them to official sources. And more than anything, they provided a consistent message of hope and optimism even during the darkest hours.

"It was incredible to see the hope that was springing out of the darkest places," Marsh said. "That was the one thing that kept us going, the hope."

Some of that hope was provided by Marsh, whose skill with words is not limited to speaking. He wrote his feelings about the tornado, sharing them both on his blog and on air.

The post, simple titled "Hope," concludes in this fashion:

We will still have our sorrow and grief to share. But eventually that bright summer will come when we can shed it. Until then we will wear it together and share our tears and our stories. Emotion will pour out and we'll let it come, til it comes no more.

Hope is alive and well. It remains in the hands and hearts of our neighbors. It is a belief in each other. It is the trust we place in our neighbors. It is the expectation that we will heal.

(Note: The Zimmer Group provided wall-to-wall storm team coverage for nine days on all six of its radio stations.

On-air staff involved were Josh Marsh, Chad Elliott, Rob Meyer, Steve Kraus, Randy Brooks, Hank Rotten, Jr., Joe Lancello, Chris Hayes, Darrin Wright, Kyle Thomas, Sam McDonald, Ryan Keith, Jennifer Wilson, Brett James, Michael Johnson, Daron Harris, and Audie Renee. Support staff included Christie Ogle, Kris Bullard, Mel Williams, Pat Whatley, Lauri Lance, Kathy Stockdale, Sherry Cable, Larry Boyd, and Tina   Robertson.)

LUCKY TO HAVE A HOME

"THREE BLOCKS FROM TOTAL DEVASTATION. I WAS LUCKY TO BE ALIVE."

BY DENTON WILLIAMS

Just after tidying up our house and finishing some chores on that fateful Sunday afternoon, I sat down to look over my Communication Arts papers, along with my Missouri Driver's Guide PowerPoint for my Reading teacher. I sat myself down on the couch, when I heard a loud noise. It was strange ... but familiar. It was the first of the two tornado sirens. Not being in any hurry, because the sirens have sounded and nothing happens time and time again, I walk toward the back door, where my parents are sitting outside, enjoying the weather, oddly enough, under the circumstances.

But I was seeking reassurance, and instructions.

"Relax," my mother replied to me, "It's all towards the west of us."

I tend to be very cautious anyway, so I put on my tennis shoes, and grabbed my phone, and other small things that I may need if we take cover. I sat them all in a pile, and once I did, the sirens turned off. My friend, Rylee Hartwell, was shopping at Wal-Mart with his mom, and he called my cell phone once the employees began to escort the shoppers into the back of the store. He wanted me to check the weather. I turned on the speakerphone, and I played the Severe Weather Alert, "Foxcast", and his last response over the phone, other than goodbye, was: "Well, the way it sounds, it sounds like it is moving away from us..."

Which it was, until the massive tornado changed its direction of destruction.

I returned outside to talk with my parents, when my dad was standing up, and announced that he was going inside to check on the

95

weather. I looked up at the sky, and I saw these really dark clouds, almost black. My dad glanced at it and told my mom, "Watch that cloud, that looks kind of funny."

"I remember just standing there, kind of mesmerized, the cloud was sort of spinning, but I thought, *that is too big to be a funnel cloud*, and just after that, I heard a train. Not in the distance, but as if it was rolling up our street."

As soon as she said that, my dad told us to get into the closet, my mom first, than myself, and my dad ... didn't get in. We were by the window, watching the storm, saying things like: There goes the light pole, and a huge limb just blew down from our tree to the other side of the road! I sat there praying the only two prayers that I could get out through the fear: "Protect me, O Lord, now and at the hour of our death," and the Lord's Prayer. After about five minutes, which seemed like 45 minutes, the storm ever so slightly calmed down, and so we got up, and went to look through the windows at our backyard, and front yard.

Once most of the heavy wind was gone, and heavy rain remained, we went outside. One light pole was blown over, had knocked down our fence, and was lying on our poolside. The light pole attached to it, on the other side of my house, was blown toward my house; the cord was the only thing keeping it from blowing into our house. Our patio furniture was blown over upside down, and every which way, and our table was in two pieces, and on different sides of the yard. I remember thinking: Thank you, O powerful God. You have proved that you are a very merciful God.

I walked down my street, and the most damage that I could see was one house that lost all of their shingles, (the only one on our street), and one house had a tree fall, and a branch damaged the roof. But a few days later, I was going for a walk to look around, and I realize: One block away, they have fairly bad roof damage. Two blocks away, people have to replace their roofs, and windows. And from there, on for one more block, each house you walk by gets a bit worse and worse, until the end of the block, where people have nothing. Three blocks from total destruction.

I am very lucky to be alive, with a home.

LIFE OF WILL NORTON CELEBRATED

"DEATH DOESN'T GET THE LAST WORD."
- REVEREND AARON BROWN

(BY RANDY TURNER FROM THE JUNE 5, 2011, *TURNER REPORT*)

When it comes to Will Norton, Rev. Aaron Brown told hundreds who gathered at Christ's Church in Oronogo this afternoon, "Death doesn't get the last word."

And for those who came to mourn for the Joplin High School graduate who lost his life two weeks ago in the tornado that devastated Joplin, the tears were mixed with smiles and often with heartfelt laughter.

As they were seated, his friends saw a large screen montage of photos of Will Norton. Photographers never had to ask him to smile; the smile was a permanent fixture on the teenager's face.

The highlights of the service, which was termed "a celebration" of the life of Will Norton, were provided by Will himself, in one of his YouTube videos chosen by his parents and in a collection of snippets from his "Willdabeast" You Tube channel, which had thousands of followers around the globe.

Testimonials to the young man were provided by Rev. Brown, Joplin High School Principal Kerry Sachetta, and business teacher Kristy McGowen.

"Will, in every way, was the type of student and young man of whom we can all be proud," Sachetta said. After Will transferred to JHS, the principal said, he immediately fit in.

"His personality lit up a room."

Though Will became a YouTube sensation starring in his videos, when the high school Constitution Team represented Joplin in the national competition in Washington, D.C. earlier this year, Will turned the camera on his fellow team members, not on himself, Sachetta noted "He chronicled their experience."

When a national accreditation team visited JHS this year, one of the highlights of their visit was watching a video compiled by Will Norton. "It was the last video we have from that building," Sachetta said.

When Will graduated, just a short time before the tornado, Sachetta said, "I was able to shake Will's hand for the last time." The principal presented Will's parents with their son's diploma.

Mrs. McGowen related stories of how Will made a special effort to see to it that everyone shared in the good times. "He always wanted you to have your moment," she said.

"Boy, did he ever make a big impact," she "Celebrate your life like Will Norton did."

Rev. Brown concluded the ceremony by saying, "Will would not want to be remembered as a young man killed in the Joplin tornado. He would want to be remembered for how he lived.

"Will knew how to enjoy life, didn't he?"

THE STORY THAT AFFECTED ME FOR LIFE

"WILL NORTON'S STORY IS ONLY ONE OF THOUSANDS, BUT FOR REASONS UNKNOWN TO ME, HIS HAS AFFECTED ME FOR LIFE."

BY SHANTI NAVARRE

O f all the stories that have broken my heart and made me cry, this one has torn me up in a way I can't even explain.
I volunteered Tuesday night and I was assigned to "missing persons." I knew I couldn't handle the phones so I volunteered for data entry, inputting the information on the missing folks.

Will Norton's name was on the list multiple times. I'm sure many of you are familiar with Will, as he was one of the horror stories that made national news. Will was literally torn from his father's arms and sucked out the sun roof of his Hummer. He was reported missing by numerous people. When I was working he was coded as "found" but apparently had gone missing a second time because, as we were down to one hospital, injured folks were being farmed out to hospitals far and wide, and often the loved ones were unaware where their people were. The entire town - hell, the nation - believed that Will was one of those. So he was on our missing persons list as "found" and became somewhat of a beacon of hope and light for our ravaged town. It appeared that Will Norton had survived.

A couple days ago, we were in a constant quest to find ways across town to storage units and not be in the way of the thousands of emergency responders and clean-up volunteers. Streets were open one minute and closed the next. We were ignorant early on as to the complete extent of the damage. Remember, we had no internet or cable - all of our news was via texts and calls from people, like Cheyla, in Tennessee, or my friend Carol in Arkansas who kept us posted on the second storm that came through and sent us scurrying to our basement. We thought we could come across the west end of town on Schifferdecker. At that point we were unaware of the damage to that area, much as we were unaware for days of the destruction on Main. We thought the worst of it was the length of 20th Street.

As we traveled north on Schifferdecker, the destruction became more and more obvious. There were police officers directing traffic, which was backed up, but we were able to get through. As I pointed out the duck ponds to my brother, Dad and I were mourning the loss of the "duck crossing" sign and sad for the "displaced ducks." The wreckage was not as severe as further east but still phenomenal and very, very moving.

Here comes the part that I will have trouble with for years to come. Last night I saw the news report that Will Norton had been found. He had never been transported to a hospital. He had never been "found" in the first place. It was all misunderstanding or miscommunication.

One of our bright lights in this horrific tragedy is extinguished. His body was in the duck pond literally as I was pointing the pond out to my brother. I feel somehow personally responsible, like I should have somehow intuitively known that he was there. He was there and I was there and if I'd known he was there he would still be alive. I know that's ludicrous but there it is.

Cheyla called me at midnight in tears, accused me of being wrong. "You said he'd been found." And so I had. We cried together, but she was more than upset. "You didn't know him, Mom. You didn't sit with him in classes." Cheyla told me that Will was "really smart," and funny, and talented, and friendly with everyone, and that he was going somewhere with his life.

Cheyla will have to grieve Will in her own way. I can't help her. They weren't close friends, but she knew him and liked him. I will grieve in my own way, and I never even met him. Will Norton's story is only one of thousands, but for reasons unknown to me, his has affected me for life.

Joplin High
Tornado Victim Was
a Shooting Star

"The budding filmmaker loved the absurd and nothing could have been more absurd than for Will Norton to have become the face of the tragedy."

(The following essay, written by Randy Turner, was originally published on the May 31, 2011, *Huffington Post*)

Will Norton had an eye for the absurd.

In a series of 67 well-received YouTube videos, the 18-year-old gleefully shared his life, not only with friends from Joplin High School, but with thousands of teens across the nation.

Calling himself Willdabeast, Will began posting his videos three years ago, finding material in everything from snow days to prom to renting videos from Walgreens.

I never had a chance to meet Will Norton, but my former students were fans and encouraged me to check out his YouTube site. In those videos, I saw what they saw, a free spirit who never took anything seriously (at least judging from the videos' content), but what I also saw was a budding filmmaker who apparently had a deep respect for the directors and stars of long ago.

At times, you could almost see elements of Chaplin and the Marx Brothers, or at least how you might have imagined them developing had they been born in these days of the internet, in his vignettes.

The budding filmmaker loved the absurd and nothing could have been more absurd than for Will Norton to have become the face of the tragedy that hit my community of Joplin during this past week.

The tornado hit just a short time after Will reached a major milestone in his life, striding across the stage at the Leggett & Platt Center on the Missouri Southern State University campus and receiving his Joplin High School diploma, a symbol of his passage to adulthood, a steppingstone in his goal to do much more with cinema. Naturally, he accepted his diploma with the same million megawatt smile that made him a news media star.

Two hours later, his life had ended, as a tornado had ended his life. Will was taken through the sun roof of the Hummer H3 he was driving, a vehicle whose virtues he had extolled in a YouTube video made on his 16th birthday.

Though the end came quickly for Will, his body was not found immediately. For the next six days, the hunt for the teenager took on a national importance, a desperate hope that somehow, something positive could come out of this tragedy which has changed the face of Joplin forever.

We learned of how Will's father, a passenger in the same vehicle, had desperately tried to hold on to his son when the tornado hit, an unsuccessful effort which resulted in a broken arm for the father. Family members called one hospital after another, after receiving an unintentionally cruel glimmer of hope when someone incorrectly reported Will had been taken to a hospital. In the confusion that followed the tornado, as in any such horrendous event, much misinformation was spread.

The family's hopes, already diminishing, were dashed forever today when they learned that Will Norton had been identified as one of those who perished during the tornado.

When word was released to the public, the outpouring of grief was intense and immediate. Facebook sites that had been established to help in the hunt for Will became a vehicle for his friends, and for people who had only been exposed to Will through the media coverage this week, to offer their condolences to the family and express what they felt about the passing of someone whose videos provided the purest definition of youthful exuberance.

We will never know if his future would have included fame and fortune, but one thing is certain.

Thanks to modern technology and the wonder that is YouTube, we will always have a record of the cheerful young man that Will Norton was, a shooting star who passed through our lives far too quickly.

How Will Norton Led Me to Joplin

"I feel that Will made me so upset and connected to him because he was guiding me to Joplin."

By Rose Fogarty

It was May 25th and I had finally collapsed in bed from yet another fast paced, stress-filled day at work. I had heard about the tornado in Joplin, Missouri, which happened three days before, but because of my schedule I had not been able to sit down and read or listen to a single news story. Until tonight.

As I do most nights I pulled out my iPhone as I lay in bed and started to catch up on the news. I started reading about Joplin and began to pay attention. Then75

, I read about Will Norton and became overwhelmed with sadness.

Will Norton, an 18 year old with a promising future in film production ahead of him, died tragically on his way home from his high school graduation. I can now expand on the initial story I had read because I had the fortunate pleasure of meeting Will's Aunt Tracey, which I will go into later.

It was Sunday afternoon and Will had just walked across the stage to receive his diploma from Joplin High School. He wanted to stay back with his father Mark to take pictures with his friends, which tragically would be his last photos. His mother and sister Sara headed home in the car before them to get ready for guests who were arriving for his graduation party. As Will was rushing home with his father Mark they were frantically trying to avoid the storm and ended up driving right into it. Being the exceptional human being that he was, Will, even though terrified, started quoting scripture to his father to calm him, who was also terrified and in the passenger seat of his Hummer SUV. They were a Christian family who read the Bible, yet Will's father had never heard Will recite those exact scriptures before. The family feels that it was God speaking through Will during his final moments on this earth.

As the tornado grew fiercer there was no way around it, Will turned to his father and said, "I'm scared." And then he was gone. The tornado had sucked out the sunroof and pulled Will out with it. His father's arm was severely injured trying to hold on to him. The SUV still had Mark in it and was being flipped around like a toy car. Mark had to be cut out and rushed to the hospital with severe injuries. Will was missing.

To think of this happening to my own son, who is 11 years old, I found myself overcome with emotion. As I read article after article I read about Will being a YouTube star and went to his site: www.youtube.com/user/willdabeast88883333.

I discovered here hundreds of videos that Will had made over the years which led him to want to pursue a film career. He was on the way to this dream by getting accepted to Chapman University in Southern California. As I watched video after video I found a beautiful, energetic, funny, charismatic, talented and handsome young man who brought life to any situation. Will lived life to his fullest and shared his spirit with everyone he touched.

After watching for about 20 minutes, I found myself sitting up in my bed bawling like a baby. I knew I had to do something to help these poor people, whose town had been completely obliterated. I felt connected to Will now, as so many people all over the world felt after watching his videos. If there were one purpose to Will creating those videos, it was to bring Joplin to the world's stage. He certainly got my attention and made it personal for me. I was completely devastated for this boy who did not deserve to lose his life.

I started watching on CNN and paying close attention to the destruction, to the people looking for loved ones. I saw Will's Aunt, Tracey (Norton) Prossler on CNN with Anderson Cooper. She was pleading for people to look and find Will; she just knew he was still alive. I had reached out to Tracey on the "Help Find Will Norton" Facebook page. I felt I needed to connect with her personally but I still didn't know why. By now, there were 50,000 people on this page so I was not getting through all the comments, I didn't even know if she saw or read all of my posts on the threads of hundreds.

Within a week, Will's body was found in a pond near the accident site, which was less than three-quarters of a mile away from his home. It was about this time that I received an email from a friend of mine, who started brainstorming about a mission trip to Joplin. I immediately joined and told myself whatever I was going to do was going to be in honor of Will Norton. There were other victims of course, but Will's story haunted me.

Within a span of about 5 days the St. Lou Crew for Joplin (https://www.facebook.com/pages/St-Lou-Crew-For-Joplin/176174329106856) was formed, united and ready to drive to Joplin with two 53-foot 18 wheelers full of donations, a 24-foot trailer, and about 10 cars filled with approximately 30 people. We had gotten radio and TV coverage, and the people of St. Louis really came together to drop off much-needed items for the people of Joplin. Not only did they drop off, some got out of their cars and stayed to help load for hours upon hours. It was incredible to watch the city come together.

We were told by many not to go down, stay out of the way, they don't need help … but we went anyway. We were on a mission and nothing was going to stop us from stepping up and helping those people.

As I left my house in the early morning of June 3rd, I had Will on my mind. I was leaving my kids for the weekend, missing their school picnic, but I knew there was someone else's child who needed my help more. I went to Will's Facebook page and snapped a picture for my iPhone screensaver. I wanted to look at Will's smiling face all weekend as I worked. I knew my phone would be connected to my hip, because I had made several contacts in Joplin and they were all stored in my phone. In those contacts were the members of Baby Skyular's family, who we were able to fill two garages full of goods which we pulled from the collections on our trucks.

As the caravan started to pull away out of Dierberg's parking lot, I was rushing around still hanging signs on people's cars. Everyone was yelling, "Let's go, let's go," so I jumped in my friends RV and off we went. We got onto the main road and I went to grab my phone to start working and making calls. It was not there. I panicked. This was BAD. I was in charge of the delivery to Skyular's family, and their phone numbers were all stored in there. I needed contact with my children, and I had a following on Facebook that were waiting for pictures and posts, and it was so important to share our experience.

The people who were traveling with me started making calls to other members in the caravan. Someone in a car even drove back for me and checked the parking lot and store. We kept calling it and could not hear the ring so we knew it was gone. I was completely devastated and inconsolable. Of all days to lose my phone, God decided to pick this one? I was so upset, I was crying all the way to Rolla, Missouri, which was a 100 mile, hour-and-a-half leg of the trip. I felt sorry for the people who were riding with me, because – believe me - it was a spectacle in that RV. I felt like I failed Will and Skyular and we had not even arrived in Joplin.

We stopped in Rolla to get gas and I jumped out of the car. By that time, I had prayed about it and decided I needed to let it go or my trip would be ruined. I figured I would be able to track down Skyular's family through Facebook, on someone else's iPhone so I was comfortable with my backup plan, yet still distraught. Then a miracle happened.

As I got out of the RV my friends little girl came up to me and said "Rose is this phone?" Time froze for a second as I was trying to make sense of it all. How in the world was she holding my phone and where was it this entire time? As I grabbed it with elation, Will's picture immediately showed up as my screensaver I had placed that morning. The voices were in a fog as I was trying to process and I could not believe what I was hearing. My phone was on the outside of the car, on the step, for 100 miles on a very windy and bumpy highway, all the way from St. Louis to Rolla, with Will Norton's picture as my screensaver. Will Norton protected my phone all the way there, no doubt in my mind.

There were hugs and laughter and disbelief. What a miracle it was and what a wonderful way to start off our trip. Will was definitely with us and guiding us safely to Joplin.

As we headed back on the highway I knew I had to make contact with Tracey, Will's aunt. She had since accepted me on her personal Facebook page, and knew the St. Lou Crew was heading to Joplin, but we had yet to speak. Although I was worried to infringe on her privacy, I took the liberty to call her personal cell phone, because I absolutely had to tell her this miraculous story. She answered, in her sweet angelic voice (yes, she really is that sweet) and I started sobbing telling her the story. She immediately said, "Rose please contact me when you get here and I want to come meet you in person." This was the beginning of the engine running full speed ahead for the St. Lou Crew for Joplin.

There were many other miracles that happened once we were down there, which I personally felt was my guardian angel in Will. Like when the St. Lou Crew for Joplin were walking into ground zero, with everything bombed out for miles, no plant or animal life around us. Suddenly, a Cardinal bird flew right across our front row. That was Will Norton.

Like when I was searching through rubble with tears in my eyes. I knew we were short on tools and something told me to search in this particular spot. I uncovered the one and only tool I found the entire weekend; a saw, which was needed at that very moment, by a man who was trying to get to some personal items buried in the rubble. As I passed it to him and watched him cutting through a tree to get to these items, I thought in my mind "that was Will Norton." Like the poor girl who just wanted to help our Mission, who got 6 barbeque pits donated from Anheuser-Busch. She was so worried because one of the lids flew off on Interstate 44 on the way to Joplin. We found the lid, on the side of the highway, unscathed on the way home two days later. That was Will Norton.

Like the man who drove our injured crew members to get a tetanus shot. He said "I will take anyone who needs to go, I work for the Lord." That was Will Norton.

Tracey, her husband Jeff, and sons, Matthew and Dilon, came to our barbecue Saturday night, directly across from St. John's Hospital. As soon as she walked up to me we hugged and cried. What was supposed to be a few minute meeting turned into a several hour visit, from someone who has become a sister to me in one short week. We have great plans going forward and the St. Lou Crew headed back for a second mission the weekend of July 22nd.

Will Norton will always be in my heart. I feel that Will made me so upset and connected to him because he was guiding me to Joplin. If I had not lost my phone, I don't know that I would have ever met Tracey in person and we would not be able to collaborate on the amazing things we hope to accomplish going forward, united in Will's memory and honor.

God must have needed a special one, as Will Norton is clearly as special in heaven as he was on this earth.

TORNADO ENDS SCHOOL YEAR FOR MOST INSPIRATIONAL TEACHER

"IT WOULD BE NO UNDERSTATEMENT TO SAY THAT I LEARNED FAR MORE FROM HER THAN SHE DID FROM ME."

BY RANDY TURNER
(FROM THE MAY 23, 2011, *TURNER REPORT*)

" She's racist."

I blinked twice and reread the beginning paragraph of a two-page paper one of my eighth grade students had written about the teacher across the hall from me.

That word did not describe the Andrea Thomas I know, my colleague and friend for the past four years.

Eighth grade reading teachers have a short shelf life at the school where I teach. The first one I taught beside, eight years ago, a tiny young woman with the look and voice of a teenager, became the first teacher at the school to have the embarrassment of having students throw furniture out of her second story window.

I didn't expect anything different when Andrea took the job. She, too, looked like she would have fit in easily with a high school class. That was where the resemblance ended. Of all of the young teachers I have worked with over the past dozen years, I have never met one who was so prepared to be in a classroom.

She knew what she wanted to accomplish and constructed a plan that would enable her to achieve that goal. I was designated her mentor for that first year, but it would be no understatement to say that I learned far more from her than she did from me.

Over the course of the next four years, I had the privilege of watching her thrive as one of those teachers who goes the extra step for her students, no matter what their race or social status.

This was a woman who put her stock in her God, her family, and her students. By no stretch of the word could she be labeled a racist.

So I kept reading. It did not take long for the student, an African American girl, to get to the point." She initially considered Andrea to be racist, but it wasn't the teacher who was the problem.

The problem, she wrote, was not with the teacher. "I was the one who needed to grow up."

The student changed her attitude and work habits and reading became her favorite class. "Mrs. Thomas wanted to make sure I didn't fail," the girl wrote.

"That is why Mrs. Thomas should be named the Most Inspirational Teacher at East Middle School."

Each year, my eighth graders write a paper declaring their choice for Most Inspirational Teacher. The students vote on the winning paper, not their favorite teacher, but for the essay, the one that does the best job of extolling the virtues of a teacher who has made a difference.

And for this young woman, that teacher was Andrea Thomas.

That award would have been presented a week from this Friday, June 3, on our last day of school. Mrs. Thomas would have received a certificate and a copy of the winning essay.

The auditorium in which that ceremony was to take place is no longer standing. The winning essay, which was on the desk in my classroom, may no longer exist, and if it does, it is highly unlikely it is in a presentable condition. From what I have been told, my room and Mrs. Thomas' room were hit the hardest by the tornado that caused extensive damage to the building, which had only been standing for two years.

In the grand scheme of things, an essay and a certificate do not mean much, especially compared to the horrible devastation that Joplin has suffered from the tornado that tore the heart out of the city and has cost at least 116 people their lives and countless others their homes and property.

But it would have been nice for Andrea Thomas to have been named the Most Inspirational Teacher...on her last day at East Middle School.

It would have marked the perfect ending for a frustrating year for Andrea, who reluctantly came to her decision to resign after she realized her long, exhausting hours of work before and after school were taking away from her time for family and church.

Andrea has bigger problems to worry about. She and her husband lost their home to the deadly tornado, but even that never caused her to waver in her faith.

After the tornado hit Sunday night, she did not ask her Facebook friends to pray for her, "Please continue to pray for our city," she wrote. As for the problems faced by Andrea and her husband, Joe, she brushed off their new homeless state. They can stay with family. "Our needs are being met."

With so many suffering, I can't help but think I am being selfish, but it would have been great to have taught alongside Andrea Thomas for nine more days and for her students to have another two weeks with this young teacher with the tough exterior and the marshmallow heart.

It would have been nice to have had a chance to say goodbye.

CALM IN THE STORM

"[GOD] HAD WRAPPED US UP AND PROTECTED US FROM THE STORM, FROM DOWNED POWER LINES, FROM IMAGES FAR WORSE THAN COLLAPSED HOMES .... WE HAD SO MUCH TO BE GRATEFUL FOR, BUT WE ALSO HAD SO MUCH TO MOURN."

BY ANDREA THOMAS

On Sunday evening, when Joe and I had planned to be with some of the youth from our church celebrating the approaching arrival of summer, we sat huddled in our bathtub as a tornado demolished the world around us.

At about five thirty, we learned that a storm was approaching and let another youth leader know we were going to wait out the storm at

home. Moments later the sirens sounded. We remained on the couch watching the TV. The anchors were saying that a funnel may have been spotted, but they could not confirm that a tornado was headed our way. Then, what I would guess was five minutes later, the woman said, "I think those in the Joplin area should probably take cover."

At this point, we went to a bathroom, which was a central room in our home. Joe joked about toilet water flying on us, and we both left the bathroom again to watch the TV. I sat in the hall for a few minutes, and then, we both

112

returned to the bathroom. The world was silent, but the power went out. I knew then that something was very wrong. I lit candles, but the candles made Joe nervous. He blew them out. We sat. Joe said, "My ears are popping." I said, "We are in a tornado." And then, we heard it.

The storm was loud; the cracking and popping of our house was louder. I remembered hearing the story of a woman flying in a bathtub with her children and surviving. I thought the roof was going to be ripped from above us, and we would fly too. I prayed aloud, "God, command your angels concerning us. God, now. God, you are our refuge. You are our stronghold. You are protector." Then I listened. Joe and I both laid lower in the tub. The house shifted. Glass was breaking. I wondered, "How much longer?"

Then it ended.

I wanted to get out then. Joe was concerned. I finally convinced him that the worst must have been over. He said he felt cold air and dirt. I felt cold water. He began to open the door. I asked him to let me light a candle; I thought we would open the door to the bathroom and see the backyard. I couldn't have imagined outer walls would still be standing, but they were. I didn't see the debris and glass at first, but Joe did. He reached for my shoes, which were near. We found him some shoes in our room, which appeared to be undamaged. Then we went to our living room and kitchen.

Glass was everywhere, water was pouring in, metal pipes and pieces -not from our home - lay scattered around our home. We opened the front door. The frame of the glass door was present, but the glass and metal handle from the door were no longer there.

Across the street, our neighbors' homes had two walls standing and no roofs. We went out into the pouring rain, turned right, and ran up the street to check on other neighbors. Everyone appeared to be okay. We ran back, jumping over downed power lines, which were everywhere. We went back into our home. We changed clothes because we were completely soaked, and we didn't know what to do. We grabbed coats and went back out. Joe went across the street because we could not see our elderly neighbor. I called to other neighbors, asking them to seek shelter under what remained of our roof. Some came but others walked around dazed. Then others appeared. Joe returned. The neighbor was not found - we learned later she hadn't been home. Joe started grabbing for coats and blankets. Then I did the same. We had something to give to people that had nothing. A couple took shelter in our garage. I asked Joe to find something for them to sit on. We tried to help them by calling their family, but the phones weren't working. We tried and tried.

Our next door neighbors wanted to flee. We helped move massive trees from their driveway. We never went past their home. If we had, we would have known a damage much more severe. Literally, three houses down, there is nothing. Nothing. We smelled gas and decided we needed to find family. We gave a neighbor the keys to what remained of our home and the keys to my car. We didn't know if we'd ever see my car or some of our more expensive items again, but it didn't matter. We had something to give.

Somewhere in the midst of it all, I realized that I had taken off my wedding ring to fold laundry. I had set the ring on a table that was sitting under one of the shattered windows. The only thing I wanted from my home was my ring. At first, I thought it wasn't even worth looking for, though. I went to help others. I thought of the ring again and went back inside. Then, I prayed, "God, please help me." Within minutes, I had the ring in my hand. In the midst of the darkness and shattered glass, I recovered my ring.

We grabbed a few clothing items, still in laundry baskets, and we headed out the door. My grandparents pulled in the driveway then. They had come to find us. They couldn't reach us; no one could. We told them we were leaving. They got back in their car and headed to find other family members, which proved to be difficult. Joe and I made it to my aunt's home. We couldn't connect with the rest of my family. They knew I was "okay" but at that time didn't know that we had experienced the tornado.

I thought my brothers were okay, but then, learned that no one could connect with them. Joe's family didn't really know how we were; we headed to their house. I tried to stay in contact with my parents as they tried to reach my brothers and tried to get to me. Soon, I learned that my oldest brother was okay. Three hours after the tornado, I learned my youngest brother was fine. Four hours later, my parents made it to me. It was a joyful reunion.

We took my parents back to my home; it was, then, I learned the devastation was beyond what I had known. We left and headed to my parents' house. I couldn't sleep that night. Every time I closed my eyes, I heard the walls crack around us. I prayed and gave thanks for what I saw as God's provisions.

· ✦ ·

I really didn't sleep much the first night, Sunday night. When the sun rose, I did too, ready to go to my home. My parents and Joe made a plan. Joe, my mom, and I headed for the house. My dad headed to Carthage to get supplies. We went through Duquesne, around the roundabout, and took 20th Street.

I couldn't believe what I saw.

I drove 20th in the direction of my school everyday; nothing looked the same. Buildings were gone; cars were overturned, mangled, stacked. Trees had disappeared. We made it to our neighborhood. One man stood across the street at what had been his mother's home - our elderly neighbor Joe could not find the day before. He told us he had spent the night on her driveway. He stayed to defend our

114

neighborhood. We were overwhelmed with what we saw, but began to salvage our belongings. Soon other neighbors arrived. I learned, then, that we had lost a little boy from our street.

About an hour after we arrived, the skies grew dark again. I wanted to seek shelter. My mom drove me to her parents' home while Joe and my brothers, who had come to help, tried to cover the massive holes in our roof. Time moved so slowly; my grandfather Hal - "Pawdad" - made me some breakfast, which was fruit because they had no power. Then he found a radio and batteries for me.

Time moved so slowly; finally, Joe and my dad arrived. Then one of my aunts and her girls came. Soon, we all had a plan and places to go. We were off again. Joe and I went to his parents. They had

power, TV for news updates, and running, clean water; their home was like returning to a normal world for us. No one was home when we arrived, but we fed ourselves, showered, and tried to talk, for really the first time, about all that had taken place.

When we had rested enough, we returned to our home. I found a few more items and left in my car, which had been spared, to go to my parents. Joe continued working. Time continued to move slowly. Finally, Joe arrived at my parents, and we decided to spend the night at his parents'. We returned to their home, and they shared their dinner with us. They also watched TV with us. Lisa, Joe's sister, who had come from Texas to help prepare for and attend a wedding for Becca, Joe's youngest sister, gave up her bed for us. I finally felt I could try to sleep. Before I fell asleep, I found a Bible and I read. I needed to hear from my Savior. He had wrapped us up and protected us from the storm, from downed power lines, from images far worse than collapsed homes, but other lives had ended. I wanted to be reminded that He understood. We had so much to be grateful for, but we also had so much to mourn.

JOPLIN FOREVER CHANGED OUR HEARTS

"IT WARMED MY HEART TO SEE THE RESIDENTS OF JOPLIN GETTING UP, STANDING STRONG, AND REBUILDING THEIR GREAT CITY."

BY TANYA SNEDDEN

I have to start out by saying there was no question in my heart whether or not there was going to be a mission down to Joplin. But what could we really do once we were there?

However, my husband and a neighboring couple decided to pull what resources we could together. We then staged a plan of action to buy as much breakfast, lunch and dinner items as we could, thinking we might be able to help at least a handful of people once we arrived in Joplin.

I had not been there in so long; things had changed over the many years. Yet I couldn't even begin to orient us. So we slowly pulled into town not sure what direction things got bad at or even just where to go. We found ourselves silently pulling down the road in complete disbelief of what we were seeing.

Mainly, we had no idea of what was hit what wasn't and to find ourselves pulling into what we would come to understand to be a landmark of safety. The hospital. Not knowing just a short week before it had been through such things mentioned in "Code Gray," according to the *Kansas City Star*. However, we wouldn't learn the things that it had been through till a good time later.

Curfew had just lifted at 6 am. It seemed as if it was going be hard to find somewhere to put the tents and start feeding. We had found our way upon the only green grass in sight that had not been littered with debris. A security officer stood there looking at the job at hand.

We asked, "Are you hungry?"

He responded with a laugh. "Of course." He had mentioned they were eating MRE's the past week. So we knew there was a service that could be done here. We then explained what we had planned. He was extremely excited to have just started his shift next to a pancake and sausage breakfast, along with a cookout for lunch and dinner. There was a huge need for some kind of food service or something on the hospital campus. We just had no idea they did not have enough time to get outside of the destruction, eat and return on time.

We found everyone from doctors, surgeons, nurses, MASH unit coordinators, national security, construction workers, you name it. They were in our line multiple times a day sharing their brave stories with us. Each one amazed us with their strength, courage and care for others. At that point it sank in, a lot of them had lost family, friends, and things, yet still day after day they returned to their jobs, doing whatever it was they could do. We had served close to a couple hundred.

That is when the donations started to roll in. Along with two very cute kids who came from over a hill with arms full of food with their family. It was great; we were able to get lots of food through money and food donations. With the local family's help, we were able to get the word out on what a great thing had developed. So we were able to run the tent for the next three days. At that point, we had to return home.

We left everything from the grill Sutherlands donated us to food with the family to carry on for another two weeks. From the point we left, there had been many foods brought, prepared and served. There came a point where the women left in charge had no idea what she might be feeding the crews that day. It warmed my heart to see the residents of Joplin getting up, standing strong, and rebuilding their great city.

Joplin, you have forever changed our hearts.

Joplin's *Apocalypse Now*

"For the most part, you don't talk, you just listen. They have a story and they want to tell it. They need to tell it."

(This essay, written by Randy Turner, first appeared in the June 5, 2011 *Daily Kos*.)

I n a few hours, it will be exactly two weeks since a tornado ripped through my city and changed it forever.

I was one of the "lucky ones." The tornado missed the apartment complex where I live by about three blocks. When I look outside the window, everything appears the same. It is an area that is seemingly untouched by the disaster.

Appearances can be deceiving, and in this case, are very much so.

When I listened to the radio coverage during the 10 or 15 minutes before the tornado hit, I thought it was coming my way, and there was not

much I could do since I live on the second floor. I covered myself with an old blanket and a pillow and waited for fate to deal its hand.

The radio announcer continued to follow the path of the tornado as it moved away from where I lived and tore its way through the central part of Joplin.

Since that time, I have blogged almost non-stop, a coping mechanism. A reporter covering the tragedy described it as survivor's guilt. That would probably be an accurate description.

For the first 36 hours after the tornado, I did nothing but offer my own thoughts, link to the best articles and videos and try to offer a service to those who were seeking information, any information, about the disaster.

Midway through the second day, I wandered into what once had been the heart of Joplin. In the school district where I teach, there are three middle schools. The one where I teach lost its gymnasium, auditorium, band room, and commons area, while classrooms suffered damage and much of the roof was blown away.

That damage was nothing compared to what I encountered when I went to the apartment complex behind the 15th Street Wal-Mart, one of the dozens of business structures that were destroyed.

I was serving as a guide for someone else who needed information about the tornado as part of her job, but I felt more like Martin Sheen's Benjamin Willard in *Apocalypse Now* as he continued a search that grew more nightmarish with every step. For as far as the eye could see, structures that had once stood proudly over Joplin's landscape had been shredded. Every once in a while, I saw a sight that reminded me that this area had once served as home to hundreds of people, a matching pair of red flowers hundreds of feet from each other, a child's doll, somehow intact in contrast to its surroundings.

My apartment was fine and I was grateful for that, but this was

the area of town where my students lived ... I correct myself, the area of town where my students once lived. The existence we all had taken for granted was no more, my students were uprooted now and maybe forever.

Through Facebook conversations with my students, I had learned that one of them, a tall redheaded eighth grader who was unfailingly polite in non-classroom settings, but occasionally a bit overzealous in class, had not been accounted for since the tornado. His apartment was one of those that would never again serve as a home.

I asked a few people about him and, as you might expect, in a large apartment complex with hundreds and hundreds of tenants, the people I talked to did not know the eighth grader.

Finally, I came across a man and his daughter quietly removing belongings from the remnants of an apartment. It was an apartment that was clearly damaged, but it appeared to be in a bit better condition that some of those surrounding it.

I asked about my eighth grader. "I don't know him," the man said, as he loaded a box into the back of his car. I thought it was another dead end, but he kept talking. "The apartment manager said everyone was accounted for and nobody was killed."

As hard as that was to believe as I looked at the kind of scene I had only seen before in post-nuclear holocaust films, I felt much better. My student was undeniably suffering from the loss of a home, but he was safe.

The man continued to talk, volunteering information I had not asked for, but information that he clearly wanted to tell.

"My son was killed," he said, leaving the four words hanging in the air.

I said nothing, but the exhilaration I had felt seconds earlier had vanished.

"He was the manager at Pizza Hut," the man said, stopping once again. I had heard the story. Chris Lucas, 27, a veteran, had sacrificed his life, saving customers and workers at the restaurant as he guided them into a cooler.

"He has two little girls," Terry Lucas said, adding that another child was on the way.

He talked for a while longer, about everything from his son's acts of heroism to the young man's love of fishing.

It reminded me of the time 17 years earlier as a newspaper reporter when I had interviewed the mother of a murdered eight-year-old boy. For the most part, you don't talk, you just listen. They have a story and they want to tell it. They need to tell it.

When I returned home, it was back to blogging; it wasn't much, but it gave me the feeling I was contributing something, adding a touch of understanding to something that clearly is not understandable.

That night, I received a phone call from one of my eighth grade students, a tiny brown-haired girl who always seemed on top of the world. It was clear a few moments into the conversation that, despite her bravado, she had been deeply affected by the events of two days earlier.

While her home was untouched by the tornado, it was clear she did not fall into that category. She had been in the middle of the city when the tornado hit. She talked of having to walk by people who had been killed by the tornado.

"It didn't bother me," she said. "I'm going to be an EMT. I will have to get used to it."

For the next 30 minutes or so, she told me how much it did not upset her.

Clearly, it did.

What upset her the most became clear. Many of her friends had lived in the apartments where I had been only a few hours earlier. Those friends were alive, but they had moved in with relatives or friends, away from Joplin, some even out-of-state. She was hurting because she might not see her friends again. The people she had counted on for support through hundreds of problems that now paled in comparison were scattered, likely never to be together again.

I was grateful that she had someone to talk to about it, and even more grateful that I was that someone. Again, it gave me a feeling that I could be of some use.

In the two weeks since the tornado hit, I have blogged one obituary after another, more than 100 of them. I have linked to stories of courage and bravery, links to sad stories of those who did not survive, inspirational stories of the way a city, a state, even a nation, came together to support Joplin.

Though I was sitting in my living room blogging my way through it, I felt hope when I heard the words offered by Rev. Aaron Brown, Gov. Jay Nixon, and President Obama at the memorial service one week after the tornado.

After a time, I continued to blog about the tornado, but I no longer felt guilt about having the St. Louis Cardinals game in the background.

The blogging will continue for the time being, lasting well past the time, I am sure, that the nation's eyes are focused on my city.

It's what I do.

THE VOLUNTEER SPIRIT

"IT HAS BEEN INCREDIBLE TO SEE ALL OF THE PEOPLE WHO HAVE COME FROM ALL OVER THE U.S. TO HELP. EVERY DAY HAS BEEN A BLESSING."
- DELLA BERGEN

BY JOHN HACKER

During the time she coordinated volunteer efforts for Samaritan's Purse, there was a certain kind of volunteer that stood out.

She recorded the names and directed the efforts of hundreds of volunteers, some from the Joplin area, some from other states.

The ones she will remember most are those who were already suffering from the wrath of the May 22 tornado.

"I had people who came in to volunteer and I asked them, 'Were you in the tornado?' and they would say, 'My home was completely destroyed, so I thought I would come in and help someone else.'

"I cried every time."

Manning the gates for the Joplin effort of Franklin Graham's international relief organization, Samaritan's Purse, brought a lot of tears for Della Bergen, but also much laughter and satisfaction.

The one thing she did not see during her time volunteering in the tornado-ravaged community was selfishness.

Even among the children, people were putting others first, she said. "We had a toy giveaway at Forest Park early on. Kids came in. There were toys all over. You would think the kids would be grabbing five or six toys, but they were reluctant to take one.

It is so hard to imagine the spirit of these kids."

One child, she said, was not concerned about toys, but about the Bible he had lost. Mrs. Bergen was able to locate a Bible for the boy and when he left, his mother was holding a toy, while he was clutching his Bible.

"That made me cry."

The Bergens' tornado story started with their volunteer help, but it could have easily been different. On Sunday, May 22, they were having a special dinner at their Carthage home to celebrate their future daughter-in-law Kelsi Loyd's graduation from Missouri Southern State University. Both Kelsey and the Bergens' son, Micah, were planning to head back to their Joplin homes after the dinner, but Mrs. Bergen, seeing the beginning of the storm, convinced them they should stay in Carthage.

The Bergens knew that everyone was safe, but with communications spotty in Joplin after the tornado, Kelsi's mother was frantic about her daughter's whereabouts until she located them at the Bergens.

The volunteer work began from Stephen and Della Bergen the next day after getting the call from Samaritan's Purse. And with that work came the stories, one after another.

"Speaking with the survivors and listening to them tell their stories and telling how God protected them.

"Two days after the tornado, a man showed up. His daughter was pregnant with twin boys." She and her mother had hidden in a closet when the tornado hit, saving their lives, but everything else was lost, including all the gifts from the baby shower and the nursery they had worked on as a labor of love was no more.

Mrs. Bergen and Lindsay Blue took this case on as a personal mission, collecting car seats, cribs, and anything else they could get for the young family.

After the babies were delivered by C-section, Mrs. Bergen and Ms. Blue took the materials to the family, which got everything it needed.

Stephen Bergen has also collected stories, working out in the field, coordinating volunteer efforts.

"We had an elderly gentleman who wanted something in his basement. His son said not to go because the basement was filled with sewage."

The intensity with which the man wanted what was in the basement piqued Bergen's curiosity. "When they were gone, I put plastic bags on, went down there, and found a trunk floating."

In that trunk, Bergen said, were dozens of letters. "They were love letters written from his dad to his mom in World War I.

It wasn't just the elderly who had belongings that held special meaning to them. One of Bergen's favorite stories concerns a 15-year-old boy named Chase who had one item he had lost that he dearly wanted to recover - his wrestling medal.

Chase's searches had been unsuccessful, but when a number of Samaritan's Purse volunteers joined the hunt, the medal was located 15 minutes later in a tree.

Another favorite story concerned an old family Bible lost in a swamp-like area, but found totally intact under a piece of furniture - the only place in which it could have remained undamaged.

Though the work has been hard, and it has nearly completely eliminated their personal lives, the Bergens would not trade a minute of their volunteer efforts.

"Every day is a challenge. It has been incredible to see all of the people who have come from all over the U. S. to help out." Mrs. Bergen said.

"Every day has been a blessing."

A RETURN TO
EAST MIDDLE SCHOOL

"GOD WILLING, THERE WILL BE A NEW EAST MIDDLE SCHOOL STANDING SOMEDAY SOON AND THE CREATION OF NEW MEMORIES WILL BEGIN."

BY RANDY TURNER
(FROM THE MAY 25, 2011 *TURNER REPORT*)

As I circled around East Middle School, where I was teaching eighth grade communication arts (English) until our school year ended nine days early due to the horrific tornado that ripped through Joplin Sunday evening, I dreaded each step, knowing I would see something that would increase the pain I was feeling.

I had walked with *Daily Beast/Newsweek* reporter Terri Greene Sterling from where we had parked in a driveway close to 13th and Duquesne to the roundabout. The sound of sirens that had punctuated the night air Sunday had been replaced by a chain saw symphony as homeowners and those who rushed

to the area to do whatever they could do to help, began the slow, painstaking process of clearing a landscape that would have seemed unthinkable ... still seems unthinkable ... just two days earlier.

As we turned onto 20th, heading east toward my school, we came across a couple celebrating one of the small victories that have served as a counterpoint to the death and destruction, a beloved pet cat had been found alive and uninjured, hiding in a small crawlspace beneath the rubble of what once had been a home. It wasn't all good news for the couple, which had slipped into the bathroom for protection when the tornado hit. They were okay, the kids were okay, the cat was okay ....but the family has two cats. The second was still among the missing.

As we talked to them, they unearthed a precious family picture, unharmed by the forces of nature. Earlier, they had been able to salvage irreplaceable photos of the wife's sister, who died a few years ago.

The scene was the same as far as the eye could see, on both sides of the street. Homes were leveled; debris was scattered. What appeared to be some kind of costume was hanging precariously at the top of what was left of an oak tree.

We gingerly stepped around any wires that were strewn across the street, though they were not likely to still pose any kind of danger. Finally, after stopping to talk to a few more survivors and workers, we turned into the driveway at East Middle School.

My room, at the end of the eighth grade hallway, is at the first corner of the building we reached. I could tell nothing about its condition; boards were covering where windows had once been. I had been told Monday that my room and the room of eighth grade reading teacher Andrea Thomas at the end of the hall had

128

suffered the most damage, primarily from the sprinklers, which had been activated.

It seemed silly in the midst of such devastation and destruction, at a time when at least 122 people had lost their lives, but I confessed to Terri Greene Sterling that the only things I worried about as far as my classroom was concerned, were the papers on the Writers' Wall of Fame, where the best work of my students is displayed each year, the older papers from my top writers of the past, which I display at the beginning of each year to give my new students examples of excellent writing, and my collection of books on the American civil rights movement, which students use each year when we do our third quarter research project.

None of those things really mattered, but I could not help thinking of them.

There was nothing to see from our vantage point outside of the building, so we walked to where our gymnasium once stood. The floor was still there, as was a fierce Joplin Eagle standing guard on the back wall, but the other walls had vanished.

I did not even want to think about the auditorium, which has been the pride and joy of East Middle School. How was I going to be able to gaze at the debris of a place where so many memorable moments had been packed into two short years?

It was the place where Lara Stamper and her drama students had staged the school's first ever musical, "Disney's The Aristocats," just a few weeks earlier, the place where concerts were performed in the last two weeks by Kylee Tripoli's orchestra, Nick Moore's band, and on the last performance ever given in the auditorium, just five days ago, Julie Yonkers' choir and the Joplin East Middle School Show Choir.

I thought about the two benefit shows we had staged to raise money for the school the past two Novembers, with performances from history teacher Rocky Biggers' group, the Victorymen, Stone's Throw Theatre's "Godspell" cast, Hannah and Tammy Cady, my band, the ironically named Natural Disaster, and scores of middle school and high school students.

It was apparent when I turned the corner - the auditorium was in ruins.

And then I saw the American flag, a source of pride in good and bad times, and an incredible thing of beauty when it stands proud in the center of such desolation. I remembered how that flag stood proud in the auditorium during our Veterans Day Assembly and our observance of 9-11. It is remarkable how much meaning such symbols have in times of despair.

There is nothing like the majesty of the American flag.

God willing, there will be a new East Middle School standing someday soon and the creation of new memories will begin. The EMS I had grown to love in its two short years of existence was no more, but the memories remain forever.

Finding "Hi" in My Joplin Classroom

"I turned it over and there, slightly dirty, but still intact, was one of the best gifts any teacher ever received."

(The following essay, written by Randy Turner, comes from the June 12, 2011, *Huffington Post*.)

It was one of those days all teachers have.

It started with a few admonitions for students to stop talking. Once one student stopped, the next would start, and soon there were outbreaks all over the classroom … and this was my fourth hour class, the class that came through for me on those days when all of my other classes were afflicted with that contagious wildness that comes from changes of weather, cycles of the moon, or vast right-wing conspiracies depending on which veteran teacher is doing the talking.

It was almost impossible to get anything going for more than a few minutes, and in the middle of this tsunami of adolescent conversation, the right hand of the one girl who had not been talking, the one girl who almost never talked, thrust forward with the urgency of someone who had a vital message to deliver.

"Sabrina," I said, looking in her direction.

She smiled and said, "Hi."

The rest of the class looked at me. If anything was going to cause this cranky old-timer to snap it would be that one-word rebellious statement.

And looking back on that day, nearly two years in the past, I recall that my first instinct was to chastise Sabrina for wasting my time. But the face that was looking at me was not one of someone who was to trying to irritate me or to provoke me in any fashion.

It was the face of a thoughtful, considerate eighth grader who knew just when her teacher needed someone to offer a friendly "Hi."

My growing anger dissolved in a blink and somehow I was able to steer my class back to learning how to develop their writing skills so they could succeed in high school and later in life.

That simple word would have remained a "hi" point of the 2009-2010 school year for me, but it became a scenario that repeated itself often throughout the year. On a few occasions, Sabrina's "Hi" came when the class was slightly unruly. Most of the time, it was just an acknowledgment that everything was okay. The one thing I never considered it to be was an interruption of class.

The 2009-2010 school years, the first in our new East Middle School building, ended much too soon, and on that last day, Sabrina didn't disappoint me. The right hand darted out, I called her, and she smiled and said, "Hi."

I was going to miss that word of encouragement.

Sabrina realized that, too. After class, she presented me with one of the most cherished mementoes I have from my dozen years in the classroom - a multi-colored wooden frame with Mr. Turner written in black letters on the top and a cute blue creature saying "Hi," surrounded by 20 "Hi's."

A big smile covered her face. "Now I'll be able to say 'Hi' to you every day," she said.

I am sure the damp spots on my face at that moment were due to the humidity.

Every day during the 2010-2011 school year, I glanced at that gift that kept on giving. On the normal days when the stream of education was flowing in the proper direction, it brought a smile to my face. On days when the storm clouds were brewing over my corner classroom, it made me realize that this, too, shall pass.

When I received word after the May 22 tornado that decimated the city of Joplin that East Middle School had been severely damaged, I imagined the worst and my first visit to what was left of the campus did nothing to dispel my fears. The auditorium, the gymnasium, the band room, the commons area, all were gone, leveled by nature's fierce fury.

I was unable to get into my classroom that day, but I had heard that it was one of those that received the most damage. Last week, the East Middle School faculty was called in to remove personal belongings.

I did not recognize the room that I had called home for two years. My Writers' Wall of Fame, posted papers of my students' best work had somehow survived, except for a few that had slipped off the wall and fallen into the small lake that had been created when the sprinkler system was activated.

My collection of books that I used each year during the third quarter for our research project on the American Civil Rights Movement had not been damaged at all.

Other items were unsalvageable. The first I noticed, which had somehow broken away from the others in a cosmic act of irony was a copy of the school's tornado procedures.

I walked over to my desk, skimmed through the books and papers that had been strewn about. The one thing I did not see was Sabrina's gift. I looked at the floor. If it were there, it would be damaged beyond repair.

There was no sign of it.

Again, I looked at my desk and on the front right-hand corner; I saw a portion of the frame, buried under papers and a couple of textbooks. I lifted those items and, there it was, face-down on the desk. I turned it over and there, slightly dirty, but still intact, was one of the best gifts any teacher ever received.

Despite the destruction that surrounded me, that collection of "Hi's" was enough to put the smile back on my face.

When East Middle School reopens in August, and the construction process has already begun, I will be surrounded by an entirely new room, a new teacher's desk, new furnishings, all interchangeable with all of the other classrooms in my building.

The one thing that I will have that my fellow faculty members will not is that gift that will hold the same position of importance in my new classroom, as it did in my old one, the gift that even a tornado could not destroy.

I will still have my daily reminder that it is a good thing for a teacher to get "Hi" in the classroom.

THE SCHOOL YEAR THAT NEVER ENDED

"THE EVENT MAY HAVE SERVED TO BRING SOME SORT OF CLOSURE TO STUDENTS, BUT IT HAD THE OPPOSITE EFFECT ON ME."

BY RANDY TURNER

The final gathering of the 2011-2012 school year at Joplin East Middle School was not in the auditorium as originally scheduled.

That auditorium, the pride and joy of our new building, was in ruins, along with half of the school following the May 22 tornado that destroyed a large section of our city.

Instead of the awards assembly and talent show, traditions we brought to East from the old South Middle School, we met at the Fourth Street Bowl, 18 days after our school year ended early.

For the seventh and eighth graders, it was the first opportunity they had to see their friends since the tornado. Many of them had wondered if they would ever see those friends again. In the days immediately following the tornado, many were not sure if their friends had survived.

So the first order of business, even before they picked up their belongings, which had been removed from lockers and placed in black trash bags, were hugs and in what immediately became a Joplin tradition after May 22, the tornado story.

Some of the students told harrowing tales of survival, while others almost apologized as they revealed that they were not in the tornado's path.

One student, seventh grader Zach Williams, did not survive the storm. Somehow the rest of them had made it through.

134

After the hugging, the next stop was the table where eighth grade reading teacher Andrea Thomas and seventh grade math teacher Areke Worku were distributing yearbooks.

The books did not contain the event which has come to symbolize the school year, but they were a much-needed chronicle of better days.

One student returned a book she had borrowed from me during our third quarter research project, a biography of Martin Luther King.

I put the book and other things I had been carrying on the table and snapped some photos of students bowling, playing games, or just sitting at tables talking, a simple activity they had always taken for granted, but one that meant so much to them now.

The two hours passed quickly and soon the goodbyes started. Though it seemed like I had seen nearly all of my students, that was nowhere close to the truth. A quick glance at the side room showed stacks and stacks of trash bags, the belongings of students who were not able to make it, teenagers who had literally scattered to the winds, books, clothes, pencils, photos, mementoes that would most likely never be reclaimed.

I always feel sadness at the end of a school year. There are always a few students who have almost worn out their welcome by the end of the school year, but when the last few days come, I always hate to let those students go.

My eighth graders from the 2011-2012 school year had been spared my traditional last day speech, when I tell them they may not be in my class any more, but they will always be my students.

Hopefully, they know that, but there is no way for knowing for sure.

I helped carry the trash bags to a couple of trucks to take back to North Middle School, the center of operations for East until we move into our new building in August.

The event may have served to bring some sort of closure to students, but it had the opposite effect on me. It was great to see the students who had been able to make it, but the overall atmosphere was depressing.

When I reached my apartment, I put the Martin Luther King biography on a table and for the past few weeks, it sat there. Finally, last night, 40 days after that last goodbye, I picked up the book to put with the rest of my collection which I had salvaged from my classroom.

As I lifted it, I saw what I thought was a bookmark, but upon closer examination, I realized it was an envelope. I opened the letter and started reading.

One of my eighth graders had written a goodbye message, one which mentioned many things that happened in the class and even made mention of my status as one of those privileged few who only has a birthday once every four years.

It ended this way:

"I hope you keep teaching until you're 25 (or 100, since you are really only 13 ¾). I'm so glad I got to have a teacher like you! I hope you have had as good of a year as I have. I will come back and visit someday to check in on my favorite writing teacher."

It was just one letter, but at that moment, it was the one letter I needed, closure on the school year that never ended.

JOPLIN TORNADO MEMORIAL SERVICE

"WE ARE NOT A PEOPLE WITHOUT HOPE. WE ARE PEOPLE FROM WHOM HOPE AND LIGHT AND LIFE SHINES TO THE ENDS OF THE EARTH."

- REV. AARON BROWN

T EXT OF REV. AARON BROWN'S SPEECH
SUNDAY, MAY 29, 2011

FATHER JUSTIN MONAGHAN, ST. MARY'S CATHOLIC CHURCH:

Heavenly Father, we take time to pause, reflect, and pray. Amidst the pain and heart of this devastation we have no doubt about your presence among us. You are infusing in each of us from near and afar a strength and resilience that is a special gift. You are calling our already close-knit community to new heights and determination and purpose. We hear the mission you have entrusted to us, and with your help we will put our hands to the plow. We are grateful for the support you are sending us and for the backing of our governor and state and for the enormous support from our president and our country at this time of renewal and restoration. Father, we open to your will. Amen.

Please be seated.

REV. RANDY GARRIS, COLLEGE HEIGHTS CHRISTIAN CHURCH:

Welcome and thank you for coming to today's memorial service.

Customarily, a greeting would include such words as "ladies and gentlemen" and "honored guests." But when there has been deep shared pain, when a community has suffered greatly and cried much together, and when the compassion and the kindness extended to one another has gone far beyond the scope of words, a more tender language than "honored guests" or "ladies and gentlemen" is heard. Words like "friends" and "neighbors" and "family" and "brothers and sisters." Words like "us." That's who gathers here today with us.

Thank you for your coming. Thank you for your role in each other's lives. Thank you for what you mean to one another.

A prayer which was led by Father Justin Monaghan who by the grace of God in a stout bathtub survived the destruction of the church of St. Mary's, a congregation of the Lord, on 26th Street. And physically and metaphorically the cross still stands.

(APPLAUSE)

There's a three-fold purpose to this gathering. The first is to grieve. The loss of even one human life is a tragedy. And we have lost scores.

We also gather to pray God's blessings as we rebuild our lives, asking God to lead us as we rebuild around the things that matter most. And we gather to celebrate the kindness that people have and are giving to one another.

Our foundation has not moved. It's still in the same place. We still have a solid place to stand. In Romans, the eighth chapter, Apostle Paul wrote these -- these words, "What, then, shall we say to these things? If God is for us, who can be against us? He who did not spare his own son, but gave him up for us all -- how will he not also, with him, graciously give us all thing?

Who shall separate us from the love of Christ? Shall tribulation or distress or persecution or famine or nakedness or danger or sword?

No, no. In all these things, we are more than conquerors through him who loved us. For I am confident that neither death nor life, nor angels nor rulers, nor anything present nor anything to come, nor powers, nor height or depth or anything else in all of creation will ever be able to separate us from the love of God in Christ Jesus, our Lord."

And now with the hymn of promise, the chancellor choir of the First United Methodist Church under the direction of Larry Sandburg (ph).

(CHOIR SINGING)

(APPLAUSE)

GARRIS:

Pastor Aaron Brown has been a good friend of the four-state area, a faithful partner in the gospel, and a shepherd of St. Paul's United Methodist Church. It, too, is a congregation that has lost much, including its worship center. He'll have our message this afternoon.

REV. AARON BROWN, ST. PAUL'S UNITED METHODIST CHURCH:

We're all trying to -- trying to process our stories and understand them in the context of what's happened, and I thought I'd take the liberty of telling you about mine about Sunday. Our family lives south of the city of Joplin. And after the tornado, I drove as far as I could into town and ran to the home of one of my closest friends. His house was gone but he and his family were safe.

From there, I was able to run to our church on 26th and Monroe, and found that about a third of it was gone, and I just had to know if everybody inside was safe. And there was one person in the church at the time the tornado hit, and she was safe. She hid under a dishwasher in our kitchen.

I went out to the street and what I saw was that people were just running. I didn't know what else to do, so I just ran alongside people and I said, "Can I help you find somebody?" And I dug through houses. And I prayed with a young couple whose friends didn't make it out of their house. And across the street from there, there were two elderly people that had died in their own backyard. I don't know their names.

But there was just a lot of running and digging and hoping and praying. That's what I remember.

I got called back to the church and the kids' wing of our church miraculously was still standing and it became a triage center. It's ironic, the classrooms that the children had played that morning, laughed around and learned about Jesus around, they became the place where wounds were being treated, and broken bones were being set, and emergency surgeries were being performed. Tables where kids had been making crafts a few hours earlier became beds of comfort and rest for the wounded.

We have all spent the last seven days looking for family and friends. We've all had of moments of unbelievable relief at hearing somebody's voice, and we've all had those moments of heart-sickening pain and hearing that somebody that we know didn't make it.

Late Friday night, I deliver the news to Mark and Trisha Norton that their son Will, his body had been identified. Eighteen years old, absolutely overflowing with life and faith. He had just graduated from high school hours before he was killed. Will is one of -- from what I've heard recently -- one of 142.

What is the word of comfort for us today? The word of comfort today for Will's family and all of those grieving comes from the God of the universe, the God who took human form and walked among us. He suffered. He knows what it's like for us when we suffer.

And Jesus said this. He said, "Do not let your hearts be troubled. Trust in God. Trust also in me."

He said, "In my father's house, there are many rooms. If it were not so, I would haven't told you."

He said, "I'm going to prepare a place for you. And if I go and prepare a place for you, I will come back and take you to be with me, so that you also can be where I am."

He said, "Before long, the world will not see me anymore but you will see me. And because I live you also will live."

And then he also says, there's few verses later, he says, "Peace I leave with you, my peace I give to you. I do not give as the world gives, so do not let your hearts be troubled and do not be afraid."

To these families who died, I think God is saying right now is death does not get the last word. I think God is saying to those families right now, this is what I wanted you to see in the resurrection of Jesus, that death doesn't win ever. Even when you think it does —

(APPLAUSE)

God is saying to you families who lost someone, even if it looks like death wins, it doesn't get the last word. Life wins. Life wins.

(APPLAUSE)

And I'll be honest. I don't know the faith stories of all those that have died. I don't know their faith stories.

But I know this -- that God's grace is wider than we can ever imagine, that heaven is real, and that this life is not the only life that we see.

I need to be honest and confess, some of us are asking, why? Why did God do this? Why did god allow this, so much death so, much destruction?

But, listen -- Jesus never promised to protect us from the storms of life. He never promised that life would be easy or convenient if we chose to follow him. In fact, almost all of his disciples, they were tortured to death.

What he did promise was very simple and powerful: to be with us. To be with us through the storm, to be with us as we grieve, to be with us as we stand at the grave site of our loved ones, to be with us and listen to us and guide us. And our challenge is: will we let him?

As hard as it may be, pray, as hard as it may be, talk to God. As hard as it may be, listen to his words. Let him love you. Let him love you.

Listen, God didn't do this to Joplin to punish us. Read the book. Jesus took our punishment for us. Read the book.

(APPLAUSE)

This happened -- this happened because life on this side of eternity is unpredictable. It's chaotic and it's broken. God says this, "For God so loved the world he gave his one and only son and he hasn't stopped loving the world."

You may wonder at times, but the fact is that God loves you and God loves Joplin and God is walking through this tragedy today and he will make a way where it seems like there is no way. You know, when Jesus was crucified, everybody -- I mean, everybody, they thought it was the end. The disciples had forgotten everything that he told them, that their world had come crashing down around them. There was this eerie darkness that covered the land. And for parts of three days, there was no hope.

But then, but then -- then Easter. Death is swallowed up in victory. Light crushes the darkness. Life wins.

Life won then. And life wins now. And now, what do we do?

We get busy. Jesus didn't come back from the grave just to point us to heaven. He came back from the grave to give us a mission that those who call on his name would be the light of the world. His mission is for us to get busy, get busy serving, get busy rebuilding our city which I love.

And by the way, I think it is the center of the universe right here in Joplin, Missouri.

(APPLAUSE)

Let's get busy. Let's get busy loving more deeply than we ever have loved. Let's get busy taking care -- you get busy taking care of your soul. Get busy connecting to God, the God who knows you by name and loves you more than you could ever imagine or believe.

And for those of you who have lost loved ones, get busy living out their legacy. They may have lost their lives, but none of them would want you to stop living yours. Get busy living.

We are not a people without hope. We are people from whom hope and light and life shines to the ends of the earth because God is good all the time. And all the time, God is good.

(APPLAUSE)

In the name of Jesus, the Lord of life, and the Lord of light, and the Lord of hope, and the Lord of new beginnings, that is the good news, amen.

JOPLIN TORNADO
MEMORIAL SERVICE
"WHAT OUR NATION HAS WITNESSED THIS WEEK IS THE SPIRIT OF JOPLIN, MISSOURI. AND WE ARE HUMBLED AND AWED BY IT."
- MISSOURI GOVERNOR JAY NIXON

T EXT OF GOVERNOR JAY NIXON'S SPEECH
SUNDAY, MAY 29, 2011

Thank you, Pastor Gariss. To the families of those who were killed and injured; to the families of those who are still unaccounted for; to the people of Joplin who have endured this terrible tragedy; to the thousands of Missourians and citizens across the nation who have opened their hearts to help us heal; to the hundreds of firefighters and emergency responders who came without hesitation to climb over piles of rubble in search of survivors; to Pastor Garris, Pastor Brown, Father Monaghan, Lieutenant Colonel Kilmer, and the wonderful choir from First United Methodist Church of Joplin; and to President Obama who is with us today – thank you all for coming.

Missouri State Photo

It is an honor to be here, joining the thousands of Missourians observing this special Day of Prayer. We stand on hallowed ground, to bear witness to the destructive power of Nature and the invincible power of faith.

We have come to mourn what the storm has taken from us, to seek comfort in community, and to draw strength from God to build anew.

It seems inconceivable that just one week ago, the people of Joplin were going about their daily lives, doing the ordinary things people do on a Sunday evening: Cooking supper. Watching TV.

Walking the dog. Attending their sons' and daughters' graduation. And then came the whirlwind. Nearly a mile wide and six miles long, with 200-mile-an-hour winds – churning and roaring, tossing cars and toppling trees, pounding homes, businesses, schools and churches to rubble.

But that storm, the likes of which we have never seen, has brought forward a spirit of resilience –the likes of which we've also never seen.

What our nation has witnessed this week is the spirit of Joplin, Missouri. And we are humbled and awed by it.

You have given "Love thy neighbor" new meaning. The parable of the Good Samaritan in Luke, Chapter 10: verses 25 to 37, begins with a conversation between Jesus and a student of religious law. It starts with a legal question, and ends with a moral imperative.

The student asks Jesus, "What shall I do to inherit eternal life?" And Jesus turns the question around and asks: "What is written in the law?"

And the student, who is well-versed in the Talmud and the Torah, replies: "Thou shalt love the Lord thy God with all thy heart, with all thy soul, with all thy strength and with all thy mind. "And thou shalt love thy neighbor as thyself."

And Jesus replies: "Thou hast answered right. This do, and thou shalt live."

But then the student, wanting greater clarity than the law provided, asks Jesus, "And who is my neighbor?" And Jesus tells him the story of the Good Samaritan.

From that parable, our charge is crystal clear. Good Samaritans do not pass by those who are suffering and in need. They show their compassion with action.

In Joplin, you see Good Samaritans everywhere you turn. You see them over in the gym at this university, where hundreds of volunteers make sandwiches every day.

You seem them passing out blankets and pillows, sunscreen and flashlights to our neighbors made homeless by the whirlwind.

You need a flashlight. Because it gets pretty dark here at night – especially when you're standing in the street, staring at the lonely pile of matchsticks that was once your home.

If you had been in the ER at St. John's Mercy Medical Center last Sunday evening, mere moments after the tornado struck, you would have seen Good Samaritans rushing frantically to reach the wounded and the dying.

Shattered glass and bleeding patients everywhere, water and gas spewing from burst pipes, one doctor stumbled through the darkness with a flashlight in his teeth, following the wail of a wounded child.

You see Good Samaritans at every checkpoint in the destruction zone, where police officers and citizen soldiers of the Missouri National Guard keep watch over wet socks, teddy bears, cherished wedding photos and crumpled wheelchairs – all that is left of our neighbors' worldly goods.

You see them in the churchyard, men sleeping on cots under the stars, after driving all night to get here from Tuscaloosa. These men were so touched, so moved by the kindness of strangers in their hour of

need, that they just had to come to Joplin. Good Samaritans – on a mission from God.

God has chosen us for a mission, too: to grieve together, to comfort one another, to be patient with one another, to strengthen one another – and to build Joplin anew. Not just to build it back the way it was, but to make it an even better place.

We know that all those who perished here are already in an even better place. But for us, the living, there is work to do. God says: "Show me." Show me.

The people of Missouri were born for this mission. We are famously stubborn and self-reliant.

Practical. Impatient. But whatever may divide us, we always come together in crisis.

And once our resolve is set, no storm, no fire or flood can turn us from our task.

In the pale hushed stillness before dawn, when the chainsaws have fallen silent, if you listen very closely – you can hear the sound of that resolve, like a tiny silver hammer tapping, tapping, tapping inside our heads.

In the days to come, the satellite trucks will pack up, leave town and move on. Joplin's story will disappear from the front pages. But the tragedy will not disappear from our lives.

We will still be here in Joplin – together – preparing for the long journey out of darkness into light. And we will need more hands, more tools, more Good Samaritans at every step.

This tragedy has changed us forever. This community will never be the same. We will never be the same.

The grief we share at this moment is overwhelming. That sorrow will always be part of us, a stone upon our hearts. But those we love – those we lost – are safe with God, and safe in our hearts. And in our hearts, the joy they gave us lives on and on. Nothing can take that from us.

We can, and we will, heal. We've already begun. Together, we can, and we will, rebuild – upon a granite foundation of faith. What we build on this hallowed ground will be a living monument to those we lost: mothers, fathers, our precious children.

It will be a monument to the will and determination of the hundreds of men, women and yes, even children, who helped their neighbors dig out of the ruins – a monument to the search and rescue crews who came swiftly to aid the quick, and the dead.

By God's grace, we will restore this community. And by God's grace, we will renew our souls.

One year from today, Joplin will look different. And more different still in two years, and in three years, and in five.

But as the years pass, the moral of our story will be the same: love thy neighbor. May God bless.

Joplin Tornado Memorial Service

"There's no doubt in my mind that Joplin will rebuild. And as President, I can promise you your country will be there with you every single step of the way."

— Barack Obama,
President of the United States

Text of President Barack Obama's speech
Sunday, May 29, 2011

THE PRESIDENT:
Thank you. Thank you so much. Please, please be seated.

AUDIENCE MEMBER: I love you, Obama!

THE PRESIDENT: I love Joplin! (Applause.) I love Joplin.

AUDIENCE MEMBER: We love Joplin!

THE PRESIDENT: We love Joplin. (Applause.)

Thank you, Governor, for that powerful message, but more importantly, for being here with and for your people every step of the way.

Official White House Photo by Peter Souza

147

We are grateful to you, to Reverend Gariss, Father Monaghan. I'm so glad you got in that tub. (Laughter and applause.) To Reverend Brown for that incredibly powerful message. (Applause.)

To Senator Claire McCaskill, who's been here, and Congressman Billy Long; Mayor Woolston. To Craig Fugate. It doesn't get a lot of attention, but he heads up FEMA, our emergency response at the federal level. He's been going from Tuscaloosa to Joplin and everywhere in between tirelessly doing outstanding work. We're grateful for him. Gail McGovern, the President of the National Red Cross, which has contributed mightily to the rebuilding efforts here.

Most of all, to the family and friends of all those who've been lost and all those who've been affected.

Today we gather to celebrate the lives of those we've lost to the storms here in Joplin and across the Midwest, to keep in our prayers those still missing, to mourn with their families, to stand together during this time of pain and trial.

And as Reverend Brown alluded to, the question that weighs on us at a time like this is: Why? Why our town? Why our home? Why my son, or husband, or wife, or sister, or friend? Why?

We do not have the capacity to answer. We can't know when a terrible storm will strike, or where, or the severity of the devastation that it may cause. We can't know why we're tested with the loss of a loved one, or the loss of a home where we've lived a lifetime.

Missouri State Photo

These things are beyond our power to control. But that does not mean we are powerless in the face of adversity. How we respond when the storm strikes is up to us. How we live in the aftermath of tragedy and heartache, that's within our control. And it's in these moments, through our actions, that we often see the glimpse of what makes life worth living in the first place.

In the last week, that's what Joplin has not just taught Missouri, not just taught America, but has taught the world. I was overseas in the aftermath of the storm, and had world leaders coming up to me saying, let the people of Joplin know we are with them; we're thinking about them; we love them. (Applause.)

148

Because the world saw how Joplin responded. A university turned itself into a makeshift hospital. (Applause.) Some of you used your pickup trucks as ambulances, carrying the injured -- (applause) -- on doors that served as stretchers. Your restaurants have rushed food to people in need. Businesses have filled trucks with donations. You've waited in line for hours to donate blood to people you know, but also to people you've never met. And in all this, you have lived the words of Scripture:

We are troubled on every side, yet not distressed;
we are perplexed, but not in despair;
Persecuted, but not forsaken;
cast down, but not destroyed;

As the governor said, you have shown the world what it means to love thy neighbor. You've banded together. You've come to each other's aid. You've demonstrated a simple truth: that amid heartbreak and tragedy, no one is a stranger. Everybody is a brother. Everybody is a sister. (Applause.) We can all love one another.

As you move forward in the days ahead, I know that rebuilding what you've lost won't be easy. I just walked through some of the neighborhoods that have been affected, and you look out at the landscape, and there have to be moments where you just say, where to begin? How to start? There are going to be moments where after the shock has worn off, you feel alone. But there's no doubt in my mind what the people of this community can do. There's no doubt in my mind that Joplin will rebuild. And as President, I can promise you your country will be there with you every single step of the way. (Applause.) We will be with you every step of the way. We're not going anywhere. (Applause.) The cameras may leave. The spotlight may shift. But we will be with you every step of the way until Joplin is restored and this community is back on its feet. We're not going anywhere. (Applause.)

That is not just my promise; that's America's promise. It's a promise I make here in Joplin; it's a promise I made down in Tuscaloosa, or in any of the communities that have been hit by these devastating storms over the last few weeks.

Now, there have been countless acts of kindness and selflessness in recent days. We've already heard the record of some of that. But perhaps none are as inspiring as what took place when the storm was bearing down on Joplin, threatening an entire community with utter destruction. And in the face of winds that showed no mercy, no regard for human life, that did not discriminate by race or faith or background, it was ordinary people, swiftly tested, who said, "I'm willing to die right now so that someone else might live."

It was the husband who threw himself over his wife as their house came apart around them. It was the mother who shielded her young son.

It was Dean Wells, a husband and father who loved to sing and whistle in his church choir. Dean was working a shift at the Home Depot, managing the electrical department, when the siren rang out. He sprang into action, moving people to safety. Over and over again, he went back for others, until a wall came down on top of him. In the end, most of the building was destroyed, but not where Dean had directed his coworkers and his customers.

There was a young man named Christopher Lucas who was 26 years old. Father of two daughters; third daughter on the way. Just like any other night, Christopher was doing his job as manager on duty at Pizza Hut. And then he heard the storm coming.

It was then when this former sailor quickly ushered everybody into the walk-in freezer. The only problem was, the freezer door wouldn't stay closed from the inside. So as the tornado bore down on this small storefront on Range Line Road, Christopher left the freezer to find a rope or a cord or anything to hold the door shut. He made it back just in time, tying a piece of bungee cord to the handle outside,

wrapping the other end around his arm, holding the door closed with all his might.

And Christopher held it as long as he could, until he was pulled away by the incredible force of the storm. He died saving more than a dozen people in that freezer. (Applause.)

You see, there are heroes all around us, all the time. They walk by us on the sidewalk, and they sit next to us in class. They pass us in the aisle wearing an orange apron. They come to our table at a restaurant and ask us what we'd like to order.

Just as we can't know why tragedy strikes in the first place, we may never fully understand where these men and women find the courage and strength to do what they did. What we do know is that in a split-second moment where there's little time for internal reflection or

150

debate, the actions of these individuals were driven by love -- love for a family member, love for a friend, or just love for a fellow human being.

That's good to know. In a world that can be cruel and selfish, it's this knowledge -- the knowledge that we are inclined to love one another, that we're inclined to do good, to be good -- that causes us to take heart. We see with fresh eyes what's precious and so fragile and so important to us. We put aside our petty grievances and our minor disagreements. We see ourselves in the hopes and hardships of others. And in the stories of people like Dean and people like Christopher, we remember that each us contains reserves of resolve and compassion. There are heroes all around us, all the time.

And so, in the wake of this tragedy, let us live up to their example -- to make each day count -- (applause) -- to live with the sense of mutual regard -- to live with that same compassion that they demonstrated in their final hours. We are called by them to do everything we can to be worthy of the chance that we've been given to carry on.

I understand that at a memorial yesterday for Dean, his wife decided to play a recording of Dean whistling a song he loved -- Amazing Grace. The lyrics are a fitting tribute to what Joplin has been through.

> *Through many dangers, toils and snares*
> *I have already come;*
> *'Tis Grace that brought me safe thus far*
> *and Grace will lead me home…*
> *Yea, when this flesh and heart shall fail,*
> *And mortal life shall cease,*
> *I shall possess within the veil,*
> *A life of joy and peace.*

May those we've lost know peace, and may Grace guide the people of Joplin home. God bless you, and God bless the United States of America. Thank you.

NATIONAL WEATHER SERVICE REPORT ON THE MAY 22ND JOPLIN TORNADO

PUBLIC INFORMATION STATEMENT ISSUED MONDAY, JUNE 13, 2011, BY THE NATIONAL WEATHER SERVICE OFFICE IN SPRINGFIELD, MO.

...UPDATE ON THE JOPLIN DEVASTATING EF-5 TORNADO...

"Date...May 22, 2011. Maximum EF-scale rating...EF-5. Estimated maximum wind speed...in excess of 200 mph. Estimated maximum path width...3/4 to 1 mileEstimated damage path length...22.1 miles. Approximate start point...1/2 mile southwest of the intersection of JJ Highway (south Central City Road) and West 32nd street (Newton Road). Approximate end point...4.8 miles north northeast of Granby, Missouri. Start time...5:34 p.m. End time...6:12 p.m. Fatalities...150+ Injuries...1000+

This preliminary information was determined by a National Weather Service survey team and is subject to change pending final review of the event and publication in National Weather Service Storm Data.

Through June 3, 2011, the National Weather Service damage assessment team has had more time to collect additional information to better detail some of the most severe damage and assign other lower-end EF scale ratings to other portions of the Joplin tornado track. However, the six-mile track within the city of Joplin was by far the most intense and devastating.

The total path length was about 22.1 miles long. This marks the first EF-5 tornado in southwest Missouri since records have been maintained for such events. Our deepest thoughts and prayers continue for the excellent people of Joplin and to those that are not with us today. God bless Joplin.

Future updates for this historical EF-5 tornado will be available on our web page at weather.gov/springfield. Local and national print and electronic media groups in Joplin and Springfield and across the country have posted numerous stories, video and photos on their respective web pages concerning this very tragic event. Much about this event has also been captured through social media.

To arrive at an EF-5 rating for a portion of this tornado, it took the National Weather Service damage survey team a couple of days. Additional time was also spent with several wind and structural engineers from various government and private organizations. I want to thank each group for their expert assistance. A large volume of data and high-resolution aerial flights have documented the damage from this event. In the coming weeks and months, this event will be examined in greater detail.

The violent nature and destruction this tornado caused was indicative of past F-5 and EF-5 tornadoes including the recent southeast United States EF-5 tornadoes. Some of the damage indictors used to rate a portion of this tornado track an EF-5 was the sheer destruction of well-built homes and businesses swept from foundations, crushed in place or piled into other destroyed structures. Numerous vehicles of various sizes and weight including buses and truck trailers being tossed over 200 yards to a few blocks and some crushed beyond recognition. Some vehicles were compressed and wrapped around trees, and some were rolled into balls. Main steel roof support trusses were rolled like paper, and main support beams twisted or curved. Trees totally debarked and denuded. In one parking lot west of the Home Depot, asphalt was torn from its base.

Wind rowing or debris packing of heavy building and other materials was evident in several areas along the most destructive portion of the path. There were also some interesting features such a chair with four legs embedded in an exterior wall with not much damage, and a rubber hose impaled through a tree.

Over the coming months and years, here is much more to be examined in great detail by meteorologists, structural engineers, wind engineers, architects, city planners, builders and social scientists. I hope their efforts and findings are employed to make all communities weather-ready and to save lives.

The following damage assessment account of the track of the tornado and associated wind strength along various portions of the track are limited to the areas the survey team was able to examine before making a final rating, along with estimating the length and width of this deadly tornado. High resolution and civil air patrol aerial surveys provide a complete look at each and every damage point, and also provides a full view of the entire track.

Estimated through May 31, 6954 homes were destroyed, 359 homes had major damage and 516 homes had minor damage. Numerous small to large businesses were either destroyed or damaged. Several public buildings were either destroyed or damaged. This included several churches, elementary schools, high school, vocational school, two fire stations, a Wal-Mart, Home Depot, large construction company with heavy equipment, nursing home, banks, Dillon's and other grocery stores, Cummins building, electric sub-station, major cell

and power transmission towers, and numerous one; two- and three-level apartment buildings.

In the coming days and weeks, more detailed and accurate lists will be available from local, state and federal officials. This does not include the additional homes and structures affected by the tornado outside the city limits.

The initial damage was about one-half mile southwest of the junction of JJ Highway (south central city road) and West 32nd Street (Newton Road) where several large trees were toppled.

This initial portion of the track was rated EF-0.

Storm chasers and spotters reported seeing multiple vortices rotating around the parent circulation near the beginning of this tornado. This was documented by

154

various video and photos from several locations, and through eyewitness and spotter reports. Their information and more scientific accounts concerning this tornado are posted at various web sites and social media groups and through standard media outlets.

From the initial damage location the tornado became stronger and widened some as it reached EF-1 strength while moving east-northeast to just south of the intersection of 32nd.

And south Alfalfa Street, from here to south Country Club Drive...numerous trees were toppled and uprooted...power poles were snapped off...and several outbuildings were damaged just south and along 32nd street. Numerous trees continued to be uprooted and power poles snapped as the tornado moved east along 32nd street.

From just to the north of 32nd street from South Ashwood Lane east to Even Avenue, Heartland Avenue and South Country Club Drive, the tornado was about one-quarter mile wide and causing EF-1 to low-end EF-3 damage to well-built brick and wood homes. Roofs were removed and some homes destroyed with walls missing and portions swept away. Damage to homes and outbuildings was also occurring south of 32nd.

At about Catnip and 32nd...the tornado crossed 32nd and continued east-northeast. Once again, numerous trees and power poles were destroyed. On South Day Road, several homes were severely damaged. From Iron Gate Road east to Schifferdecker Avenue, numerous well-built homes had roofs and walls removed or totally destroyed. Vehicles were tumbled into some homes. Some of this damage was rated in the EF-2 to low-end EF-3 categories. Just west of Schifferdecker Avenue some low-end EF-4 damage was evident.

As the tornado crossed Schifferdecker Avenue just south of Sunset Drive, it started to widen more and increase in intensity. The forward speed of the tornado through most of Joplin was less than twenty miles per hour. The tornado moved east-northeast crossing 29th and Winfield Avenue. Numerous homes, businesses, and medical art buildings were destroyed by high-end EF-4 to low end EF-5 wind speeds. Vehicles were tossed from parking lots and steel-framed roofs were lifted and wrapped around trees and other objects. Some vehicles were crushed and some flattened and wrapped around trees. Concrete walls were toppled and moved several feet and also crushed into foundations.

By the time it moved to 26th and McClelland Blvd, the tornado was moving east and causing EF-4 and some low end EF-5 damage. In a medical arts parking lot just west of St. Johns hospital, 200 to 300 pound concrete parking stops attached by rebar into the asphalt were lifted and tossed up to 60 yards. A large sturdy concrete step and floor structure leading to a completely destroyed medical arts building was deflected upward several inches and cracked. Metal trusses from some of the buildings were rolled up like paper and concrete walls toppled. Some steel main support beams were curved, twisted or distorted.

Debris piling or wind rowing was also evident along some portions of the main damage path.

EF-3 to EF-5 damage continued to just east of Range Line Road. The outer portions of the track were rated from EF-1 to EF-3 damage.

At St. John's, more parking stops were tossed several feet. Numerous vehicles of various sizes and weight were tossed several hundred yards. Some vehicles were crushed beyond recognition. Some St. John's medical workers and people affected by the tornado could not locate their vehicles. A St. John's medical vehicle was tossed north of 26th, and the life flight helicopter was blown off the roof and destroyed.

The St John's structure had just about every window blown out on three sides. Once the wind was inside the interior...there was severe destruction of walls and ceilings on every floor. A portion of the top roof was removed or heavily damaged. It was also reported a portion of the hospital's foundation underpinning system was compromised. This has not been confirmed as of yet. However, engineers have determined the entire structure will need to be taken down and replaced with a new building.

North of St. John's and 26th, Cunningham Park was leveled. Large old hardwood trees were toppled and uprooted, and structures destroyed. Hundreds of homes north and east of this area were leveled or crushed.

East of McClelland Boulevard and along 26th, the tornado was now at full strength and over three-quarters of a mile wide. Hundreds of homes were totally destroyed and some swept from their foundations or crushed. Concrete porches were lifted and tossed several yards. Numerous vehicles were tossed into neighboring homes or across to other streets. Many were also rolled up and crushed. This was the case along the rest of the primary damage path to just east of Range Line Road.

Also along most of the primary damage track, it was very common to find boards, limbs and even small twigs embedded into wood siding and stucco walls. In some cases, even cardboard was embedded into stucco walls.

This occurred at the high school.

The wood framing from most homes disintegrated into small pieces. This caused thousands of deadly projectiles. Many open fields were covered with wood and other material, including steel beams, embedded into the ground like tossed spears. At one location, the four legs of a wooden chair had been embedded into a wall.

As the tornado moved slightly east-northeast along and north of 26th, it destroyed many businesses. The most intense track started shifting north and east at 26th and Moffat Avenue. St. Mary's church and school on 25th were severely damaged. The only thing left standing was the steel cross and a portion of the metal structure.

The tornado crossed 25th and South Main Street causing total destructions to homes, apartments and businesses. Three-story apartment complexes had their top two floors removed. Other two story complexes were partially leveled.

As the tornado reached the Franklin Technical Center and Joplin High School near 20th and Indiana, it continued to show EF-4 and EF-5 strength. The newer section of the high school was destroyed and outer walls of the old section were severely damaged. The technical center was also destroyed. A bus had been tossed on top of the destroyed bus garage just to the west of the technical center.

Based on how steel fence posts around the high school's ball field were bent and positioned, the center of the tornado may have crossed this area. East of the high school on Indiana, a large church was destroyed.

The main force of the tornado continued total destruction three-quarters of a mile wide centered between 26th and East 20th street. A bank was totally destroyed with portions of the walls swept from the foundation. The only thing left in place was the concrete and

steel vault. To the east of the bank, two-story apartments were just about leveled. The Dillon's grocery store had significant roof and exterior wall damage.

The tornado continued eastward between 22nd and 20th where it crossed Connecticut Avenue. The damage continued to mount with hundreds more homes and businesses destroyed. When the tornado reached south Range Line Road and 20th, it destroyed several well-constructed buildings along with the Academy Sports, Wal-Mart, Home Depot, Pepsi distribution building, Cummins building, a large construction firm located east of Home Depot, and tore apart a large apartment complex east of Wal-Mart. Two large cell towers were toppled northward on top of the apartment complex. A couple of Wal-Mart tractor-trailers were tossed over 200 yards on top of the debris of what was left of the Pepsi distribution building.

A parking lot west of the Home Depot had scoured asphalt. Vehicles in the Home Depot were tossed several hundred yards, one into the Home Depot.

From South Range Line Road to South Duquesne road north and south along 20th street numerous warehouse-style facilities and many more homes and businesses suffered severe damage or destroyed. Along this track, the tornado was just over one-half mile wide and producing some EF-4 to EF-3 damage.

Near South Duquesne Road to near the Interstate 44 and 249/71 junction, the tornado began turning right and moving southeast. However, EF-2 to low-end EF-3 damage was evident along 20th street east to Markwalk Drive. As it passed across Interstate 44, damage was related more to a high-end EF-2 rating. Cars and trucks were blown off the interstate. Interstate 44 was closed for several hours to remove those cars and trucks.

Across and east of Interstate 44 and to where it lifted about 4.8 miles north northeast of Granby, Missouri. The tornado continued to damage homes, trailers, and outbuildings and topple trees. At this part of the track, the tornado was about 500 yards wide and produced low-end EF-1 to EF-0 damage.

For reference, the enhanced Fujita scale classifies tornadoes into the following categories:

EF0...wind speeds 65 to 85 mph.
EF1...wind speeds 86 to 110 mph.
EF2...wind speeds 111 to 135 mph.
EF3...wind speeds 136 to 165 mph.
EF4...wind speeds 166 to 200 mph.
EF5...wind speeds greater than 200 mph.

To conclude, from the national weather staff at Springfield, Missouri, we offer our deepest condolences and heartfelt sympathy to all that were affected by this devastating event.

Our thoughts and prayers will be with those that lost their lives during this tragic event, and for all citizens of Joplin affected by this tornado. I offer my deepest thanks and gratitude to emergency management, public safety officials, law enforcement and the many volunteers who are assisting the citizens of Joplin.

I also offer my thanks to all those that assisted our office staff during several days of damage surveys. The tragic 1974 tornado outbreak launched the research for new technology to better provide the public with more lead time on tornadoes. For the most part, we are achieving that goal. This, and the recent late April events in the Southeast, will certainly launch another era of research, especially in the science of how people respond to warnings."

MIC - William Davis
National Weather Service
Springfield, Missouri

IN MEMORY OF LIVES LOST
OBITUARIES

JOSE ALVAREZ
(The following information is taken from JoplinMemorial.com.)

José O. Alvarez received his bachelor's degree in Anthropology from Colombia National University, master's degree in Hispanic Studies, and Ph.D. in Latin American Literature, from Florida International University.

He is a former editor of one of the first literary online magazine of University of Miami, and a pioneer in the application of educational online platforms like Blackboard, WebCT, and Moodle. He has a genuine enthusiasm and commitment on finding solutions to the digital divide problem.

He was a Professor with the Department of Modern Languages in Miami-Dade College, University of Miami, and Florida International University. Dr. Alvarez published five volumes of his students' short stories. Dr. Alvarez was the author of the books "Cuentos de vida, muerte y resurrección," "Vivir del cuento", "Poética de la brevedad en Borges." He also created the first online Anthology of Latin American Literature, the first online Short Stories Anthology, movie reviews, literary reviews, and has participated in several short stories anthologies, International Book Fairs, and lectures in several countries. He was nominated "Faculty of the Year 1999" by the Federation of Black Greeks, the Interfraternity Council, and the Panhellenic Association, and Excellence in Teaching Award Instructional Advancement Center 2000" of the University of Miami. José Alvarez was an assistant professor at Missouri Southern State University. He was teaching Spanish.

BILL and SARAH ANDERSON
(The following obituary information is taken from the Ozark Funeral Home website.)

William Austin "Bill" Anderson, 53, and Sarah Lee Anderson, 46, of Joplin, Missouri departed this life suddenly on Sunday evening, May 22, 2011 at their home from injuries sustained in the devastating Joplin tornado.

Sarah entered this life on April 20, 1965 in Phoenix, Arizona to the late Todd Dean and Lois (Faux) Sherfy. At age thirteen she moved with her family to Branson, Missouri. She graduated from Branson High School in 1983 and has resided in Joplin, Missouri since 1985. She was employed by the Joplin School District as a secretary at South Middle School for the last ten years.

On August 25, 1985 in Branson, Missouri, Bill and Sarah were united in marriage and to this union two children were born. They both enjoyed reading and were members of the 26th and Connecticut Church of Christ in Joplin, Missouri.

They are survived by their two children, Grace and Quinton Anderson both of the home. Bill is also survived by four siblings, Stuart Anderson of Neosho, Missouri, David Anderson of Tipton, Iowa, Marti Crawford of Granby, Missouri and Kay Anderson of Neosho, Missouri. Additional survivors for Sarah include her three siblings, John Sherfy of the state of Iowa, Sharon Sherfy of Branson, Missouri and Ellen Wiebelhaus of Waddell, Arizona. They are also survived by several nieces and nephews; as well as a host of other family and friends.

GRACE AQUINO
(The following obituary is taken from the Mason-Woodard Mortuary website.)

Grace Layug Aquino, age 46, of Joplin, Missouri, passed away on May 22, 2011, at Harmony Heights Baptist Church, from injuries sustained in the catastrophic tornado.

Grace was born on October 6, 1964 in Florida Blanca, Philippines, the daughter of Armando Layug and the late Elena Punzalan. She has been a resident of Joplin for the past nine years. She received a bachelor's degree in business. She was a member of Harmony Heights Baptist Church. She worked as a hostess for the China Pantry. Grace unselfishly covered and protected her twelve-year-old son during the tornado, and as a result his life was spared. She will be greatly missed by all of her family and friends.

She married Rizaldy Aquino on March 19, 1986 in the Philippines, and he survives. Additional survivors include her son, Malachi Jacob Aquino, of the home; two daughters, Divine Aquino, Overland Park, Ks., and Eunice Aquino, Manhattan, Ks.; three brothers, Cezar Layug, of Germany, Noel Layug, and Eugene Layug, both of the Philippines.; her twin sister, Divina Villaruel, of the Philippines; sister-in-law Liberty Nicholas and husband Bernard and family, Seattle, Wa.; great-aunts, Corazon Mangio and Ofelia Oakley; cousins, Leni and Robert Welch, Joplin, Lerma and Orlando Castaneda, Sacramento, Ca., Jerwin and Eden Signa, Joplin, Miranda and Perry Taylor, Joplin, Noreen Jean Smith, Ann & Robert Mathews, Joplin; many nieces and nephews; and her grand puppies, Orly and Klassy.

CYRUS ASH
(The following obituary is taken from the Parker Mortuary website.)

Cyrus Edward (Ed) Ash, age 87 of Joplin, passed away on May 22, 2011 from injuries sustained in a tornado.

Born September 21, 1923 in Monett, Missouri, he was a U.S. Navy Veteran of World War II. He worked in the receiving department of Lozier, from the first day the company located in Joplin and remained over 20 years, before retiring. He was an avid Joplin Flea Market dealer, and remained active there until the age of 83. He was a member of College Heights Christian Church. He was an expert billiards player and went fishing at Shoal Creek every evening to "unwind".

On December 28, 1941, he married Emma Landreth in Joplin. She survives.

Additional survivors include two daughters, Brenda Nichols and husband Danny of Carl Junction, Shirley Elliott and husband Norman of New Hampshire; four grandchildren, Chad, Matt, Lisa and J.W.; five great-grandchildren; two sisters, Maxine Latimer and Evelyn Leedy, both of Wichita, Kan.

Ed was preceded in death by two daughters, Helen Judith Ash in 1973, and Patricia Sue Miller in 2010; and three brothers, all of Kansas.

ROBERT BAKER
(The following obituary is taken from the Mason-Woodard Mortuary website.)

Robert W. Baker, age 54 of Joplin, Missouri passed away Sunday May 22, 2011 from injuries sustained in the Joplin tornado.

Robert was born April 23, 1957 in Michigan to John W. and Katherine (Sanders) Baker.

Robert worked at the parts desk for Cycle Connection. He married Sandra Woodworth; she survives.

Additional survivors include two daughters, Trisha Cortinas of Emperial, Missouri, and Brandy Baker state of Texas; two brothers, Kenneth Baker of Alto, Nm., and Daryl Baker of Joplin; two sisters, Shirley Randleman of Joplin and Jackie Beatty of Blue Springs, Missouri and four grandchildren.

BRUCE BAILLIE
(The following information came from the *Joplin Globe*.)

Bruce W. Baillie, 56, of Joplin, was a page designer for the *Joplin Globe* and the father of a college-age daughter. Born in British Columbia, he worked for several Canadian newspapers before buying a bed-and-breakfast in Sedona, Ariz. He later worked for the Benton County (Arkansas) Daily Record and joined the Globe in 2003.

ROB BATESON
(The following obituary is taken from the Parker Mortuary website.)

Robert E. "Rob" Bateson, Jr., age 47 of Joplin, has gone to be with His Lord and Savior as the result of injuries received in a tornado on May 22, 2011.

Born April 14, 1964 in Bowling Green, Ohio, he lived in Joplin most of his lifetime. A licensed master plumber, he was both self-employed and did some contract work. For the past eight months he was employed at Modine. A Christian, he was a member of Central Christian Center in Joplin.

Survivors include his parents, Karen and Dan Mitchell of Joplin, Robert E. Bateson, Sr. and Donna of Sevierville, Tenn.; three children, Eric Davis, Jamie Peavler and Mariah Bateson; three grandchildren; five sisters, Diane Wood and Jack of Miami, Okla., Teresa Worley of Neosho, Kim Kemp and Brian of Columbus, Ohio, Julie Hudson of Pineville, Missouri, Ruth Buxton and Curt of Webb City; two brothers, James T. Brummett and Eric A. Brummett; paternal grandmother, Thelma Mitchell of Webb City; many aunts, uncles, cousins and extended family.

Robert was loved by his family and he loved his family. Rob, we'll miss your beautiful smiling face and twinkling eyes…We love you so very much.

DORTHEY BELL

Dorthey C. Bell, age 88 of Joplin, died as a result of injuries received in a tornado on May 22, 2011.

She married Edwin M. Bell April 28, 1950, in Joplin. He died Sept. 29, 2000.

Survivors include three sons, David Bell, Joplin; Dan Bell, Plano, TX; Steve Bell, Fairfax, VA; and five grandchildren: Frances Bell, Florida; Ian Bell, Houston, TX; Lauren Bell, Plano, TX; and Christopher and Leanne Bell, Fairfax, VA. Born Oct. 15, 1922 in Barnsdell, OK, she had lived in Joplin for many years. She attended Joplin Junior College and graduated Pittsburg State Teachers College. Later she taught school and was a farm woman. She was a member of the Order of the Eastern Star and Central City Christian Church, and she was active in the Joplin Y. She enjoyed travel, bird-watching, reading, genealogy and water walking.

BARBARA BOYD

Barbara Boyd, 87, Joplin, was a resident of Greenbrier Nursing Home. She worked more than 20 years in the burn unit of a Veterans Administration hospital in Richmond, Va. She liked to crochet and belonged to the First Baptist Church in Joplin.

She is survived by two sons, two daughters, and six grandchildren.

LATHE BRADFIELD

(The following obituary is taken from the Parker Mortuary website.)

Lathe Edward Bradfield passed away at St. John's hospital on Sunday, May 22, 2011 during the tornado that swept through Joplin. He was a husband, father, grandfather, brother, and uncle. He was an avid fisherman in his youth and enjoyed all animals and children. He was Uncle Lathe to many and a stranger to none. He would often greet people with "hello friend", and he meant it.

He was proud of his service in the Army during WWII and was honorably discharged on December 25, 1946. He was injured in the war and received a purple heart.

He was a life-long member of the Teamster's Union and the Disabled American Veterans. He also belonged to the American Legion and the Veteran of Foreign War Organizations.

He married Florence Ellen Clifton in Columbus, Kansas on June 24, 1947. Lathe and Florence raised a family of two daughters and one son. They lived, laughed and cried together for 64 years.

Lathe worked as an auto mechanic all of his life. He spent a number of years at the old 408 Cab Company, at Joplin Police Station and he retired from Fleming Foods where he worked as their head mechanic for a number of years. He was sent to Indiana to a technical institute on repairing Thermo King units. He worked every day of his life and then would often come home and work on cars or build on his home. He would offer his help to anyone that needed it.

He is survived by his wife, Florence Ellen Clifton Bradfield; his daughter, Sharon Bradfield of the home, his daughter, Karen Bradfield and Ernie Blackford; his son Steven Bradfield and daughter-in-law Shelley Bradfield; his two grandchildren, Samantha Bradfield and Cole Bradfield, who were his pride and joy. We miss him dearly every day.

Lathe was the oldest of six brothers and two sisters. All survive him; Leroy and Earleen Bradfield, James and Joanne Burtrum, Bill and Mary Burtrum, Ray and Jolene Burtrum, Rex Burtrum, John Burtrum, Etta Morgan and Mary and Pauly Hembree, Cecil Weber, a cousin who grew up with Lathe and was always regarded as a brother.

BURNICE BRESEE
(The following information was taken from the Mason-Woodard Mortuary website.)

Burnice M. Bresee, age 91, of Joplin, Missouri, passed away Wednesday, June 22, 2011, at McCune Brooks Hospital from complications with her health following the Joplin tornado.

She was born Dec. 14, 1919, in Springfield, Missouri, to Edward A. and Mary (Everly) Alexander.

She was a homemaker. Burnice was a member of Christ Point Church in Joplin.

She married Willie Bresee Sr. on May 24, 1940, in Joplin. He preceded her in death on Nov. 10, 1980.

Survivors include two sons, Willie Bresee Jr. and wife, Pat, of Carl Junction, and Homer Bresee and wife, Merna, of Rockford, Ill.; four daughters, Norma Jean Enlow and husband, Charles, of Joplin, Bernice Irene Smith and husband, Gene, of Joplin, Margie Goetz and husband, Stanley, of Joplin, and Teresa Thomas and husband, Ben, of Seneca; one daughter-in-law, Marsha Bresee, of Joplin; one sister, Wilma Bresee, of Galena, Kan.; 18 grandchildren; 34 great-grandchildren; and four great-great-grandchildren. She was preceded in death by one son, Bobby Bresee on April 24, 1991; one daughter, Donna Bresee on Jan. 25, 1998; four brothers; and two grandchildren.

RAMONA BRIDGEFORD
(The following obituary is taken from the Campbell-Biddlecome Funeral Home website.)

Ramona (Pevey) Bridgeford passed into eternal rest May 22, 2011 from injuries sustained in the tornado that devastated Joplin, Missouri.

Ramona Mae Pevey was born February 18, 1934 in Waseca, MN the daughter of Alvin Hugh and Violet Lilly (Sanders) Pevey. Ramona had formerly taught pre-school in California. She married Leo Russell Bridgeford Sr., July 15, 1952 in Yuma, AZ and he preceded her in death in December of 2001.

Additional survivors include two sons, Leo Bridgeford Jr., Seneca and Robert "Bob" Bridgeford, Gravette, ARK; one daughter Brenda Lindo, Seneca.

LEO BROWN

(The following obituary was taken from the Parker Mortuary website.)

Leo E. Brown, 86 of Joplin, Missouri, passed away Sunday May 22, 2011 as a result of the tornado that hit St. John's Regional Medical Center, where he was a patient.

Leo was born April 18, 1925, the son of the late Wilburn and Mary Kingston Brown.

He was a graduate of Joplin Senior High School class of 1943. He graduated from Manhattan Bible College and Phillips University at Enid, Okla. He was a retired clergyman of the Christian Church (Disciples of Christ) having served churches in Kansas, Missouri, Arkansas and Illinois.

He is survived by his wife, Katherine of the home; one daughter, Debra Brown of Springfield, Missouri; one son, Earl Brown of Fort Scott, Kan.; two grandchildren, Travis and Dixie; one great-grandchild, William; two brothers, Paul E. Brown of Joplin, Ivan Merle Brown of Eugene, Ore. In addition to his parents, he was preceded in death by a brother, Carl W. Brown.

HUGH BUTTRAM

(The following information is taken from Lucas Funeral Home, Hurst, Texas.)

Hugh Odell Buttram, age 85, passed away Sunday night, May 22, 2011, after sustaining injuries from the tornado that struck Joplin, Missouri that evening.

Odell, as he was known by friends and family, was born February 2nd, 1926 in Hillsboro, Texas. He was a veteran of WWII, serving as a chaplain's assistant in the Armed Forces. He subsequently received his bachelor's degree from Southwestern Assemblies of God University in Waxahachie, TX and did graduate studies in marketing at Texas Wesleyan College and Texas Christian University. He was an accomplished salesman receiving many significant sales awards over more than fifty years in the insurance business.

Odell was a devout Christian and lifelong member of Bethel Temple Assembly of God in Fort Worth, TX. His family and friends are comforted that he is with the Lord and they will see him again. He was much loved and will be sorely missed.

Survivors: He is survived by his wife, Evelyn Buttram of Joplin, Missouri; three daughters, Judith Rylee, and husband Tom Rylee of Springfield, Missouri, Lisa Satterfield, and her husband Rev. Dallas Satterfield of Baxter Springs, Kansas, and Cathy Buttram of Joplin, Missouri: two siblings, James Buttram and wife Lou, Sims Buttram and wife Fern; five grandchildren, Meredith Cunningham, Shannon Hachman, and husband, Chris Hachman, Paige Giarrizzo, and husband, David Glarrizzo, Morgan Satterfield, and Drew Satterfield; and one great-grandson, Dominic Ochoa.

TAMI CAMPBELL

(The following obituary is taken from Hafemeister Funeral Home of Watertown, Wisconsin.)

Tami L. Campbell, 28, of Joplin, Missouri, passed away on Sunday, May 22, 2011, as the result of the tornado in Joplin. An Angel on Earth is now an Angel in Heaven.

The former Tami Leigh Moldenhauer was born on Aug. 30, 1982, in Watertown, the daughter of Randy and Kathryn (Schuett) Moldenhauer. She attended St. Mark's Lutheran Grade School in Watertown and was a 2001 graduate of the Watertown High School. On June 24, 2006, Tami married Steven Campbell at St. Mark's Evangelical Lutheran Church in Watertown. She was employed at Wal-Mart in Joplin as a photo lab technician. Tami was a member to St. Mark's Evangelical Lutheran Church. She enjoyed photography and loved tigers. She was an avid collector of tigers in various arrays.

Tami is survived by her husband, Steven, of Joplin; two sons, Jordan C. Campbell and Caleb J. Campbell of Joplin; a step-son, Austin M. Powell of Joplin; her parents, Randy and Kathryn Moldenhauer of Watertown; her maternal grandmother, Esther Schuett of Watertown; a sister, Angela (her son Christian) Moldenhauer of Watertown; a brother Jeffrey Moldenhauer of Watertown; her mother-in-law, Diana Mclallen of Joplin; her father-in-law, Jim Campbell of Kansas City, Missouri, as well as other relatives and friends. Tami was preceded in death by her maternal grandfather, Clarence Schuett and her paternal grandparents, Roy and Elaine Moldenhauer.

MOISES CARMONA and ARRIYINNAH CARMONA

Moises Carmona, age 42, and his daughter, Arriyinnah, age 8, of Joplin, passed away Sunday, May 22, 2011 from injuries sustained in the Joplin tornado.

Moises was born September 12, 1969 in Jabonera, Chihuahua, Mexico. He had lived in Joplin since 2001, moving here from Albuquerque, New Mexico. Moises was a heavy equipment operator with Anchor Stone Co., east of Joplin. He was a member of the Joplin Full Gospel Church.

Moises married Kari Patten October 24, 2001 in Albuquerque and she survives. Additional survivors include two daughters, Marisela, and Adriennah "Audrey" Carmona, both of the home, three brothers, Abraham, Juan, and Pachino Carmona, all of Mexico, and six sisters, Manuela, Kick, Teo, Lula, Genoveva, and Lorenza, all of Mexico.

Arriyinnah Savannah Carmona, age 8, was born March 1, 2003. She was a 2nd grade student at Royal Heights Elementary School. In addition to her Mother, and sisters, Arriy is survived by her Maternal Grandfather, Joe Garcia Padilla, Elgin Ill., and her Maternal Grandmother, Carol Ballard, Joplin.

SHANTE CATON

(The following information is taken from the Lakin Funeral Home website.)

Shante Marie Caton, age 10, of Joplin, Mo., died on Sunday, May 22, 2011 as a result of the tornado. Shante Caton was born in Joplin, MO on Thursday, April 05, 2001. She was the daughter of Moses Caton and Crystal Whitely. She was a student at Eastmorland School in Joplin.

Surviving are her mother and dad, one sister: Keana Caton of the home, her maternal grandparents Felix and Aleta Whitely of Baxter Springs, KS. and paternal grandmother Mary Caton of Joplin, Mo.

TRENTAN CATON
(The following information is taken from the Lakin Funeral Home website.)

Trentan Maurice Steven Caton, age 6, of Joplin, Mo., died on Monday, May 23, 2011 at Children's Mercy Hospital in Kansas City, Mo., as a result of the tornado. Trentan Caton was born in Joplin, Mo., on Wednesday, March 23, 2005. He was the son of Moses Caton and Crystal Whitely. He was a student at Eastmorland School in Joplin.

Surviving are his mother and dad one sister: Keana Caton of the home, his maternal grandparents Felix and Aleta Whitely of Baxter Springs KS and his paternal grandmother Mary Caton of Joplin.

RAYMOND CHEW
(The following obituary is taken from the Campbell-Biddlecome Funeral Home website.)

Rev. Raymond LeRoy Chew Sr., 66, Joplin, MO, passed into eternal rest Sunday, May 22, 2011 from injuries sustained in the tornado that devastated Joplin, Missouri.

Rev. Raymond LeRoy Chew SR. was born July 30, 1944 in Joplin, MO the son of Rev. Dudley R. and Rev. Lenora D. (Riley) Chew. Raymond was a veteran of the United States Marine Corps serving his country from 1961 to 1965. Raymond was a heavy equipment operator he had worked for Webb City Special Road District. He was a member of the Cornerstone Church in Carterville. Raymond married Helen (Cauthren) Chew August 25, 1962 in Reno, Nevada and she survives.

Additional survivors include two sons, Raymond Chew II and wife Carla, Neosho, MO and Kevin Chew and wife Crystal, Seneca, MO; one daughter Carol Gibby, Carterville, MO; His mother Rev. Lenora D. Chew, Galena, KS; 5 brothers, Dudley Ray Chew Jr., Sacramento, CA, Pastor Frank R. Chew, Galena, KS, Terry U. Chew, state of Al, Jeff Chew, Joplin, MO, and John Chew, Shelby, MT; 5 sisters, Barbara Mullin, Joplin, MO, Susan Edward, Sacramento, CA, M. Jean Evans, Carterville, MO, Kendra Seymore, Shelby, MT and Samantha Hawkins, Carl Junction, MO; 11 grandchildren and two great-grandchildren.

Raymond was preceded in death by his father Rev. Dudley Ray Chew Sr.; 2 brothers, Sammy L. Chew and Danny M. Chew and one sister, Donna Kay Bedsual.

CLYDE COLEMAN
(The following obituary was taken from the Derfelt Funeral Home website.)

Clyde Coleman, age, 72, passed away on May 22nd, 2011 in the tornado that struck Joplin, Missouri. He was born July 16, 1938 in Paxton, NE to Austin D and Wanda Coleman.

He graduated from Hayes County High in Hayes Center, NE in 1956 and married Carolene Yonker on Nov 4, 1956 in Dickens, NE. She survives at the home in Galena, KS.

He went to work for the Singer Sewing Machine Company in McCook, NE. He managed stores in several locations in Nebraska before being transferred to Wichita, KS. In 1975 he made his final move to this area. He owned and operated Coleman's Upholstery Shop in Galena, retiring in 2005. He then worked for USD 499 as a bus monitor and most recently a crossing guard.

He was of the Catholic Faith. He was a member of the Joplin Elks Lodge #501 for 35 years. He served on the Galena KS City Council from 1997 – 1999. He had also served on the Planning and Zoning Committee. Among his interests were reading, gardening, storytelling, and community service.

He is also survived by two daughters, Melanie Tyler and Kelly (husband, Jack) Evans, Joplin, MO; 5 grandchildren, Heath Richmond Tyler (wife, January), Sarah Coleman Burkybile (husband, Travis), Megan Paris Tyler, Jared Kingston Worley (wife, Kim) of Gardner KS, Clinton Bradwell Worley (wife, Brittany) Joplin, MO; 6 great-grandchildren, Quinton Tyler, Madison Worley, Phil Dean Burkybile, of Joplin, MacKenly, Ellie and Molly Worley, of Gardner, KS; 4 Great Step Grandchildren, Alisa, Christian, and Jerrid Ireland, and Landon Tyler of Joplin, MO; one brother, Vance Coleman, State of Nebraska, one sister Phillis Phyllips and son, Dwight, State of Nebraska.

In addition to his parents, he was preceded in death by one brother, Walter Coleman.

CAROLANE COLLINS

(The following information is taken from the Grand Lake Funeral Home website.)

Carolane Jean Collin, 62, of Eagle Rock, MO, passed away Sunday, May 22, 2011 in Joplin. Carolane was born May 9, 1949 in Southwest City, MO to Otis and Mildred (Easter) Burton.

Carolane graduated from Jay High School in Jay, OK. She married Thomas in Joplin, MO on Dec. 6, 1991. Carolane worked as a Quality Control Tech for Eagle Picher Technologies for over thirty years before retiring. She was a member of the Lighthouse Pentecostal Church in Eagle Rock, Missouri. She enjoyed cooking, spending time with family, canning, and antiques.

Carolane is survived by her husband Thomas of the home, one daughter; Shiela Merriman of Joplin, MO, one step-son; Nathan Collins of Ft. Scott, KS, one brother; Don Burton of Disney, OK, one sister; Marilyn Turner of Greenwood, AR, five grandchildren; Tasia Lyn Simms, Matthew Tyler Merriman, Tiffani Nicole Renne Merriman, Trevor Brandon Merriman, Jamie Collins, one great-grandchild; Aliviah Simms, several nieces, nephews, other relatives and friends.

Carolane is preceded in death by both her parents and one brother; James Burton.

LOIS COMFORT

(The following obituary information is taken from the Simpson Funeral Home website.)

Lois Ada Comfort, age 66, of Webb City, went to be with the Lord May 22, 2011, as a result of the tornado.

Lois was born January 27, 1945 in Doniphan, MO to Orison and Virda (Jones) McKinney.

Lois was a member of the Emmanuel Baptist Church of Webb City. She married Larry Comfort May 24, 1991, at the Bethel Baptist Church, her death coming 2 days before their 20th Anniversary. Larry survives of the home.

She worked for Eagle Picher for 30 years. Lois enjoyed working in the yard with her flowers and loved fishing at the river. Her first love was for God, her family and her many friends. Her greatest concern was to help those who could not help themselves. She was a wonderful wife, mother, grandmother, sister and friend who will be greatly missed.

Lois is also survived by her sons, Acel Little of Carl Junction and Clayton Bickford and wife Shannon of Joplin; daughter, Katrina Feller and husband Rick of Joplin; brothers, Henry McKinney, Mansol McKinney and wife Kathy and Lindle McKinney; sisters, Thelma Brown, Norma Dudley and husband Bob, Faye Darnell and husband Cecil all from Doniphan, MO and 5 grandchildren, Kandice Gilliam, Kaycia Feller, Lauren Miller, Jordan Miller and Chad Miller.

KEENAN CONGER
(The following information came from the Simpson Funeral Home website.)

Keenan Krise Conger, age 49, of Carl Junction, went to be with the Lord on May 22, 2011, as a result of the tornado that went through Joplin, Missouri.

Keenan was born on April 12, 1962 in Detroit, MI to Aaron and Barbara (Tucker) Conger. During the tornado, Keenan gave his life trying to protect his dogs, Sissy and Sally, who survived the storm. Sissy and Sally gave Keenan great happiness. Also surviving the storm was Keenan's fiancée, Cheryl Hardin, whom he loved with all of his heart.

Keenan enjoyed working at a boat yard in his youth in Wyandotte, MI but was disabled in his later years. Keenan worked all his life to gain knowledge and was always working on motorbikes and found happiness in his grandchildren and pets.

Keenan cared deeply for his family and friends. Keenan is survived by his mother, Barbara Jean Porter; one brother, Bryan Conger; and two sisters. Brenda Cook married to Michael Cook; niece, Brandy Morton, her two children, Jayzier and Jozelyn all of Carl Junction, Mo. Lisa Prater married to Jeff Prater; niece, Megan Prater her daughter Annalyse; and nephew, Jordan Prater all of Bronaugh, Mo.

Keenan's relatives in Michigan include Phil and Teresa Conger, and cousins Paul, Rebecca, Steve, and Jenny whom he thought the world of on his father's side and a Great Aunt and Uncle on his mother's side, Lavaughn and Lloyd Wethington.

Keenan's adopted grandchildren, who gave Keenan the most happiness includes Jocelyn, Jacie, Brayden and their families, Cheryl's son and daughter and by Cheryl's mother who meant the world to him.

Keenan accepted Christ as his savior and was a member of the Pentecostal Church of God. No services will be held.

JIM COOKERLY
James V. "Jim" Cookerly, age 49, Joplin, passed away on Tuesday, June 14, 2011 at 2:52 a.m. at Joplin Health and Rehabilitation Center.
Jim was born July 6, 1961 in Carthage, Missouri, son of the late Eugene James Cookerly and Elizabeth Fay Smith Cookerly. He graduated from Grove High School, and attended NEO Votech for two years before beginning his career in

HVAC. He worked in Grove, Oklahoma City, and Joplin. He had lived in McDonald County for the past 12 years before moving to Joplin a year ago.

Survivors include his wife, MaryBeth Wilson Cookerly whom he married January 24, 1998 in Joplin; daughter, Amanda Werner and husband Brian of Seneca, Missouri; son, Carl Cookerly of Grove, Oklahoma; grandchildren, Jake, Kyle, and Brianna; sisters, Karyl Conard and husband Robert of Wichita, Kansas, Debi Sparks of Joplin, April Parcher and husband Roy of Oklahoma City, Oklahoma, and Denise Kramme and husband Dave of Carl Junction, Missouri; several nieces and nephews.

EDMON COOPER

Edmon A. Cooper, age 88, Joplin, passed away on Thursday, June 16, 2011 at Freeman West Hospital.

Edmon was born June 15, 1923, in Wheaton, Missouri, son of the late Charles and May Cooper. He worked as a mechanic with farm equipment for Massey Ferguson from 1950 until 1988. He then went to work at Vollenweider Orchid in Exeter, Missouri which he did until retiring in 1995. He was an Army Veteran of World War II with the 96th Division.

In addition to his parents, he was preceded in death by his wife, Anna Cooper who died January 4, 2011, a daughter, Pamela Sue Murdock, brothers, Olen Cooper and Cecil Cooper; sisters, Elsie Phillips, Bernice Charles, and Blanche Lee.

Survivors include a son, Karl Cooper of Overland Park, Kansas; daughter, Vicky Weaver of Clarksville, Tennessee; 11 grandchildren, 13 great-grandchildren, one great-great-grandchild; and a brother, Glenn Cooper of Purdy, Missouri.

VICKI COOPER

Vicki L. Cooper at 58 of Joplin, Missouri passed away Sunday May 22, 2011 during the Joplin tornado.

ALICE COPE

(The following information is taken from the Clark Funeral Home website.)

Alice L. Hudson Cope, 79, Neosho, died Sunday, June 19, 2011, at Freeman West Hospital, after being in the Joplin, tornado on May 22. She was born June 2, 1932, in Cassville.

Alice had been a member of College Heights Christian Church in Joplin. She attended First Christian Church in Neosho before her long illness, and was active in their annual apple pie baking program. She loved Bible studies and participated in them at the church and at Graystone Apartments.

She was a fine seamstress and made beautifully appliquéd dresses, drapes and stylish clothes. She was a voracious reader and enjoyed books on history and religion.

She graduated from Cassville High School and attended Southwest Missouri State College, now Missouri State University. After her children were grown, she returned to Springfield and completed a degree in archeology. She worked on an archeological dig in Israel.

Alice is survived by her son, Steve, and wife, Heather, Bella Vista, Arkansas; her daughter, Judy Cope and husband, Gary Rasmussen, Woodcliff, N.J.; a sister, Dorothy Knoblauch, Joplin; three grandchildren, Stephanie Cope, Cara Cope and

Alex Rasmussen; two great-grandchildren, Gavin James and Maddie Rose; and the father of her children, Stan Cope, and wife, Linda, Anacortes, Wash.

TEDDY COPHER
(The following obituary is taken from the Parker Mortuary website.)

Teddy Ray Copher, age 71 of Joplin, passed away from injuries sustained in a tornado on May 22, 2011. He has been a resident of Joplin all of his life.

Born June 24, 1939 in Joplin, he was the son of the late Benny F. Copher and Margaret Smith Copher. He was an employee for Tamko as a Paper Hydro-Pulper Operator for 31 years.

He is survived by one son, Richard Ray Copher and his wife Angela of Joplin; one brother, Larry Copher and his wife Carolyn of Webb City; and six grandchildren.

In addition to his parents, he was preceded in death by one brother, Benny Copher Jr.

MALISA CROSSLEY
(The following obituary is taken from the Mason-Woodard Mortuary website.)

Malisa Ann Crossley, age 36, of Joplin, Missouri, passed away on May 22, 2011, at her home, from injuries sustained in the catastrophic tornado.

Malisa was born on January 29, 1975 in Joplin, Missouri, the daughter of Jerald Lynn Gaston and Peggy "White" Gettler. She has been a life time resident of Joplin. She worked as a customer service representative at Wal-Mart on 7th Street the past two years. Malisa unselfishly covered and protected her nine year old son during the tornado, and as a result his life was spared. Malisa was a loving mother. She was always smiling and she loved to make others smile. She will be greatly missed by all of her family and friends.

She is survived by her mother Peggy Gettler, Grand Praire, Texas. Two sons, Thomas Crossley, Joplin, Missouri and Chaz Martin of the home, one daughter, Shantal Crossley of Joplin, Missouri Her fiancé Bryce Coleman. Two sisters, Jennifer Gordon and husband David of Irving, Texas, Lindy Molina and husband Freddy of Irving, Texas. Her best friend, Angela Baumann, who was a sister to her. She is also survived by Aunts and Uncles and nieces and nephews. Her father Jerald Lynn Gaston preceded her in death in 1980.

ADAM DARNABY
(The following obituary is taken from the Derfelt Funeral Home website.)

Adam Dewane Darnaby, age 27, passed away Sunday May 22, 2011, as a result of the tornado that ravaged Joplin, Missouri, that evening.

Adam was born May 26, 1983 in Joplin. His parents were Ronald Wayne and Janet (Moore) Darnaby. He was raised in the Galena-Riverton KS area. He had earned an Associate of Electrical Technology Degree at Pittsburg State University. He was employed as an electrician at Jasper Products.

He attended the House of Prayer and the Riverton Friends Church. He enjoyed fast cars, including racing and going four-wheeling. He loved doing anything outdoors especially Cat Fishing.

Adam was married to Kaitlin E Kissee on September 6, 2008 in Riverton, KS. She survives. Additional survivors include his parents Ron and Janet Darnaby, Riverton, KS; his maternal "little Grandma", Galena, KS, 2 brothers Matthew Darnaby, Joplin, Missouri, and, Aaron Darnaby, Riverton, KS ; his father and mother in law, Ron and Debbie Kissee, Galena, KS; Nieces and Nephews, Kaleigh, Sanna, Dayton, Kaden, Madison, Courtney, Dawson, Bryson, Brandt, Victoria, Madelynn, Kaylee, and Carter.

He was preceded in death by grandparents, Carl R. Moore, Herbert and Hazel Darnaby.

PATRICIA DAWSON
(The following information is taken from joplinmemorial.com.)

Patricia Dawson, age 74, of Joplin, Missouri, died on Sunday, May 22, 2011, at her home as a result of the tornado in Joplin. Mrs. Dawson was born in Kansas City, Mo. on Friday, January 01, 1937. She was the daughter of Jack and Ruth (McKinley) Sears. She was a homemaker and a member of the Temple Baptist Church in Springfield, Missouri

She is survived by the following: three sons, Jerry Dawson of Springfield, Mo., John Dawson of Pierce City, Mo., and James Dawson of Saint Louis, Mo.; three sisters, Jane Wimer of Joplin, Mo., Nancy Fox of Springfield, Mo., and Barbara Taylor of Buffalo, Mo.; her former husband, Donald Dawson of Springfield, Mo.; three grandchildren; and one great-grandchild.

MICHAEL DENNIS
(The following obituary is taken from the Parker Mortuary website.)

Michael Wayne Dennis, age 52, of Galena, Kan., passed away at 11:57 p.m. on Friday, June 10, 2011, at St. John's Medical Center in Springfield, from complications due to injuries he sustained in the May 22nd Joplin tornado, while he was a patient at St. John's Regional Medical Center in Joplin.

Born April, 7, 1959, in Parsons, Kan., he was the son of the late Wayne Dennis and Shirley Cowley Dennis and lived in the Columbus and Baxter Springs, Kan. areas most of his lifetime. Michael was disabled. He graduated from Columbus Vo-Tech studying graphic arts. He enjoyed comic books and Playstation.

He was a resident of Emerald Pointe Health and Rehab Centre, Galena.

Survivors include his uncles and cousins.

NANCY DOUTHITT
(The following obituary is taken from the Parker Mortuary website.)

Nancy Elizabeth Douthitt, age 94 of Joplin, passed away from injuries sustained in a tornado on May 22, 2011.

Born September 5, 1916 in Newtonia, MO, she was the daughter of the late Virgil A. Thornberry and Ether Virginia Hendrickson. She is a member of St. Paul's

United Methodist Church, St. John's Prestige, and also a former member of Surviving Spouses.

She married Curtis W. Douthitt on January 12, 1937 and together they owned and operated Douthitt Grocery Store on 202 N. Gray in Joplin from 1947-1987. Curtis preceded her in death on November 27, 1989.

She is survived by one son, Robert (Bob) Douthitt and his wife Jean of Tulsa, OK; one brother, Walter Thornberry of Mt. Vernon, MO; one sister, Lenore Rhodes of Homer, IL; three grandchildren, James, Thomas and Cathleen; and eight great-grandchildren.

In addition to her parents she is preceded in death by her daughter Barbara Douthitt, and one sister, Genevieve Robinson.

ELLEN DOYLE
(The following obituary is taken from the Mason-Woodard Mortuary website.)

Ellen Jeanette Doyle, age 75, of Joplin, Missouri, passed away on May 22, 2011, at her home, from injuries sustained in the catastrophic tornado.

Ellen was born on November 29, 1935 in Carthage, Mo, the daughter of the late Raymond C. Kennell and the late Mary Virginia Pace. She has been a resident of Joplin Area her entire life. She was a homemaker. She was a member of College Heights Christian Church. Ellen loved spending time with her family, going out to eat, and shopping. She will be greatly missed by all of her family and friends.

She married Keith Doyle on February 19, 1954 at Forest Park Baptist Church in Joplin. He preceded her in death September of 2003. Survivors include two daughters, Susan Brookshire and special friend Mario Morales; Terri Branham and her husband Randy, five grandchildren, Jason Brookshire and his wife Stephanie, Lesa Branham, Stephanie Sargent and husband Jeremy, Jamie Fort and husband Matt; five great-grandchildren, Tamerik Branham, Jasmine Sargent, Lilly Sargent, Kaden Fort and Jarett Fort; three brothers Jerry Kennell, Grandview, Missouri, Bud Kennell and wife Dolly, Harbor City, Ca., and Johnnie Kennell, Kansas City, Missouri; two sisters, Carol Davidson and husband Galen, Pittsburg, Ks., and Linda Salmans husband Randy, Topeka, Ks. She was preceded in death by granddaughter Kelly Jo Brookshire, son-in-law John Brookshire and a sister, Nola Randall.

FAITH DUNN
(The following obituary is taken from the Mason-Woodard Mortuary website.)

Faith Constance Dunn, age 71, of Joplin, Missouri, passed away Sunday, May 22, 2011 at her home from injuries sustained in the Joplin tornado. Faith was born November 27, 1939 in St. Thomas, Ontario, Canada. She moved to Joplin in 1964 when she enrolled at Ozark Bible College. Following her graduation from Ozark she was employed by the College for almost 20 years in the Music Department. She also taught sign language.

Faith was a member of the Park Plaza Christian Church. She was an avid horseman for many years, and rode with two separate drill teams.

Faith is survived by one sister, Judy Dunn, rural Jasper, Missouri, two nieces, and a nephew. She was preceded in death by her parents, Fred and Connie Dunn, and a brother, Steve Dunn.

AMANDA EASTWOOD
(The following information is taken from the Paul Thomas Funeral Home website.)

Amanda Sue (Brashear) Eastwood, 49 of Joplin, Missouri formally of Miami and Commerce passed away May 22, 2011 in Joplin, Missouri.

Amanda was born May 6, 1962 in Miami, Oklahoma to Leonard and Sondra Sue (Turner) Brashear.

She graduated from Commerce High School, and received her Registered Nurses License from Northeastern Oklahoma A&M College. She was employed by Freeman Hospital for several years.

Family: father: Leonard Brashear of Picher, OK, mother: Sondra and the late Clifford Crabtree of Miami, OK, one son: Robert Hiram Eastwood of Miami, OK, two daughters: Amber Helen Eastwood of Commerce, OK, Erika Lynn (Eastwood) Mitchell, Galveston, TX, three sisters: Leona Ceclie (Brashear) Lewin, Tulsa, OK, Peggy Sue (Brashear) Schneoring, Corpus Christi, TX, Bonnie Ann (Brashear) Hall, Miami, OK, three grandchildren and a host of nieces and nephews.

RICHARD ELMORE
(The following obituary is taken from the Parker Mortuary website.)

Richard Allen Elmore went to be with his Heavenly Father May 22, 2011. He was a resident of Greenbrier Health Center, and was killed in the tornado.

Born in Memphis, Tenn. November 4, 1940, he was a foreman at Cole Steel in Tulsa for many years, retiring in 2003.

Richard loved to go to his Church in Saginaw. He was a member of Saginaw Baptist Church.

He married Velta Hamilton May 13, 1993. She survives.

Additional survivors include five sons, Richard, Jr., Nick, Tony, Chris and Gary; five grandchildren; one great-grandchild; three stepchildren, Jason Hamilton, Brad Hamilton and Amber Sachetta; six step grandchildren; one sister, Betty DeGraffenried of the Memphis area; two brothers, Donny and Ronnie, both of the Memphis area.

RANDY ENGLAND
Randy Edward England, age 34, of Granby, Missouri, Beloved Husband, Father, Brother, Uncle, and Friend, was born October 25, 1976 in Joplin, Missouri Randy left this world on May 22, 2011, one of the many victims of Joplin's devastating tornado. Randy leaves behind his wife of 14 years, Kelly Ann Barwick England; and their two wonderful children, Julie England, age 12 and Justin England, age 8. Randy was preceded in death by his parents, Raymond and Ruby Greer England.

Additional survivors include three brothers, Ricky England of Joplin, Danny and Gary England, both of Neosho; three sisters, Tereasa Neal of Seneca, Sherry Johnson and Carolyn Jarmin, both of Neosho; as well as many nieces, nephews, and great-nieces and great-nephews.

Born and raised in the Newton County area, Randy attended Seneca High School. After leaving school, he joined the workforce, working for several years as a diesel mechanic and working for the past seven years as a La-Z-Boy employee at Neosho.

Randy loved his family, friends, and life with a great passion.

When he wasn't attending his children's activities or off on an adventure traveling or trading, he could be found at home with a group of family and friends Barbequing, watching movies, playing Rock-Band, or reading.

Randy always had time to help a child or a friend. He was always working on a project vehicle, including a panel van that had belonged to his father. Rand was a great organizer to plan fun trips with his family and friends, most recently, a Deep-Sea fishing trip to Texas. Randy had also taken up the game of Golf and he loved it. Randy will be missed by many.

MARK FARMER

(The following information is taken from the *Joplin Globe*.)

Mark Farmer, 56, Joplin, had worked at Joplin Workshops for more than 20 years. His friends and roommates, Rick Fox and Tripp Miller, died with him in the storm.

IDA FINLEY

(The following information is taken from the Clark Funeral Home website.)

Ida M. Finley, 88, Joplin, passed away on May 22, 2011, as a result of the tornado. Mrs. Finley was born May 12, 1923, in Logan County, West Virginia. She had worked at Continental Can in the warehouse for 31 years and moved to Missouri in July 2009 from Proctorville, Ohio.

She married James A. Finley on July 8, 1942, at Huntington, W.V., and he preceded her in death on Aug. 16, 2006.

She is survived by a son, Clinton R. Finley, Joplin; three grandchildren, Christina R. Finley, Arin Lunsford and Joseph Holtzman; a great-grandchild; and two great-great-grandchildren; a brother, Wm Raymond Cartmill, Hurricane, W.V.; and a sister, Nellie Mae Hutchison, Huntington, W.V. In addition to her husband and parents, she is preceded in death by a son, Jan Robin Finley; a daughter, Marsha Kay Finley; and grandson, George Arthur Osborne.

BETTY JO FISHER

(The following obituary is taken from the Parker Mortuary website.)

Betty Jo Burrington Fisher, age 86 of Joplin, died Sunday, May 22, 2011, a casualty of the tornado.

Born January 27, 1925 in Lubbock, Texas, she was the daughter of the late Henry McKinley and Mamie Hunter McKinley. She was a long-time resident of Joplin where she owned and operated Betty's Beauty Shop for many years in her home. She was a member of Blendville Christian Church, a 4-H leader, a volunteer at St. John's and enjoyed square-dancing.

Her first husband, Roy Burrington, preceded her in death Nov. 14, 1975.

Her second husband, Jim Fisher, preceded her in death Dec. 12, 2010.

Survivors include three daughters, Shelia Tasker and her husband, Larry, Janet Townsend, and her husband, Damond, and Sandy Blizzard, and her husband, Ron, all of Joplin; a son, Tom Fisher and wife, Patty, state of South Carolina; a brother, Harvey McKinley, Post Falls, ID; four sisters, Jean Love, Sahuarita, AZ, June

Boelsen, Spring, TX, Jo Murdock, Lubbock, TX, and Henrietta Wilson, Olvsmar, FL; eight grandchildren; 10 great-grandchildren; and 1 great-great-grandchild. She was preceded in death by a son, Jim Fisher Jr., and a brother, Payton McKinney.

ROBERT FITZGERALD
(The following obituary is taken from the Clark Funeral Home website.)

Robert S. Fitzgerald died at his home in Joplin, Missouri, as a result of the tornado on Sunday, May 22, 2011.

He was born in Granby, Missouri, to Shelby and Freda (Nunn) Fitzgerald on Dec. 22, 1949. Robert graduated from Granby High School, attended Crowder College and MSSU.

He was an army veteran from the Vietnam era and an avid St. Louis Cardinals fan. His great nephew, Tyler, plays ball for the local Food-4-Less team in Joplin, and his great-uncle, Robert was his greatest fan. He also loved putting on the "Santa Hat" and being Santa Claus to the nieces and nephews. He was a collector of music and loved to read. If you made friends with Robert he was your friend for life.

Robert was a 10-year cancer survivor. He had battled cancer two different times.

Robert is survived by his wife of 33 years, Marti (Cupps) Fitzgerald.

Additional survivors include his brother, Max Fitzgerald and wife, Kathy, of Lowell, Arkansas; sisters, Donna Fullerton, Granby, and Lana Deadmond, of Branson, and Gordon and wife, Mary Jo Cupps, of Branson; nephews, Nathan Deadmond and wife, Michelle, of Kansas City, Chad Deadmond, Branson, Brian Fitzgerald and wife, Christal, of Sinking Springs, Pa., JR Fullerton, Granby, and Will Cupps (Amanda Daugherty), of Joplin; nieces, Melissa Cupps, Branson, and Serena Tinsley and husband, Kendon, Joplin; great-nephews, Tyler Tinsley, Fletcher Cupps and Luke Fitzgerald; and great-niece, Addison Cupps.

Robert worked over 27 years for Wal-Mart and called them his "Wal-Mart Family." Through his cancer battles the "family" was wonderful and gave great support.

He was preceded in death by his parents; nephew, Ben Cupps; and his mother-in-law, Phyllis Cupps Darby.

RICK FOX
(The following obituary is taken from the Parker Mortuary website.)

Rick E. Fox, age 56 of Joplin, passed away May 22, 2011 as a result of injuries sustained in the tornado.

Born October 20, 1954 in Joplin, he graduated from Eagle-Picher Training Center in 1975. Since 1976, he has worked at Joplin Workshops. A Christian, he was a member of Calvary Baptist Church and attended First Presbyterian Church. Rick enjoyed all sports and was an accomplished bowler, participating on the Special Olympics Bowling Team.

His father, Richard E. Fox, preceded him in death on March 2, 2005.

Survivors include his mother, Doris Fox of Joplin; his aunt, Joann Chapman of Grand Prairie, Tex.; cousins, Gary and Teri Selby, Steve and Kim Selby, John and Larrah Selby, Matt and Mike Selby, Jason and Chad Chapman, Aimee and Eric

Golden, Stevie Selby, Mike & Paul Chapman, Dane and Katie Bell; very special friends, Shirley and Sheila, with whom he enjoyed many vacations which enriched Rick's life. Numerous friends will also miss him.

MARSHA ANN FROST

Marsha Ann Frost, 32, a resident of Joplin, Missouri, passed away May 22, 2011 in the tornado of Joplin, Missouri. She was born July 10, 1978 at Lincoln, Arkansas, the daughter of Larry Joe and Ruth Esther Young Winkler.

She was a member of the Christian Life Center in Joplin. Marsha had been employed by Wal-Mart in Bentonville, Arkansas.

Survivors include one son, Gabriel Frost of the home; her parents Larry Joe and R. Esther Winkler of Neosho, Missouri; one brother Larry Winkler II of Neosho, Missouri; two sisters, Bethany Burton of Joplin, Missouri and Christina Winkler of Neosho, Missouri; Paternal grandparents Willis & JoAnne Winkler of Lincoln, Arkansas; a maternal grandmother, Nedra Ann Johnson of Lincoln, Arkansas.

SEBASTIAN FROST

Sebastian Charles Frost, a resident of Joplin, Missouri passed away May 22, 2011 in the tornado of Joplin. He was born March 4, 2001 at Boonville, Missouri, the son of Marsha Winkler Frost.

Sebastian was a member of the Christian Life Center in Joplin, Missouri.

Survivors include one brother, Gabriel Frost of the home; his father Roger Frost of Moberly, Missouri; maternal grandparents' Larry & Esther Winkler of Neosho, MO; maternal great-grandparents' Willis & JoAnne Winkler of Lincoln, Arkansas; maternal great great-grandmother Nedra Ann Johnson of Lincoln, Arkansas; paternal grandparents' Gary and Connie Whitehurse of Boonville, Missouri; paternal great-grandmother Betty Wells of Boonville, Missouri.

CHARLES GAUDSMITH

(The following obituary is taken from the Knell Mortuary website.)

Charles Kenneth Gaudsmith, 21, Carthage, passed away Sunday, May 22, 2011 from injuries sustained in the Joplin tornado.

Charles Kenneth Gaudsmith was born November 7, 1989 in Glendale, California, the son of Russell Gaudsmith and Melisa Renee (Johnson) Gaudsmith. Charles and his family moved to Carthage in 1998 from California. He was a graduate of Carthage Senior High School, Class of 2009 and was a cook for the south Carthage McDonald's. He was active in Carthage Tiger sports serving as a team member of the Carthage Tiger Football squad and the Tiger Wrestling team.

Survivors include a sister, Lashawnda (Travis) Cavener, Joplin, MO; his father, Russell (Donna) Gaudsmith, Hemet, CA; girlfriend, Candice Harper, Carthage; three nieces, Cheyeanne, Kaylee, Alyssa; his grandparents, Jim (Jane) Johnson, Carthage, Mike Libby, Sunland, CA. Charles was preceded in death by his mother, Melisa, who was with him in the Joplin tornado; a brother, Jody Gaudsmith, and a grandmother, Gaye Libby.

BILLIE JOE GIDEON
(The following obituary is taken from the Mason-Woodard Mortuary website.)

Billie Jo Gideon, age 77 of Joplin, Missouri went to be with the Lord early Monday May 23, 2011 at Freeman Hospital from injuries suffered during the devastating tornado that hit Joplin on May 22, 2011.

Billie was born on December 10, 1933 in Goodman, Missouri the daughter of Conley and Bernice (Johnson) Bellamy. She worked for 32 years at the Pentecostal Church of God Headquarters and Messenger Publishing. Billie attended the First Pentecostal Church of God, which is now known as Crown of Life Chapel.

She was previously married to Delbert Gideon; he survives. Additional survivors include three sons, Dennis Gideon, Sr. and his wife Blinda of Joplin, Danny Gideon and his wife Candy of Joplin, Scott Gideon and his wife Linda of Joplin, two daughters, Debbie Patterson of Joplin and Betty Benfield and her husband Dale, Sr. of Joplin, ten brothers and sisters, twelve grandchildren and twenty-four great grandchildren. Billie was preceded in death by one sister.

ROBERT GRIFFIN
(The following information is taken from Greenlawn Funeral Home.)

Robert M. Griffin, age 61, of Battlefield, Missouri, passed away Friday, June 3, 2011 in Christian Health Care West as a result of injuries during the Joplin tornado.

He is survived by his wife Kay Griffin of Battlefield, Missouri; daughter, Bobbi Magana of Kansas City, Missouri; three step-children, Lynn Scott of Kansas City, Missouri, Todd Lisenby of Springfield, and Stacye Perriman and husband Tim of Willard; four grandchildren; and a host of family and friends.

PAUL HADDOCK
Paul E. "Gene" Haddock, Sr., age 62 of Joplin, Missouri lost his life during the tragic tornado that hit Joplin on May 22, 2011.

Paul was born at home in Spring City, Missouri on December 13, 1948 the son of Fred and Ada (Mullen) Haddock. He worked as a lead and set up welder for Lozier for 25 years before medical issues forced him to retire. Paul was well known around the Joplin YMCA where he had many friends.

He married Karen Hartje on February 10, 1974 in Webb City, Missouri, she survives. Additional survivors include his three sons, Richard Haddock of Indianapolis, In., David Haddock and his fiancé Monica of Indianapolis and Christopher Haddock and his wife Faith currently of Neosho, Missouri, three brothers, Bill Haddock of Kansas City, Missouri, Bob Haddock of Kansas City, Missouri and Fred Haddock, Jr. of Picher, Ok., two grandchildren, Ayden Haddock and Collin Haddock. Paul was preceded in death by his parents and by his son, Paul "Tiny" Haddock, Jr.

JOHNNA HALE
(The following obituary was taken from the *Kansas City Star*)

Johnna Hale, 49, a FAG Bearing Company employee, passed away Sunday, May 22, 2011.

Johnna was calm as the tornado sirens blared over Joplin on May 22. She phoned her daughter; gathered water; corralled her dog, a border collie mix named Star; and hunkered down in the bathtub. But then Star bolted. Out the door, into the storm. And Hale followed.

She called her daughter again in those final, fraught moments — crying, frantic, scrambling — but the connection severed as the tornado bore down on the city. She was found nine days later in the rubble of a building where she took shelter. Star was there with her, in her arms.

Read more: http://www.kansascity.com/2011/06/11/2943345/victims-of-joplin-tornado-wont.html#ixzz1PhBvimUU

LEOLA HARDIN
(The following information is taken from the Mason-Woodard Mortuary website.)

Leola L. (McCune) Hardin, age 76, of Joplin, Missouri, passed away Wednesday, June 8, 2011, at Freeman Hospital from injuries sustained from the Joplin tornado.

She was born Dec. 23, 1934, in Jasper, Missouri, to Howard L. and Vera (Ferguson) McCune.

Leola worked as a packer for Bagcraft retiring in 2000. She made lap blankets for Hospice Compassus.

She married Kenneth Hardin on Feb. 14, 1954, in Jasper. He preceded her in death in December 1999.

Survivors include two sons, Thomas Hardin, of Joplin, and Kenneth Hardin and wife, Lori, of Poplar Bluff, Missouri; one daughter, Kathy Robbins and husband, Wade, of Carthage, Ind.; one brother, Jim McCune, of Carthage, Missouri; one sister, Helen Carter, of Carthage; and three grandchildren. She was preceded in death by her parents and one brother, Roy McCune.

LANTZ HARE
(The following obituary is taken from the Parker Mortuary website.)

Caley Lantz Hare, age 16 of Joplin, passed away from injuries sustained in the Joplin tornado May 22, 2011.

Born September 2, 1994 in Coffeyville, Kan., he had lived in Joplin since 1998 and attended Joplin Public Schools. He was a straight A student of the junior class of Joplin High School. Lantz was an avid BMX bike rider. He rode at Autumn Ramp Park and loved spending time at The Bridge. He participated in bible studies, was a member of the BMX Team, and volunteered at both The Bridge and Autumn Ramp Park. He attended Christ's Church of Joplin with fellow Bridge staff, members and close friends.

Survivors include his mother, Michelle Hare of Joplin; his father and stepmother, Walter Mike and Shannon Hare of Broken Arrow, Okla.; his brother, Matthew Hare of Joplin; two sisters Shaylee Albee of Colorado Springs, Colorado, Jayln Mattson of Broken Arrow; paternal grandmother, CeCelia Hare of Coffeyville, Kan.; maternal grandmother, Mary Lou Green of Coffeyville; maternal grandfather, Ron Green of Edna, Kan.; maternal grandmother, Teresa West of Findley, Ohio; several aunts, uncles and countless friends.

Lantz was preceded in death by paternal grandfather, Caley Kitch and maternal grandfather Fritz Jehle.

DOROTHY HARTMAN

(The following obituary is taken from the Knell Mortuary website.)

Dorothy Viola Hartman, 91, Joplin, MO, passed away Sunday, May 22, 2011 from injuries sustained in the Joplin tornado.

Dorothy Viola Gray was born May 5, 1920 in Union, MO, the daughter of John Thomas Gray, Sr. and Matilda Clementine (Clark) Gray. She was a homemaker and for many years was a member of the Bethel Methodist Church, south of Carthage. She married George Washington Hartman on October 4, 1940 in Carthage.

Survivors include her husband of 70 years, G.W. Hartman, Joplin; a daughter, Sherrie Hartman Messer, Oronogo, MO, Jerry Messer, Oronogo; two granddaughters, Angela (Jeff) Howrey, Carthage, grandchildren, Tyler and Isabelle Howrey; Michelle (Kevin) Houser, granddaughter, Tiffanie (Matt) White; three great great grandchildren, Mathew, Ryan and Kenzye White; one brother, John T. (Neva) Gray, Carthage; two sisters, Lorraine Wright, Jefferson City, MO and Marian (Chester) Hildgedick, Ashland, MO; several nieces and nephews. She was preceded in death her parents; three brothers, Earl, Curtis and Clifford; two sisters, Laura and Pauline.

DEE ANN HAYWARD

(The following obituary is taken from the Derfelt Funeral Home website.)

Dee Ann Hayward, age 47, 302 E 22nd St, died Sunday evening, May 22, 2011 in the tornado that struck Joplin, Missouri.

Dee Ann was born August 25, 1963 in Glendora, California. Her parents were James Robert and Bernice Lee (Brady) Kelly. She had lived in Galena since 1977.

She graduated from Galena High School in 1981. She had worked the past 4 years for Hallmark Card Co maintaining card displays in area Wal-Mart Stores. She was a member of Riverton Friends Church, Riverton, KS where she had been a Sunday school teacher. She had traveled to Brazil and Jamaica on different missionary journeys. She loved music and collected several recordings. Dee Ann had a very kind heart, always looking for ways she could help people.

She was married to Jim C. Hayward on May 26, 1984 in Galena, KS. He survives.

Also surviving are two sons, Robert Glen Hayward and Caleb Grant Hayward, one daughter, Christina Gail Hayward, all of the home; her mother, Bernice Kelly, Seneca, MO; two brothers, Michael Brady Kelly, Redding , CA and Kenneth J Kelly, Seneca, MO; one sister Patricia Gail Penn, Nice, CA; and her father-in-law, Jack Hayward, Baxter Springs, KS. H

Her father preceded her in death.

JUDY HEAD

No information was available on Judy Head, except that she was age 56 and from Joplin.

KENNETH HENSON
(The following information comes from the Paul Thomas Funeral Home.)

Kenneth James Henson of Miami, Oklahoma passed away Saturday May 28, 2011 at his home. He was 56.

Mr. Henson was born November 26, 1954 in Wichita, Kansas to Earnest Arwood and Zenia (Hudson) Henson, II. He had lived in Miami for many years, he was a master machinist.

He was preceded in death by his parents, 4 brothers and a sister Evelyn Porter. Survivors include: One Son and his wife James and Jamie Henson of Claremore, OK, one Grandchild Jadyn Dihel of Claremore, OK

GLENN AND LORIE HOLLAND
(The following obituary is taken from the Parker Mortuary website.)

Glenn and Lorie Holland of Joplin, Missouri, exchanged their earthly home for a better one on the evening of May 22, 2011, having just returned from a week at Walt Disney World in Florida in celebration of their 15th wedding anniversary.

Glenn Wayne Holland was born June 21, 1951, in Joplin. He graduated from Memorial High School in 1969, and then later earned a bachelor's degree in business administration, a master's degree in health care management, and finally a bachelor's degree in computer information science. He was a retired Air Force major and a member of the Retired Officer's Association, the National Rifle Association, the American Legion and the National Skeet Shooting Association. He was currently working at Leggett & Platt.

Lorie Marie Holland was born December 22, 1962, in Joplin. She graduated from Parkwood High School in 1981 and attended Southern Illinois University in Carbondale where she was a member of the Sigma Kappa Sorority. She was a drafter for several companies in St. Louis and Joplin, having most recently worked at Allgeier and Martin. She loved scrapbooking, was an avid Disney enthusiast, a seasonal worker at OCC, and election poll worker. She was training for the Boomtown Days half marathon. She was a member of First Presbyterian Church growing up and a member of the Mayflower Society.

Lorie and Glenn were married on May 18, 1996, and were members of Central City Christian Church.

Glenn was preceded in death by his daughter Amy, grandparents Perry and Ruth Holland, and Wesley and Velma Tracy, and is survived by daughters Shannon Mills of Cibolo, Texas, and Rachel Alexander of Bryan, Texas, and grandchildren Ethan, Avery, Ryan, Taylor, Kyle. Glenn is also survived by his parents, Wayne and Mary Holland of Joplin, sister Dorothy Vaughan of Joplin, sister and brother-in-law Jenny and Rick Smith of Webb City, and numerous nephews and nieces.

Lorie was preceded in death by her grandparents, Paul and Edna Marti, and Dennis and Lois Lippoldt. Lorie is survived by her mother and stepfather, Bonnie and William Mahood of Overland Park, Kansas, sister and brother-in-law, Kristie and Steve Tusinger of Joplin, niece and nephew, Abby Marie Tusinger and Zachary Tusinger of Joplin, father Victor Lippoldt of Joplin, stepbrother and wife, William and Michele Mahood of Overland Park, KS, and their children, Kristen and Kellen Mahood.

Memorial contributions may be made to the Joplin Humane Society, Ozark Christian College, or charity of your choice.

CHARLOTTE HOPWOOD
Charlotte Hopwood, 84, Joplin, was killed in the May 22 Joplin tornado.

RUSTY HOWARD, HARLI HOWARD, and HAYZE HOWARD
(The following obituary is taken from the Mason-Woodard Mortuary website)

Russell T. "Rusty" Howard age 29, Harli Jayce Howard, age 5, and Hayze Cole Howard, age 19 months, passed away in the catastrophic tornado on May 22, 2011. Harli and Hayze were found securely in their daddy's arms.

Russell T. "Rusty" Howard was born on July 5, 1981 in Coffeyville, Ks., the son of Harry Howard and Dianne Long Nunez. He was a graduate of Cherryvale High School a member of the class of 2000. He worked as an electrician for PCS Phosphates for the past five years and previously he worked for B.E.I. He was a member of St. Peter the Apostle Catholic Church. He was a member of the Kansas Army National Guard. He enjoyed fishing and riding motorcycles. He married Edie Boss on August 10, 2002, in Cherryvale, Ks. He never met a stranger and he would talk to anyone who would listen. He will be greatly missed by all who knew him.

Harli Jayce Howard was born on February 6, 2006 in Joplin, Missouri She was known as the family chatter bug she loved to talk almost as much as her daddy did. Her mother's favorite saying of Harli's "Hi, friend".

Hayze Cole Howard was born on October 27, 2009 in Joplin, Missouri He was our sweet little baby boy and a force unto himself.

They are survived by their wife and mother, Edie (Boss) Howard, Joplin; parents and grandparents, Harry Howard, Grove, Okla., and Dianne Long Nunez, Edna, Ks.; in-laws and grandparents, Marie and Mike Boss, McAlester, Okla.; brother and uncle, Jason Niemier, Cherryvale, Ks; sister and aunt, Amanda Nunez; grandparents and great-grandparents, Marvin and Joyce Long, Cherryvale, Ks.; sister-in-law and aunt, Missy Niemier and cousins Cooper and Carson; brother-in-law and uncle Jeff Boss, sister-in-law and aunt Erin Boss; niece and cousin, Leila Boss.

IONA HULL
(The following obituary comes from Weng Funeral Home.)

Iona Lee Hull, age 70, of Carthage, Missouri, passed away Sunday, May 22, 2011, in Joplin, Missouri, as a result of the tornado.

Iona was born on July 1, 1940, in Meade, Kan., to James and Violet (Waltye) Hinsdale.

Iona was a homemaker. She was a member of the Joplin Full Gospel Church.

Survivors include: two daughters, Amanda Hull and Hannah Hull, both of the home; one brother, Bill Hinsdale of Carthage; two sisters, Mary Norris of Carthage, and Corky Bassinger of Arkansas; nine grandchildren, and 13 great-grandchildren.

She was preceded in death by her parents; two sons, Rick Hull and Bill Hull; one daughter, Tammy Patrick and one sister, Betsy.

WENDY ISTAS
(The following obituary is taken from the Mason-Woodard Mortuary website.)

Wendy Ann Istas, age 58, Joplin, Missouri, went home to the Lord on May 30, 2011, at KU Medical Center, as a result of the injuries she sustained in the Joplin tornado.

Wendy was born on April 26, 1953 in Peoria, Ill., the daughter of the late James and Ardith (Pool) Wasson. She has been a resident of Joplin, for the past twenty-one years. She was a member of St. Paul's United Methodist Church. She married Jason Istas on September 1, 2001. Together they co-owned and operated J-W Solutions for the past ten years. Wendy was an excellent accountant and Quick Books Specialist. She was an instructor of Quick Books for Franklin Technical School. Her clients quickly became her friend and greatly relied on her.

She was a director for the Stained Glass Theatre and a member of their board. She enjoyed sewing, crafts and most of all spending time with her grandchildren. Her kind nature and sense of humor will be missed by all. She is survived by her husband, Jason Istas, Joplin; her children, Tracy Happs and husband Roy, Joplin, Beth Trenary and husband Jason, Rogers, Arkansas, Brian Gleason and wife leslie, Blue Springs, Missouri, and Ashley Istas, Joplin; three brothers Michael Wasson and wife Kathy, Estero, Fla., Stephen Wasson and wife Mary, Woodridge, Ill., and James Wasson and wife Carol, Decatur Indiana; and ten grandchildren.

JANE JAYNES
(The following obituary is taken from the Parker Mortuary website.)

Jane E. Jaynes, age 86 of Joplin, passed away from injuries sustained in a tornado on May 22, 2011.

Born November 11, 1924 in Webb City, Missouri. She is a member of Joplin Heights Baptist Church, and lived in this area for her lifetime.

She married Eugene C. Jaynes on August 9, 1945 in Columbus, Kansas, and together they owned and operated Gene's Dari Jane at 26th and Main Street in Joplin from 1960-1985. Eugene preceded her in death on January 4, 1998.

She is survived by one son, Richard Jaynes and his wife Debbie of Joplin; one daughter, Carole A. Waggoner and her husband Ralph of Joplin, Mo.; one brother, William Pierce of Alba, Mo.; two sisters, Virginia Youst of Modesto, Ca., and Bobbi Holmes of Idaho.; four grandchildren, Jeff Jaynes, Christy Waggoner, Kelly Weaver, Chrisanna Jaynes; three great-grandchildren, Blake, Campbell and Owen.

In addition to her husband, she is preceded in death by her mother Josephine Pierce, her daughter Marilyn Jaynes, and four brothers, Fred Pierce, Andrew Pierce, Burt Pierce and Jack Pierce.

MELISA JOHNSON
(The following obituary is taken from the Knell Mortuary website.)

Melisa Renee Johnson, 50, Carthage, passed away Sunday, May 22, 2011 from injuries sustained in the Joplin tornado.

Melisa Renee Johnson was born June 11, 1960 in Hollywood, California, the daughter of Jim Johnson and Marilyn Gaye (Myers) Johnson. Melisa was a graduate of Verdugo Hills High School, Sunland, CA and was a homemaker.

Survivors include her daughter, Lashawnda (Travis) Cavener, Joplin; a brother, Joe Johnson, Sunland, CA; stepfather, Mike Libby Sunland, CA; three granddaughters, Cheyeanne, Kaylee, and Alyssa, Joplin; niece, Amber Failla, Springfield, MO; nephew, Dennise Johnson, Carthage and aunt Joann Baugh, Carthage. Melisa was preceded in death by two sons, Jody Gaudsmith and a son, Charley Gaudsmith, who died with her in the Joplin tornado; her mother, Gaye Myers Johnson Libby; her brother, Mickey Hunt; a sister, Debra Sprague; her grandparents Joe and Avis Myers, Cecil and Rose Johnson.

CHERYL JONES

Cheryl L. Jones, 39, of Altamont, died Sunday, May 22, 2011, from injuries sustained from the tornado at St. John's Regional Medical Center in Joplin where she was currently a patient.

She was born at Parsons, Kansas to Lloyd D. and Mary L. (Uitts) Jones. She grew up at rural Altamont and attended the Independence Bible School where she graduated in 1989. She worked as a telemetry technician at the Via Christi St. Francis Hospital in Wichita for several years.

She enjoyed playing the piano and writing in her journal.

She is survived by her son, Brendan Sean Hamilton of Sedgwick, Kansas; Her father and stepmother, Lloyd and Ruth Jones of rural Altamont; One brother, Marvin Jones of Altamont; One sister, Brenda Roark of Loveland, Ohio. She was preceded in death by her mother in 2006.

KATHY KELING

Kathy Keling, age 53, of Joplin, Missouri, died Sunday, May 22, 2011 in her home as a result of the tornado in Joplin, Missouri Ms. Keling was born in Springfield, Missouri, on March 7, 1958. She was the eldest daughter of Walter and Geneva (Garrison) Fischgrabe of Fair Grove, Missouri She was an active member of Glendale Christian Church for many years and later Southland Christian Church of Springfield. More recently she attended Alpine Christian Church in Riverdale, Utah. She was a beautiful, nurturing caregiver to all of us. She gave us the best of herself. To say that we will miss her wouldn't give her justice. The love she showed us will remain inside us forever. She also loved the Lord and shared that with us daily.

She is survived and missed by her two children, Heather and Dustin and their spouses, Russ and Michele; beloved Nonny to five grandchildren, Nathan, Ocean, Hailey, Strayker and Jeremiah; big sister to Allen Fischgrabe, Trudy Pike and her husband Wayman, and Ann Fischgrabe; aunt to Tara Fischgrabe and dear friend to Debbie Larsen and Ray Keling.

JAMES KENDRICK
(The following obituary is taken from the Mason-Woodard Mortuary website.)

James "David" Kendrick, age 63, Joplin, passed away May 22, 2011 at the Elks Club during the tornado.

David was born in Joplin on December 17, 1947 to Carl L. Kendrick and Olive "Billie" Reeves Kendrick, both deceased. David is survived by two brothers; Clyde "Don" Kendrick (wife Colleen), Neosho and Toney Kendrick (wife Pam), Cocoa Beach, Florida. He was preceded in death by a brother, Carl Allen Kendrick (widow Anita). Also surviving are five sisters: Diana Porter, Carthage; Nita Lane (husband Vernon), Diamond; Mary Jane Eichelberger, Joplin; Sharon Prauser, Baxter Springs, KS; Suzanne Mael (husband Stanley), Colorado Springs, Co.

He is also survived by a daughter, Brandi Lawson, and a grandson Jonathan Matarazzo, Joplin, Missouri.

David graduated from Duenweg High School in 1965. He served in the Army from 1968-1969 and was a Vietnam veteran.

He retired in 2010 after forty years in the explosive industry, working for the former Atlas Powder and its successive owners. He enjoyed his retirement and spending time with friends and family.

David was interested in everything, but a special interest and the source of many stories were his experiences prospecting for gold in Alaska. He loved to fish and went on a spring fishing trip with the same group of fishermen for over forty years.

He was an active member of the Elks Club and the Gold Prospecting Association of America. He also was a former member of the VFW. group of fishermen for over forty years.

He was an active member of the Elks Club and the Gold Prospecting Association of America. He also was a former member of the VFW.

ABE KHOURY
(The following obituary is taken from the Parker Mortuary website.)

Abraham H. (Abe) Khoury, age 26 of Joplin, went to be with his Lord and Savior Jesus Christ, Tuesday morning, May 31, 2011 at University Hospital in Columbia from injuries sustained in the Joplin tornado.

Born December 7, 1984 in Stillwater, Okla., he lived in Joplin most of his lifetime, attended Joplin public schools, and graduated from Joplin High School in 2004. Currently, he was pursuing his degree in Business and Entrepreneurship at M.S.S.U. He also worked as a server at Outback Steakhouse in Joplin. Abe was a Christian. He loved fishing, camping and the outdoors. He also loved to play Texas Hold-em and aspired to play professionally. He loved football, played in high school, and was a passionate K.C. Chiefs Fan.

Survivors include his mother, Teresa Worley of Joplin; his father, John Khoury of Gallatin, Tenn.; three brothers, Frank Carey of Joplin, Nicholas and Michael Khoury both of Old Hickory, Tenn.; a sister, Samantha Khoury of Old Hickory; a stepbrother, Zach Worley of Joplin; maternal grandparents, Dan and Karen Mitchell of Neosho; maternal grandparents, Robert and Donna Bateson, Sr. of Sevierville, Tenn.; paternal grandparents, Antoinette Khoury of Amman, Jordan; many aunts, uncles, cousins, nieces, nephews and countless friends. Abe was preceded in death by a paternal grandfather, Ibrahim Khoury; an uncle, Robert Bateson, Jr., who also went to be the Lord after sustaining injuries in the same tornado, and an infant sister, Nadia Khoury.

STANLEY KIRK
Stanley Dale Kirk, 62, Joplin, died Sunday, May 22, 2011, from injuries sustained in the tornado. He was born March 1, 1949, in Springfield, MO to Elmer (Hap) Kirk and Evelyne (Tosh) Kirk.

Stanley worked 38 years at Rocketdyne, Teledyne, Sabreliner and Premier Turbines as an aircraft engine technician. He was member of the National Guard and United Aerospace Workers.

Stanley is survived by his wife, Janice Lynn, a daughter Jodelle Lynn Kirk of the home, a son, Bobby Wayne Giger, Jr. of Joplin, two step sons, Eric Shoenberger, Aurora, MO, Rick Shoenberger; Siloam Springs, AR; one step daughter, Kim Cumming, Neosho, Mo., and one brother, Kelly Kirk, Shawnee, Okla.

GENEVA KOLER
(The following information is taken from the Clark Funeral Home website.)

Geneva Eutsler Koler, 84, passed away at Green Briar Nursing home in Joplin, Sunday, May 22, 2011, as a result of the Joplin tornado.

She was born Aug. 17, 1926, in Galena, Missouri, the daughter of Luther and Edna Eutsler. She was a lifelong area resident and had worked at La-Z-Boy in Neosho. She is survived by two sons, Michael Koler, Dallas, Texas, and Patrick Koler, Yakima, Wash.; two grandchildren, Sarah Ashbaugh and Aaron Koler, Yakima; five great-grandchildren of Yakima, area; four sisters, Lucille Moffett, Granby, Joan Eutsler, Neosho, Sharon Sanders, Neosho, and Lorene Myers, Ft. Smith, Arkansas; two brothers, Richard Eutsler, Granby and Larry Eutsler, Granby.

In addition to her parents, she was preceded in by two brothers, Donald Eutsler and Herbert Eutsler.

TEDRA KUHN
(The following obituary is taken from the *Joplin Globe*)

Tedra Jewell Kuhn, 69, of Joplin, was a homemaker who loved her family. She also enjoyed going to the casino, and she always had a smile on her face and cared for others before herself. Survivors include two children, two grandchildren, and several great-grandchildren.

DONALD LANSAW
(The following obituary is taken from the Thornhill-Dillon Mortuary.)

Mr. Donald Wayne Lansaw, Jr., 31, of Joplin, Missouri departed this life suddenly on Sunday evening, May 22, 2011 at his home from injuries sustained in the devastating Joplin tornado.

Don began his journey on August 21, 1979 in Joplin, Missouri born to the union of Donald Wayne Lansaw, Sr. and Beth R. (Dinwiddie) Lansaw. He was raised in Seneca, Missouri and was a 1998 graduate of Seneca High School. He furthered his education at Crowder College in Neosho, Missouri. Don was a man of great work ethic. He owned and operated Lansaw Technologies and was a licensed Realtor with Charles Burt both located in Joplin, Missouri. He enjoyed spending time outdoors where his favorite activities were camping and float trips.

On July 2, 2005 in Webb City, Missouri he was united in marriage to Bethany Ann Krudwig and she survives of the home. Additional survivors include his parents, Donald Wayne Lansaw, Sr. of Joplin, Missouri and Beth Lansaw of Seneca, Missouri; a brother, Zach Lansaw of Joplin, Missouri; paternal grandmother, Mary

Sargent of Carl Junction, Missouri; his father and mother in-law, Jim and Donna Krudwig of Webb City, Missouri; as well as a host of other family and close friends.

BRUCE LIEVENS
(The following obituary was taken from the Clark Funeral Home website.)

Bruce Allen Lievens, 48, Joplin, died Sunday, May 22, 2011, from injuries sustained in the Joplin tornado.

He was born December 18, 1962, in Moline, Ill., to James Lee Lievens and Darlene Kay (Kelso) Lievens.

Bruce moved to the Neosho area in 1975 from Illinois where he had worked in the family business of Circle L-Auctions Service as an auction clerk for over 30 years, He was an avid sports fan, loved being with his family and also buying and selling antiques.

He is survived by his parents James and Darlene Lievens of Neosho; two brother, Bart Lievens, Seneca, Brett and wife Roxanne Lievens, Neosho; two sisters, Brenda Boyd and companion Mike Larson, Neosho, Betsy and Gabe Shorter, Neosho; 13 nieces and nephews, Marquise, LaKyne, Jake, Mark, Dakota, Garrett, Cara, Carinna, Trevor, Seth, Grace, Hollie and Katlyn; and his best friends Rick and Giselle Scott.

BILLIE SUE HUFF LITTLE
(The following obituary is taken from the Simpson Funeral Home website.)

Billie Sue Huff Little, age 65, of Joplin went home to be with the Lord, Sunday, May 22, 2011 as a result of the tornado. Billie was born January 10, 1946 in Butler County, Missouri to Harry and Martha (Mitchell) Huff. She was a waitress.

Billie is survived by her daughter, Tammy Curtner and grandson, Donnie Reed both of Joplin along with other siblings. She will be missed by those who loved her.

SKYULAR LOGSDEN
Skyular Ignatius Logdson, 16-months, Joplin, died Sunday, May 22, 2011, from injuries sustained in the Joplin tornado.

He was born Jan. 19, 2010, in Joplin to Corderro I. Logsdon and Carol J. Tate.

He is survived by his parents; his paternal grandparents, Robin Logsdon and Michael Rickey of Joplin and John Logsdon and Alesha Feather, Goddard, Kan.; maternal grandparents, James Tate, Carl Junction, Milissa A. and Rusty, Carl Junction; paternal great-grandparents, Sue Crow Slaughter and husband, Ralph, Grove, Okla., Frank Reynolds, Rutledge, Ga.; maternal great- grandparents, Debbie and Lee Cummins, Carl Junction, Nancy Reynolds, Joplin, Carol Tate, Joplin; maternal great-great-grandmother, Joyce McGuirk, Sarcoxie, Missouri; numerous aunts, uncles and cousins.

The family has requested for contributions in Skyular's honor be made to the Skyular I. Logsdon Memorial Fund, in care of Clark Funeral Homes, P.O. Box 66, Neosho, 64850.

MARY LOVELL
(The following obituary is taken from the Mason-Woodard Mortuary website.)

Mary Lois Lovell, age 65 of Joplin, Missouri passed away Sunday May 22, 2011 in the tornado that devastated the city of Joplin.

Mary was born on September 30, 1945 in Joplin the daughter of the late Emmett and Alice (Cook) O'Connell. She worked for the Carl Junction School District as a cafeteria cook for many years before retiring.

Mary married Burton Lovell on May 4, 1963 in Joplin, he survives. Additional survivors include two sons, Rick Lovell and his wife Joanna of Carthage, Missouri, Emmett Lovell of Carl Junction, Missouri, one daughter, Michelle Lovell of Carl Junction, two brothers, George Himes and his wife Dollie of Joplin, Charles Himes of Springfield, Missouri, four sisters, Faye Hance of Michigan City, In., Helen Rigs and her husband Bob of Webb City, Missouri, Janie Wood and her husband Jay of Webb City and Twyla Murphy of Joplin, three grandchildren, Amanda, Josh and Rebecca, and one great-grandchild expected in June or July. She was preceded in death by her parents, two twin brothers, Emmett Lee and Jackie Lee O'Connell and two sisters, Dolly Bigbee and Joyce Vance.

CHRIS LUCAS
(The following obituary is taken from the Luginbuel Funeral Home website.)

Christopher Don Lucas, 27 year old former Vinita resident, died Sunday May 22, 2011 in Joplin. He was born November 24, 1983 in Claremore to Terry Don Lucas and Pamela Jean Parker. Chris attended Vinita Schools, then joined the United States Navy in August of 2003, and was Honorably Discharged in July of 2009. He was currently the Assistant Manager of the Rangeline Pizza Hut in Joplin.

The family includes: his two daughters, Chloe Alexandra Lucas and Emily Kay Lucas; father Terry Don Lucas and wife Angel; mother Pamela Jean Praytor and husband Michael; grandparents, Mary J. and Bill K. Parker, Alice F. and Bobby D. Lucas; his girlfriend Brooke E. Praytor and their unborn child; brothers and sisters, Jacqueline Rene Bass, Terri Jo Bass and her fiancée` D. C. Williams, Tiffanie Faye Wickliff, Terri Dawn Breger, Joshua Aaron Lucas, Jacob Ryan Lucas, Jeremy Kyle Lucas, Cody Lee Lucas, Cody Michael Praytor; the mother of his children Andrea Monique Lucas; numerous nieces, nephews, aunts, uncles, cousins and many friends.

Preceding him in death were his great-grandparents Alfred and Julia "Babe" Woolman.

PATRICIA MANN
(The following obituary is taken from the *Joplin Globe*)

Patricia Mann, 64, of Joplin, worked for Rouse Heating and Air Conditioning for about 25 years. She loved animals and enjoyed reading, particularly mystery novels. Survivors include a brother.

RACHEL MARKHAM
(The following obituary is taken from the *Kansas City Star*)

When Katy O'Keefe awoke and was pulled from the rubble of her home in the 2500 block of Murphy Avenue, she had no idea where her cousin Rachel Markham was.

The two had taken shelter in a closet to wait for the tornado to pass, but it wouldn't be until days later that O'Keefe and her cousin — Markham's brother Bobby — would locate Markham's five-month-pregnant body at a morgue.

"She was so excited about the baby," said Rachel's grandmother, Eleanor Markham, who lives in Escondido, Calif. "I just have to believe there's somewhere they're safe and together."

Eleanor said Rachel's friends and family gathered to remember her at a karaoke lounge in Escondido that she used to frequent. They sang songs to Rachel, celebrating her life.

"Everybody loved Rachel," Eleanor Markham said. "She would light up a room when she walked into it."

Rachel Markham, 33, was a hostess at the Red Onion Cafe.

NANCY MARTIN

Nancy Ann Martin, 52, Neosho, died Sunday, May 22, 2011, in Miami, Okla., from injuries sustained in the Joplin tornado. She was born June 19, 1958, in Lebanon, Mo., to Marion Kyle Grinage and Betty M. (Paulson) Grinage.

Nancy was a lifelong resident of Neosho and graduate of Neosho High School. She worked at the New Vision Group home as a caregiver.

She is survived by her two sons, Anthony Kyle Owen and Brandon Shane Martin, both of Neosho; one granddaughter Khristeena Ann Marie Owen, Goodman; a brother Michael Grinage, Kansas City, Mo.; a sister Linda Dettmer and husband Jim of Joplin and 4 nephews, David Dewitt and wife Rinatta of Mesa, Arizona; Tyler Dewitt, Neosho; Daniel Dewitt, Neosho and Christopher Dettmer of Colorado.

JANICE MCKEE

Janice Kay McKee, resident of Wyandotte, Okla., passed away Wednesday, June the 15th, 2011 at Select Specialty Hospital in Springfield, Mo. She was 60 years old. She was born December the 6th, 1950 in Webb City, Mo., to Charles and Grace (Cleveland) Yeager. She married Gary McKee, Sr., on May the 15th, 1968 in Carl Junction, Mo.

Janice was survived by her mother, Grace Lawton, of Webb City, Mo., husband; Gary, of the home., one son; Gary McKee, Jr., and spouse Jennifer, of Wyandotte, Okla., one brother; Gerald W. Yeager, of Quapaw, Okla., one sister; Joyce Goodpasture, of Carl Junction, Mo., and one granddaughter; ShaKetha Lei McKee, of Commerce, Okla. She was preceded in death by her father, Charles, and one grandson; Kacee Lynn Star McKee.

JESSE MCKEE
(The following information is taken from the Clark Funeral Home website.)

Jesse Len McKee., 44, Neosho, died Sunday, May 22, 2011, from injuries sustained in the Joplin tornado. He was born May 17, 1967 in St. Louis, Missouri to Lee Roy McKee and Irma (Rayfield) McKee.

Jay and Susan Johnston were married on June 15, 1991 in Ellington, Missouri. They moved to Neosho in 1998. He served in the United States Air Force. Jay was a self-employed master electrician and a member of the Set Free Ministries in Wyandotte, Okla. He was an avid fisherman, hunter and loved playing music.

He is survived by his wife Susan McKee; his parents Irma Hampton, Seneca; his children, Jessica McKee, Justin McKee and Zachary McKee, all of the home; twos sisters, Judith Peters, Sumerland, FL and Janet McKee, Webb City, Mo.; two step brothers, Robert Hampton, St. Louis, Mo. and David Hampton, St. Louis, Mo.; step sister Tina Klesterman, St. Clarks, Mo.

JAMES and MARY MCKEEL
(The following obituary is taken from the Parker Mortuary website.)

James Edward McKeel, age 69, Joplin, passed away on Sunday, May 22, 2011 at his home as a result of injuries sustained in the tornado.

Jim was born October 22, 1941 in Warsaw, Illinois, son of the late Marvin and Ollie McKeel. He was a baker for over 30 years for several companies in the Joplin area. He enjoyed life, and was always trying to make people smile. He loved to entertain and cook for his family.

He was preceded in death by his first wife, Donna Marie McKeel in 1999. Jim was with his current wife, Mary McKeel, during the tornado, she also passed away.

Survivors include sons, Jimmy McKeel of Asbury, Missouri, and Kenny McKeel of Lebanon, Missouri; daughters, Jamey McKeel of Duenweg, Missouri and Regina McNamara of Webb City, Missouri; grandchildren, Darin Keen, Ashley Hoskins, Dylan Ward, Amber Ward, Brandi Whitehead, Jesseca McNamara, Samantha McNamara; great-grandchildren, James Micheal Keen, Brandon Hoskins, Bailyn Mercer, Zachary Whitehead, and Austin Whitehead.

No information about Mary McKeel was included in the obituary.

LADONNA MCPURDY
(Obituary information was taken from the Forbes-Hoffman Funeral Home.)

LaDonna S. (Journot) McPurdy, 68, of Joplin, Missouri, formerly of Parsons, Kansas, went home to be with her Lord at 4:57 p.m., Tuesday, May 31, 2011, at Freeman West Hospital in Joplin from injuries sustained in the tornado.

She was born October 6, 1942, in Parsons, Kansas, to Frank and Myrtle (Johnston) Journot. She grew up in Parsons where she attended St. Mary's Elementary School and was a graduate of Labette County Community High School in Altamont. Following high school graduation, she attended Ft. Scott Community College where she earned a degree in cosmetology. Later in life, she attended Independence Community College where she earned a cosmetology teaching certificate and had taught classes at Vatterott College in Joplin. She was a lifelong hair stylist in Parsons before moving to Carl Junction in 2005.

She was a member of St. Mary's Catholic Church in Joplin. She enjoyed painting, ceramics, gardening, fishing, camping and traveling. She especially enjoyed spending time with her family and friends.

She and Richard McPurdy were married in 1983 in Miami, Oklahoma. He survives of the home.

Additional survivors include: one son, Dale Gough of Parsons, Kan.; four daughters – Karla March of Weir, Kan., Lisa Dhooghe of Diamond, Mo., Debra Shields of Parsons, Kan., and Julie Ramsey of Carl Junction, Mo. Stepson, John McPurdy of Kings Mountain, N.C., 27 grandchildren, 28 great-grandchildren, one sister, Christine Jones of Valley View, Texas, and an Aunt, Ann Pontious of Parsons, Kan.

She was preceded in death by her parents and one brother, Eugene Quirin.

RANDY MELL

(The following information is taken from the Simpson Funeral Home website.)

Randall Elvin Mell, age 49 of Webb City, passed away Sunday, May 22, 2011 as a result of the tornado.

Randy was born November 15, 1961 in Joplin to Elvin E. and Peggy (Musgrave) Mell.

He was a longtime custodian and helped in maintaining Jasper County Courthouse in Carthage.

Randy was a former member of Emmanuel Baptist Church in Webb City for many years and currently attended Open Door Baptist Church in Carthage.

When he wasn't working, Randy enjoyed going to watch productions at the Stained Glass Theatre, Webb City High School, Ozark Christian College and MSSU, where he was also a lion backer season ticket holder. He loved to attend Webb City High School sporting events at every chance and enjoyed their music and drama programs.

Randy was courteous and kind and a wholesome man who will be greatly missed by those who knew him.

He is survived by his parents, Elvin and Peggy Mell of the home; his sister, Carole D. White of Mission, KS and several cousins.

ANGELINA MENAPACE

(The following obituary is taken from the Parker Mortuary website.)

Angelina Ann Menapace was born on September 18, 1958 to Leo Louis and Julia Ann Menapace in Joplin, Missouri. She passed on from this earthly life to her heavenly home on Sunday, May 22, 2011 at the age of 52 from a devastating tornado that hit Joplin, Missouri.

Angelina worked as office manager of Behavior Management and Associates for 12 years. She truly enjoyed her job there and felt as if she were part of each of their families. Angelina raised two children, Kebra Renee and Kevin Erik Menapace. Her pride and joy were her two granddaughters, Jazmine Reann and Alexis Darlene Menapace.

Some of Angelina's favorite things were cooking, shopping at consignment stores, spending time with her grand-daughters and playing with her Boston terrier, Frank Duke. One of Angelina's favorite times was the holidays. She would always prepare plenty of extra food while teasing each of her nieces and nephews, and often playing practical jokes on them. We never got through a Thanksgiving or Christmas season without her famous turkey dressing.

Angelina is survived by one sister, June V. Boyer of Joplin, Mo; two brothers, Frank L. Armstrong of Huntsville, Al and Leo L. Menapace Jr. of Joplin, Mo; two children, Kebra R. Menapace and Kevin E. Menapace; two grand-daughters Jazmine R. Menapace and Alexis D. Menapace as well as several cousins, nieces and nephews. She was preceded in death by her parents Leo L. and Julia A. Menapace; sister, Katherine M. Pence and brother Steven A. Menapace.

RONALD MEYER
(The following obituary is taken from the Mason-Woodard Mortuary website.)

Ronald D. Meyer, age 64, of Joplin, Missouri, passed away on May 22, 2011, at his home, from injuries sustained in the catastrophic tornado.

Ronald was born on August 5, 1946 in Metropolis, Illinois, the son of the late Nelville Meyer and Adele Elizabeth Bourm. He moved to Joplin in 2008 from Murfreesboro, TN. He worked as a night auditor for hotels until he became the full-time caregiver of his brother George. Ronald was an Air Force Veteran serving in the Viet Nam War.

He is survived by his three brothers, Roger Meyer of Joplin, George Meyer of Joplin and Billy Meyer, Maryland; one sister, Brenda Meyer of Metropolis, Illinois.

TRIPP MILLER
(The following obituary is taken from the Parker Mortuary website.)

Tripp Miller passed away early Monday morning, May 23, 2011, after sustaining severe injuries from the tornado that hit Joplin on Sunday afternoon.

Tripp was the son of Patricia Gray Miller and Ray Donald Miller, Jr. of Joplin and was born at St. John's Hospital in Joplin on July 20, 1961. He graduated from Collegeview State School in 1982. After graduating, Tripp began working at the Sheltered Workshop in Carthage for two years and then joined the work force at Joplin Workshop, Inc. and worked there for the last 27 years.

He was a lifelong member of the First Presbyterian Church in Joplin and attended regularly his God's Fellowship Sunday School class. Some of Tripp's many loves in his full life were living with his childhood friends, Rick Fox and Mark Farmer, at their home at 2302 Iowa; his special friends, Penny Morehouse, at Joplin Regional Center and James Newman, case worker of connections case management and Tripp's support staff of Community Support Services; bowling weekly with friends at 4th Street Bowl; meeting with friends at 1st Presbyterian Church; his title of "Number 1 Uncle" to his five nieces and four nephews; traveling to see his brother and sisters; going to Mizzou football games with his family where he was a very proud member of the University of Missouri Alumni Association; and rooting, as a life-long fan, for his St. Louis Cardinals and then calling his Dad to let him know the results of the game. Tripp loved sports. He was an enthusiastic fan of local high school sports teams, particularly the Parkwood Bears and Joplin Eagles. He was a participant in the Special Olympics since his school days.

He excelled at bowling and in his early years, swimming. He won his last of many gold medals at the State Special Olympics in the fall of 2010 at 4th Street Bowl in Joplin by bowling the best game of his life. Tripp was a happy, gentle, kind, and loving man. He didn't know a stranger. He was your friend for life even if he just met you and was always so glad to see you. He touched the lives of so many people, and we were all better people having him in our life. His family will miss him terribly every moment of every day.

Tripp is survived by his sisters, Melinda Miller Crowe and her husband, Lawrence Kerdolff Crowe, of Overland Park, Kan.; Rebecca Miller Gurley and her husband, Curtis Raymond Gurley, of Farmington, N.M., and Mary Elizabeth Williams of Galena, Kan.; brother, Thomas Gray Miller and his wife Patti O'Sullivan Miller of St. Louis, Missouri; nephews, Lawrence Kerdolff (Kert) Crowe, Jr., Nathan Miller Crowe, Jackson Miller Gurley, Davis Cummins Gurley; nieces Laura Elizabeth Crowe, Elizabeth Leigh Williams, Riley Grace Miller, Molly Ann Miller and Madison Rose Miller; uncles William R. Gray and family of New Berlin, Wis., Thomas R. Gray and family of Columbia, Missouri; aunt Patricia Miller Righthouse, of Broken Arrow, Okla. and many additional cousins and relatives.

LORNA MILLER
(The following obituary is taken from the *Joplin Globe*)

Lorna "Kay" Miller, 72, of Joplin, had lived most of her life in Kansas and was retired from the food service industry where she had worked as a waitress, grocery store clerk, and school cafeteria cook. She enjoyed sewing, reading and bird-watching, and she loved nature and cats. Survivors include one daughter and two grandchildren.

SUZANNE MOCK
(The following obituary is taken from the *Joplin Globe*)

Suzanne Mock, 39, of Forsyth, is survived by her husband, Thomas Mock, her son, Thomas J. Mock, and her daughters, Amber Mock and Amanda Mock. She also had two grandchildren.

DORIS MONTGOMERY
Doris Marie Menhusen Montgomery, age 83 of Joplin, passed away at her residence from injuries sustained in the tornado on Sunday, May 22, 2011. Born April 22, 1928 in Glen Elder, Kan., she was the daughter of the late Harold Finley and Doris Mae Shane Finley and graduated from high school in Glen Elder. She attended Kansas State University, from which she received her teaching certification. Marie was a teacher in Kansas for several years. She lived in Joplin for 20 years, before moving to be near her children in Tonganoxie for 13 years. She returned to live in Joplin with her local children two years ago. She attended Christ's Community United Methodist Church. Her first husband, Gordon Menhusen, to whom she was married for 48 years, preceded her in death.

Her second husband, Richard Montgomery, also preceded her in death.

Survivors include three daughters, Jeanie Morris and Cathy Menhusen, both of Joplin, Debbie Gravatt and husband Bob of Tonganoxie, Kan.; one son, Gary Menhusen and wife Patricia of Tonganoxie; step-children, Dick and Pat Montgomery of Kansas City, Missouri, Bill and Pat Montgomery of Tonganoxie, Kansas, and Judy Forbach of Lawrence, Kansas; one brother, Vernon Finley and wife Mary of Hiawatha, Kan.; nine grandchildren; 12 great-grandchildren and nine great-great-grandchildren; many nieces and nephews.

EDIE MOORE
(The following obituary is taken from the Thornhill-Dillon website.)

Edith "Edie" L. Moore, 48, passed away on May 22, 2011 due to injuries sustained in the Joplin Tornado. She was born in Columbus, KS. On July 18, 1962 to Herman William Froelich and Edith Emma (Henderson) Froelich who preceded her in death.

Edie was raised in Columbus, KS and then moved to Joplin where she had lived for the last several years. She is survived by her son, Bowen Daniel Greninger of Joplin; daughter, Emily Diane DeGraff of Joplin; and a brother, Herman Wayne Froelich of Parsons, Kansas. Edie was a dedicated mother to both her children, and loved her cats that she had adopted.

ESTRELLITA MOORE
(The following obituary information is taken from the Mason-Woodard Mortuary website.)

Estrellita M. Moore age 64 of Joplin, Missouri passed away May 22, 2011 from injuries sustained in the catastrophic tornado.

She was born December 4, 1946 in Angeles City, Philippines, the daughter of the late Faustino and Felisa (Mercado) Manansala. She was a hair dresser for J.C. Penney's. She was a Catholic and attended St. Mary's Catholic Church. Estrellita loved going to the casino.

SALLY MOULTON
(The following obituary is taken from the *Mascoutah* (Ill.) *Herald*)

Helping others find shelter from the approaching tornado in Joplin, Missouri, on May 22nd, may have cost a former Mascoutah resident her life.

Killed in the storm was Sally Ann (Harris) Moulton, 58, who graduated from Mascoutah High School in 1971.

A memorial service for Sally Ann (Harris) Moulton occurred June 26th at St. John United Church of Christ.

Before moving to Joplin, Moulton worked at MarKa Nursing Home here, and is remembered by friends as "a very nice lady."

Her brother, Rick Harris, was a member of the Mascoutah Police Department.

In Joplin, Moulton was a member of a theater group that had been performing "I Remember Mama," at The Stained Glass Theater, on the afternoon of the tornado. Moulton was playing the part of Aunt Jenny in the production. According to family members, the theater is just a block away from St. John's Hospital, which took a direct hit from the giant storm.

NADINE MULKEY
(The following obituary is taken from the Clark Funeral Home website.)

Georgia 'Nadine' Mulkey, 91, Joplin, died June 1, 2011 at Spring River Christian Village from injuries sustained in the May 22nd tornado. Nadine was born April 9, 1920 in Pierce City, MO, the daughter of George Morris and Myra Burton Morris.

She was a lifelong area resident and had worked in the food service of the schools and Sale Memorial Hospital, now Freeman Neosho Hospital. She was a member of the First Baptist Church in Neosho. Nadine married John Mulkey on April 9, 1939 at Cassville, Mo., and he preceded her in death on Jan. 30, 1997.

She is survived by four children, Myra Koeneke, Joplin; William 'Bill' Mulkey, Joplin; Barbara Krambeck, Denver, Co., and John W. Mulkey, Carthage; 5 grandchildren and 6 great grandchildren. In addition to her parents and husband, she is preceded in death by two sisters, Claudia Kuklenski and Goldie Miller.

EDMUND MULLANEY
(The following obituary is taken from the *Springfield News-Leader*)

Edmund Vincent Mullaney was born on March 24, 1929, in Adrian, Mich., the son of Edward Vincent Mullaney and Marie (Clancy) Mullaney. He was a veteran of the United States Marine Corps. He was a member of Our Lady of the Lake Catholic Church and was a member of the Knights of Columbus. He had been a resident of the area for the past 10 years.

He is survived by his wife, Marilyn Mullaney of Hollister, Missouri; his sister, Julie Forester and husband Stephen of Oxford, Conn.; and brother, Robert Mullaney of Huntington, Conn.

He was preceded in death by his parents.

SHARYL NELSON
(The following obituary is taken from the Mason-Woodard Mortuary website.)

Sharyl Anyssa Nelsen of Webb City, Missouri, passed away in the catastrophic tornado on May 22, 2011.

Sharyl was born on November 11, 1976 in Brownsville, Texas. She was working as a Sales Representative for the AT&T store on Rangeline when the tornado struck. Sharyl was able to help a family out of harm's way moments before the tornado struck the building.

Sharyl was a loving mother and wife, a caring daughter and sister, and a nurturing person whose heart and arms were open to everyone who was blessed to have known her.

Sharyl is survived by her loving husband, Chad Nelsen, her beautiful children, Matilyn Jade Perry (14), and Aaron Cain Nelsen (10), her step daughter Ashley Nelsen Baker, her parents Yolanda Reed and Ernest San Miguel, her stepfather Terrel Reed, her sisters Cynthia Hopkins and Sandra Mendoza, her brother Ernie San Miguel, and her step brother Tim Reed.

She is preceded in death by her grandparents Enrique and Cecilia Ybarra and Pedro and Josefina San Miguel, and her step sister Tamara Reed.

WILL NORTON
(The following obituary is taken from the Parker Mortuary website.)

William Richard Norton, known by friends and family as Will, went home to heaven on Sunday evening, May 22, 2011. Will was born and raised in Joplin, Missouri where he did so much more than just attend Joplin High School. The tragedy of the Joplin tornado has left behind his parents Mark and Trish Norton of Joplin, his sister Sara Norton, grandparents Richard and Laveda Norton, aunts and uncles Tracey and Jeff Presslor, Jane and Chuck Haver, Connie Allen, and Ralph Worster II, along with many loving cousins. Will was preceded in death by his grandparents Ralph Worster, Lora Worster-Kaffenberger, and Leo Kaffenberger.

Those who were blessed to know Will watched him live a full and joyful life in his short 18 years. Very few of us can say we've accomplished half of the things this young man has done or touched a community with a heart such as his. Will has left an endless legacy to the people influenced by his numerous YouTube videos, tweets, and outstanding contributions to those in need. To recognize the enormity of those lives he touched, he had over 2 million upload views on his Willdabeast YouTube account (which can be found at http://www.YouTube.com/Will), over 6,000 followers on Twitter, and over 800 friends on his personal Facebook page, not to mention the 50,000 people across the world who have been praying for him since the storm through the Help Find Will Norton Facebook community page.

Will has always noticed the small things in life as an excited and optimistic dreamer. With such a creative mind, we've witnessed his many clever videos as he partnered with YouTube with the ability to reach thousands. One of his videos mentioned the 50 things he had done as of 3 years ago. We can add multiple highlights to this list including graduating high school on the very day of this tragedy.

To name a few, Will loved traveling, and one of his favorite places was Africa, where he got to see the great wildebeest migration. He played on a state-level tennis team and became a private pilot this year. He traveled to Washington DC with his state-winning US Constitution Team where he rallied outside of the White House after Bin Laden was killed. Will was an avid volunteer and loved the Joplin Humane Society. He was accepted to Chapman University for Film Production, which was his lifelong dream.

Will's faith in his savior was evident in his everyday life and powerfully so, as he quoted scripture in the arms of his earthly father before being taken to his heavenly father that day.

DENNIS OSBORN
(The following obituary is taken from the Campbell-Biddlecome Funeral Home website.)

Dennis M. Osborn, 34, Seneca, Mo., passed into eternal rest May 22, 2011 from injuries sustained from the tornado that devastated Joplin, Missouri.

Dennis Melvin Osborn was born June 3, 1976 in Savannah, ILL. the son of Richard Joel and Helen Azenith (Rothenbeuhler) Osborn. Dennis had worked for

Jasper Foods and was a member of the 203rd National Guard. Dennis married Steffannie Michelle (Hufferd) Osborn, April 15, 2000 in Joplin, Mo., and she survives.

Additional survivors include one son, Matthew Osborn, Seneca; one daughter, Aundree Osborn, Joplin, His mother Helen Osborn, Seneca three brothers, Rick Osborn state of Ill., Ron Shafer, Seneca and Todd Shafer state of Ill.; four sisters, Dianne Denson, Seneca, Brenda S, state of Ill., Peggy Jackson, state of Texas, and Roxanne Smith, Seneca.

Dennis was preceded in death by his father Richard Osborn in November of 2000.

CHARLES OSTER
(The following obituary is taken from the Clark Funeral Home website.)

Charles E. Oster was born July 30, 1933 in Roads, Missouri, the son of Raymond Oster of and Velma Rosebud Hampton Oster. He entered into rest on May 22, 2011 as a result of the tornado. Charles was a lifelong area resident and had served in the U.S. Army during the Korean Conflict. He currently was semi retired, working for Share Corp, Milwaukee, WI in sales. Charles was a member of the First Christian Church in Webb City and served as a deacon.

SHIRLEY PARKER
(The following obituary is taken from the Bath-Naylor Funeral Home website.)

Shirley Ann Parker, 68 of Joplin, Mo., died Sunday, May 22, 2011 in the tornado that devastated Joplin.

She was born February 11, 1943 in Sterling, Kansas the daughter of Kenneth and Rosemary(Greene) Stange.

She was married to Ronnie G. Parker, and later divorced.

Shirley was a Mammography Technician at Loveless Health Care System in Albuquerque, NM for many years, she retired in 2008.

Survivors include a son, Greg Parker and fiancée Jennifer Willey of Pittsburg, a daughter Stephanie Woods and husband Joseph of Joplin, MO, along with six grandchildren Jessawynne Parker, Shelby Ann Woods, Alexis Kathryn Woods, Mitchell William Woods, Daniel Thomas Willey and Connor Peyton Willey.

She was preceded in death by her parents and a brother Robert Dee Stange.

NICHOLE PEARISH
(The following obituary is taken from the Mason-Woodard Mortuary website.)

Nichole Sherie Pearish, age 23, of Joplin, Missouri passed away at 3:21 p.m. Saturday, June 4, 2011 at the University of Missouri Medical Center in Columbia, Missouri from injuries sustained in the Joplin tornado.

Nichole was born July 24, 1987 in Joplin and lived in the Joplin area most of her life. She was a 2006 graduate of Sarcoxie High School and was active in FFA. She was employed as a Customer Service Supervisor with Aegis Communications.

Nichole was a member of the First Baptist Church of Sarcoxie, and was a member of the Route 66 Cloggers.

JOYCE PERRY

Mary Joyce Perry, age 76, of Joplin, passed away on Sunday May 22, 2011, from injuries sustained in the tornado.

Joyce was born November 16, 1934 in Joplin, Missouri, the daughter of John and Vivian Thurman. She was a lifelong resident of Joplin and a graduate of Joplin High School. In October 1953 she married Warren E. Perry in Joplin. He preceded her in death on October 31, 1983. She was a secretary for Prudential Insurance and KODE TV and then owner of It Figures in Joplin. She presently worked for C.J. Uniform Shop in Joplin. She was a member of Epsilan Sigma Alpha and AARP. She enjoyed spending her time with her grandchildren.

She is survived her daughter, Debbie McMurry and husband Doug, of Pittsburg, Ks.; her son, Dan Perry, of St. Louis, Missouri; grandsons, Eric Smith, of Carl Junction, Missouri and Ryan Smith , of St. Charles, Missouri; great-grandson, Cooper Smith; great-granddaughter Catie Smith, Carl Junction, Missouri; and a sister, Jean Goff, of Joplin. She was preceded in death by her husband and parents.

BEN PETERSON

James Benjamin John "Ben" Peterson, age 27, Joplin, passed away on Sunday, May 22, 2011 due to injuries sustained in the tornado.
Ben was born September 20, 1983 in Joplin, and graduated from Joplin High School in 2003. He was currently working at the McDonalds on Main St. with the night shift.

Survivors include a mother, Leilani Halvorsen of Joplin; step-father Tom Halvorsen of Joplin; sister, Myra Boatright of Joplin; grandmother, Margaret Heuer of Skokie, Illinois; nephews, Austin and Job; nieces, Quin and Laci.

He was preceded in death by his father, James E. Benham.

ANNA PETTEK

Anna Pettek, 91, a Greenbriar resident, passed away Sunday, May 22, 2011. Arrangements were entrusted to the Thornhill-Dillon Mortuary.

JAY PETTY

(The following obituary information is taken from the Clark Funeral Home website.)

John Henry (Jay) Petty, Jr., 37, Joplin, died Sunday, May 22, 2011, from injuries sustained in the Joplin tornado. He was born April 3, 1974, in Hoopston, IL to John Henry Petty, Sr. and Linda Sue (Watson) Petty.

Jay moved to the Neosho area 5 years ago and worked at Jasper Products in Joplin for the past 5 years. He spent two years serving in the Army Rangers. He loved God, his country and spending time with his family. He also loved to hunt, fish and play the guitar and had a band, Iris Road.

He is survived by his parents John Henry, Sr. and Linda Sue Petty of Gray Ridge, Mo.; his fiancé, Lisa Hartman, Neosho; two daughters, Hannah Petty, Dexter, Mo., Hayli Petty, Dexter, Mo.; his fiancés children, Leif Larson and Jedidiah Larson, both of the home; two brothers, Dallas Petty, Malden, Mo.; Nicholas Petty, Gray Ridge, Mo., and one sister, Alisha Hagy, Essex, Mo.

MARIE PIQUARD
(The following obituary is taken from the Mason-Woodard Mortuary website.)

Hallie "Marie" Cook Piquard age 78 of Joplin, Missouri passed away Sunday May 22, 2011 from injuries sustained in the catastrophic tornado.

Marie was born October 20, 1932 in Lufkin, Tx. to Arthur and Nobbil (Mossingelle) Agleton. She worked as a Deputy Collector for Jasper County, and with CFI for eight years. She was a member of the Harmony Heights Baptist Church. She enjoyed bowling and southern gospel music.

She married Elbert "Dick" Cook on December 3, 1960 in Texas, he preceded her in death on December 8, 2000. She then married Lloyd Piquard on May 3, 2003, he survives. Additional survivors include two sons, Lloyd Piquard Jr. and wife Donna of Neodesha, Ks., Chris Piquard and wife Pamela of Joplin. Three daughters, Bonita Harrison and her husband Gary of Carthage, Debbie Poole and her husband Karl of Jena, La. and Susan Tatum and her Husband Mike of Joplin; thirteen grandchildren and twenty-four great grandchildren; one niece and two nephews. She was preceded in death by one brother, Gene Agleton in 2011, one daughter Carolyn Piquard and one grandson, Joshua Harrison.

NATALIA PUEBLA
(The following obituary is taken from the Ulmer Funeral Home website.)

Natalia Puebla, 17 of Carthage passed away on Sunday, May 22, 2011. She was born on July 26, 1993 in Joplin; Mo.

Natalia was the daughter of Carey and Latina Puebla. She was a student of Ozark Christian College and had just completed her first year. Natalia was loved by her piano students, church family and college friends. She was a member of the Joplin Full Gospel Church.

Natalia is survived by her parents, two brothers, Joshua and Jacob of Springfield, and one sister Angela (Elliott) Pinkham of Webb City, Mo., four nieces Kaylene, Kristin, Kelly, and Kara, Uncle Jesse & Pam of Carthage, Missouri. Natalia is preceded by Paternal Grandparents, Jesus Puebla and Marjorie Scoville, she is also survived by two aunts, Shelly Simon of Davenport, Iowa and Ramona Lacy of Farmington, Ill.

LORETTA RANDALL
(Obituary information is taken from the Clark Funeral Home website.)

Loretta Lea Randall, 54, Webb City, died May 23, 2011, from complications of the May 22, 2011, tornado.

Loretta was born Aug. 13, 1956, in Neosho and was a lifelong area resident. She currently taught at the SEK Learning Center in Girard, Kan. She was a member of the First Christian Church in Webb City; a member of the Cardigan Welsh Corgi; National Education Association of Teachers, Smoke-Free Webb City and MSSU Alumni Assoc.

Loretta married Kyle Randall on Aug. 1, 1986, in Joplin and he survives.

She is also survived by a daughter, Krista Lee Rubottom Stark and husband, Jason, Webb City; two grandchildren, Reannon Lea Stark and James Stark; her mother, Janet Oster, Joplin; two brothers, Carey Oster, Carl Junction and Tim Oster, Joplin; and one sister, Cheryl Davis, Independence, Kan.

She was preceded in death by her father, Charles Oster, who perished in the tornado; and a brother, Mark Oster.

TROY RAMEY

Troy Ramey, age 39, was originally from Trinity, Texas. He is survived by his parents, Tom and Vicki Ramey of Trinity, TX. two sisters, Melanie Watanabe of Beaumont, Texas, and Jennifer Ramey of Houston, and four children, Allison Leech, Tommy Ramey, Trey Ramey, and Tigh Ramey.

SHELLY RAMSEY

Shelly Marie Ramsey, 42, Neosho, died Sunday, May 22, 2011 from injuries sustained in the tornado at Joplin.

Shelly was born Sept. 26, 1968 in Ft. Scott, KS and grew up in the Ft. Scott area. She moved to SW Missouri in 1991 from Ft. Scott and currently worked at Jay Hatfield Mobility in Joplin. Her children were her priority and she was a very giving person, always having a smile and positive attitude.

She is survived by her son, Blake Ramsey and daughter, Mikayla Ramsey, both of Neosho; her father, Jerry Gray and wife, Kathy, Ft. Scott, Kan.; her mother, Shorty Cooper and husband, Dan, Richards, Mo.; maternal grandmother, Marilyn Fowler, Ft. Scott, Kan.; two brothers, Scott Brillhart and Eric Gray, both of Ft. Scott, Kan.; two nephews, Johnathon and Austin; two nieces, Aura Lee and Morgan and the father of her children, Thad Ramsey and wife, Michele, Neosho.

CHERYL RANTZ

(The following obituary is taken from the Clark Funeral Home website.)

Cheryl E. Rantz, 62, Carl Junction, Mo., died May 30, 2011 at Cox South in Springfield from complications of the May 22nd Joplin tornado.

Cheryl was born Sept. 14, 1948 in Carthage, Mo., and was a lifelong area resident. She worked as a tax preparer for H and R Block and was a member of the Nazarene Church.

She is survived by a daughter, Kimberly Phillips, Springfield, Mo.; two grandchildren, Steven McReynolds and Mabel Phillips; one brother, David Spruce, Carthage and two sisters, Judy Baugh, Carthage and Karen Gregory, Altus, Okla.

She is preceded in death by her parents, Edward and Dorothy Spruce; her husband, George Rantz and brother, Gary Spruce.

DARLENE RAY

(The following information is taken from Derfelt Funeral Home.)

Darlene Kay (Hall) Ray, age 63, a former employee of King Louie Manufacturing, Baxter Springs, Kan., passed away Wednesday evening June 1, 2011 at Kindred Hospital, Kansas City, Mo., following an illness.

She was born August 18, 1947 in Joplin, Missouri. Her parents were George and Oleta Hall. She was a lifetime resident of Galena.

She graduated from Galena High School in 1965. She had previously worked as a seamstress at King Louie Manufacturing, Baxter Springs, Kan. She enjoyed going to Bordertown Casino to play bingo.

She was married to Wesley G. Ray on October 29, 1974 in Miami, Okla. He survives. Additional survivors include one son, Steven Wade Ray, Galena, Kan.; one brother, Tom Hall, Joplin, Mo.; and one sister, Barbara Fields, Galena, Kan.

One sister, Phyllis Strickland preceded her in death.

TOM REID
(The following obituary is taken from the Bath-Naylor Funeral Home website.)

Virgil "Tom" Reid 77, of Columbus, Kan., died 5:45pm Sunday May 22, 2011 at Joplin, Mo. during the tornado tragedy in Joplin.

Virgil was born May 14, 1934 in Hallowell, Kan. the son of Charles Marion "Shorty" and Melba Trucilla (Hutchens) Reid. He was a lifelong resident of the area and a graduate of Columbus High School. He was a Veteran of the Army. In 1959 he married Barbara Napier; they later divorced.

On May 22, 1992 Tom married Jesse Williams in Miami, Okla.; she survives at the home. Tom worked in construction all his life and started SEK Construction with Ivan Crossland. He also was affiliated with Maxwell Bridge Company in Columbus, Kan. Tom retired after working 50 years in construction in 2000.

Tom was a member of the Hallowell Word of Life Church in Hallowell, Kan.; enjoyed gardening, pecans, coin collecting, elephant collecting, cooking, dominos with his friends and family and finding recipes on the internet.

Survivors include his wife, children Tom D. Reid and wife Rhonda of Columbus, Kan., Cindy Davis of Columbus, Kan., Robert Cox of Columbus, Kan., Rhonda Norris and husband Mike of Owasso, Okla., and Jeri Lyons and husband Erving of Parsons, Kan.; an aunt Martha Back of Hallowell, Kan.; special friends Don and Susan Gurnee of Hallowell, Kan., who he enjoyed dominos with; grandchildren Brian Reid and wife Jennifer, Hope Von Soosten, Alexander Cox and wife Heather, Samantha Cox, Cassie Norris, MacGyver Norris, Elyjah Lyons and Aliyah Lyons; and great-grandchildren Madalyne, Monica and Copper Dean Reid.

He was preceded in death by his parents and brother Richard Reid.

JOHNNIE RICHEY
(The following obituary is taken from the Parker Mortuary website.)

Johnnie Ray Richey, age 52, Joplin, passed away on Sunday, May 22, 2011 as a result of injuries sustained in the tornado.

Johnnie was born October 7, 1958 in Webb City, Missouri, son of the late Ernie "Cork" Richey, and Joyce Mosher Richey of Joplin. Johnnie graduated from Webb City High School and attended MSSU. He has worked for Allgeier Martin and Associates for over 30 years and was currently a project engineer. He was an active member of the Joplin Elks Lodge #501 where he was a Trustee. He enjoyed volunteering his time with the youth at both Carl Richards locations, and worked with Habitat for Humanity. He was also attended St. James United Methodist Church.

In addition to his mother, Johnnie is survived by a son, SSgt. Adam Richey and wife Raygen of Jacksonville, North Carolina; a grandson, Griffin Ray Richey;

sister, Kerri Simms and husband Don of Farmington, Missouri; nieces and nephews, Kelsey Smith of Fayetteville, Arkansas, Tara Simms of Farmington, Justin Simms, Jordan Simms, and Jesse Simms all of Festus, Missouri; several aunts and uncles and cousins, and his faithful canine companion, Sugar.

VICKI ROBERTSON
(The following information was taken from the Parker Mortuary website.)

Vicki Patrice Robertson, age 66, Joplin, passed away on Sunday, May 22, 2011 as a result of injuries sustained in the tornado.

Vicki was born October 8, 1944 in Joplin, daughter of the late Clifford and Clancy Scott.

Survivors include her children, Mike Johnson, Danny Robertson, Joe Robertson, Dannielle Robertson, and Ardis Robertson.

CAYLA ROBINSON
(The following obituary is taken from the Mason-Woodard Mortuary website.)

Cayla Ann Selsor Robinson, age 64 of Joplin, Missouri, passed away early Saturday June 4, 2011 from injuries suffered in the devastating tornado that came through Joplin on May 22, 2011.

Cayla was born on October 31, 1946 in Joplin the daughter of Charles and Colleen (Conner) Selsor. She was a lifetime area resident, and was a stay at home mom caring for her family. Cayla attended Frisco Church in Webb City, Missouri and later attended Forest Park Baptist Church in Joplin.

She is survived by three daughters, Nicole Shultz and her husband Joey of Joplin, Pam Spencer of Carthage, Missouri, Donna Fisher of Springfield, Missouri, one son, Jerry Michael Fisher of Carthage, one sister, Marcy Hays of Webb City, one brother, Cary Selsor of Webb City, eight grandchildren and one great-grandchild, Karlee Laramore, with another on the way. She was preceded in by her mother, Colleen and by two sons, Billy and Matthew Fisher.

KEITH ROBINSON
(The following obituary is taken from the Mason-Woodard Mortuary website.)

Keith Derek Robinson, age 50, Joplin, passed away on May 22, 2011, from injuries sustained in the Joplin tornado, at the Greenbriar Nursing Home.

Keith was born on August 1, 1960 in Joplin, the son of Charles and Betty (Love) Robinson-Gray. He has been a lifetime Joplin resident. He worked as a CNA for the Greenbriar Nursing Home, prior to that he worked eighteen years for Freeman Hospital. Keith had a wonderful way with his patients. He would motivate them to do their rehabilitation in a stern but kind and respectful manner. He was responsible for many patients being able to recover and even walk again. He thoroughly enjoyed watching old movies.

He is survived by his mother, Betty Robinson-Gray, Joplin; one sister, Mary Katherine "KK" Robinson, Joplin; one brother, Charles Robinson, Jr.; nephews, Jeremy and Justin Robinson, and Dylan Rapp, all of Joplin; three uncles, J.D. Love, Joplin, Jerry Love, Jr. and wife Elaine, Joplin, and Robert Love, Farmington, Missouri; and many, many cousins and friends. He was preceded in death by his father, Charles D. Robinson; his step-dad William O. Gray; his grandparents, Jerry and Katherine Love, and an uncle, Raymond Love and two aunts Vera Jenkins and Helen Derrick.

MARGARET ROW

Margaret Ellen Row, 50, a resident of Joplin, Missouri, formerly of Fredonia, Kansas, died Monday, June 6, 2011 at St. John's Hospital in Springfield, Missouri, as the result of injuries sustained in the May 22, 2011 Joplin tornado.

She was born March 31, 1961 in Fredonia, the daughter of Billie (Palmer) Row Kidd and the late William A. Row. Margaret was a 1979 graduate of Fredonia High School. She attended college at Labette Community College in Parsons, Kansas, and obtained her RN nursing degree.

Margaret had worked at Mercy Hospital in Independence, Kansas and St. John's Hospital in Joplin for many years. Most recently she was employed as a hospice nurse in Joplin. She took pleasure in collecting clowns and piggy banks and enjoyed traveling.

Margaret is survived by her mother Billie Kidd of Fredonia, Kan., three brothers, William (Bill) and Karla Row of Cassville, Mo., Bob and Cathy Row of Fredonia, Kan., Jack and Renee Row of Golden City, Mo., one sister Rose Mary and Greg Rhodes of London, Ark.

She is also survived by several nieces and nephews, as well as great nieces and nephews.

Margaret's father, grandparents, aunts and uncles preceded her in death.

VIRGINIA SALMON

Virginia Mae Salmon, age 80, passed away Sunday, May 22, 2011, at her home in Duquesne, from injuries sustained in the tornado that devastated Joplin.

Virginia was born June 21, 1930, in Wichita, Kan., to John Raymond and Opal Louise (Cravens) Templeton and attended high school in Porterville, Calif.

She married Raymond Jesse Salmon on May 7, 1949, in Las Vegas, Nev. He preceded her in death on Oct. 17, 2002.

She lived in California for 34 years, moving to Joplin in 1973 with her husband and family. She was a homemaker and loved spending time with her family. She had a wonderful sense of humor and enjoyed telling stories about her childhood. She loved to shop, especially for others, and was a big fan of country and Gospel music. She was disliked by no one and will be missed by all. Rest in peace, Mom, and thank you, God, for allowing her to be with us for almost 81 years.

Virginia is survived by one daughter, Shelley Russow and fiancé Bud Ochsenbein, of Joplin; four sons, Gary Salmon and wife Mary Jane, of Joplin; Gayle Salmon, of Boise, Idaho, and Leta Salmon, of Cleveland, Okla., Stacey Salmon and wife Cindy, of Joplin, and Scott Salmon and fiance Bev Stepp, of Seligman, Missouri; two sisters, Margaret Young, of Joplin, and Roberta Miller, of Yuma, Ariz.; three brothers, Charles Templeton and wife Phyllis, of Lakeland, Fla., Frank Templeton and wife Linda, of Tigard, Ore., and Jim Templeton and wife Juanita, of Seres, Calif.; 15 grandchildren; 28 great-grandchildren; five great-great-grandchildren; many nieces and nephews; as well as many other family members and friends. In addition to her husband and parents, she was preceded in death by two sisters, Juanita Baggs, and Jenny Mayfield.

GRACE SANDERS

Grace Marie Sanders passed from this life at 3:08 p.m. Monday, June 20, 2011, at St. John's Intensive Care Unit in Springfield, Missouri, from complications following surgery.

Grace was born to Elmer and Francis Dummit on April 11, 1929, in Buhl, Idaho.

Following a tragic car accident, Grace and her sister, Elouis, now deceased, were adopted at the age of 7, by their aunt and uncle Hupperfelt, of Miami, Okla. in October of 1936.

Grace later married Robert Dale Sanders, of Carthage, on Nov. 21, 1946, and they enjoyed nearly 65 years of marriage together. Bob remains at the couple's home in Carthage.

Grace was recovering from surgery at St. John's Hospital in Joplin, on Sunday, May 22nd and was located on the west end of the upper floor when the EF5 tornado struck, destroying her room and the entire end of the floor on which she was seeking cover.

She survived the tornado but sustained multiple injuries requiring 18 stitches at the triage at Memorial Hall. She, along with 39 other patients from Joplin, was transported to Springfield, for further care. She was discharged and returned home but required further surgery on June 17th and died on Monday from various complications. Her husband and a nephew were present with her at the time of her passing.

Grace was employed for many years at the Joplin Stockyards as a bookkeeper and was always a gracious and welcoming person. She will be most dearly missed by all who loved her and respected her.

THOMAS SARINO
(From the *Joplin Globe* and *Kansas City Star*)

Thomas Sarino, 75, of Joplin, lived alone. His family, including several children and grandchildren, live in the Philippines. He had worked for Warner Brother Inc.'s finance department in New York before moving to Joplin in 1995 to work in finance for the Loma Linda Golf Resort. He was retired.

TONI SAWYER
(The following information came from Cheney Witt Memorial Chapel)

Tonja Lee "Toni" Sawyer, age 41, a resident of Fort Scott, died Sunday, May 22, 2011, as a result of the Joplin, Missouri tornado. She was born December 17, 1969, in Olympia, Washington, the daughter of Larry Goldsby and Sandra Gamache Goldsby.

Toni married Chad Sawyer on January 3, 2011. She was currently employed by Taco Bell in Fort Scott. She enjoyed painting, collecting antiques and writing poems and short stories as well as listening to the rain and sitting around a bonfire. Toni loved animals and often took in strays. She attended the Apostolic Pentecostal Church.

Survivors include her husband, Chad Sawyer, Fort Scott; her children, Dashedin Goldsby, Fort Scott, Jarred Goldsby, Shelton Washington, Makyah Goldsby and Samara Hernandez, both of Fort Scott. Also surviving is her father,

Larry Goldsby, Shelton, Washington; two brothers, Ron Larson, Matlock, Washington and Gerald Goldsby, Olympia, Washington; two sisters, Julie Goldsby and Dottie Goldsby, both of Shelton, Washington; and a granddaughter, Icysis Goldsby. She was preceded in death by her mother, and infant son, Jed Goldsby and a sister, Crissy Goldsby.

FRANCES SCATES
(The following information came from Bennett-Wormington Funeral Home)

Frances Ann (Worm) Scates, 71, of Joplin, Missouri, formerly of Monett, passed away May 22, 2011 her home. She was a victim of the recent tornado. She was born July 14, 1940 in Freistatt, Mo., to Earnest and Nora (Jackel) Worm.

Frances was a member of the St. Johns Lutheran Church in Freistatt.

Frances is survived by two sons: Brian Scates of Bentonville, Ark., and Bruce Scates of Joplin; three daughters: Bridgit Ferrell of Stella, Mo., Brenda Seward of Stella, Mo. and Brandi Parker of Monett, Mo.; one brother: Martin Worm of Verona, Mo.; one sister: Marcel Mitchell of Springfield, Mo.; 11 grandchildren and 6 great-grandchildren.

GLADYS SEAY
Gladys J. Seay of Welch, Okla., passed away Sunday, May 22, 2011 at St. John's Regional Medical Center in Joplin, Mo., during the recent tornado. She was 83 years young.

Gladys was born January 30, 1928 in Miami, Oklahoma, to William Jefferson and Myrtle Florence (Morris) Seay. She was a graduate of Miami High School.

DANIEL SHIRLEY
(From the *Joplin Globe*)

Daniel Wayne Shirley, 48, of Joplin, traveled all over the United States and Canada as a salesman with a carnival. He moved to Goodman one year ago and had been living at the Greenbriar Nursing Home in Joplin since February, up until the time of his death as a result of the Joplin tornado.

He enjoyed metal detector hunting, fishing, and collecting knives and guns. He was a member of First Baptist Church of Pineville.

GENE SMITH
Gene Smith, age 71, of Joplin, Missouri, passed away Sunday, May 22, 2011 from injuries sustained in the Joplin tornado.

Gene was born November 24, 1939, in Webb City, Missouri. He had lived in the Joplin-Webb City area all his life. Gene was employed with the Union Pacific Railroad for 24 years. He was a U.S. Army veteran and served 29 years with the National Guard and Naval Reserves. Gene was a member of the Webb City Church of the Nazarene. He was also a member of the Joplin Eagle's Lodge, and the Greater Joplin U.S. Bowling Congress. He loved Webb City Football and the St. Louis Cardinals.

Gene married Donna Gunlock August 10, 1973, in Webb City, Missouri, and she survives. Additional survivors include one son, Jeff Smith, Joplin, one daughter,

Robin Shember and husband James, Webb City, and two grandsons, Nick and John Shember.

JUDY SMITH

Judy Lee Smith, age 71, of Joplin, Mo., passed away on Thursday, May 26, 2011 at the Cassville Healthcare and Rehabilitation in Cassville, Mo.

Judy was born on May 30, 1939 in Webb City, Mo., the daughter of Lloyd and Fern (Cromer) Brown Carter.

Judy spent most of her life in Joplin and owned and operated the Second Hand Rose Consignment Store. She was a member of the St. Paul United Methodist Church and graduated from Joplin High School with the class of 1957. She enjoyed reading, watching movies, playing trivia pursuit and bridge as well as shopping.

Judy is survived by two daughters, Nikki Oliver, of Joplin and Jill Walkinshaw, of Kansas City, Mo.; four grandchildren, Jamie, Sally, Amon and Jesse; three great-grandchildren, Robbie, Eric and Havaah; one brother, Cokher Carter and wife Claudia, of Joplin; one sister, Garlanda Davis, of St. Louis, Mo.; one aunt, Emma Edie, of Bowerston, OH; five nieces and nephews; and a lifelong friend, Linda Cupp, of Joplin. Judy was preceded in death by her parents.

NICHOLAUS SMITH

(The following obituary information is taken from the *Joplin Globe*)

Nicholaus Smith, 23, of Joplin, died as a result of the Joplin tornado.

Nicholaus worked for Ozark Technical Ceramics. He moved to Joplin in February from his hometown of St. Louis. He and his brother, Chris, were interested in music and video production, and were preparing to open their own entertainment business as well as a hot dog stand. He had also recently become engaged. His friends called him "Chill."

SHYRELL SMITH

(The following obit was taken from the Timmons Funeral Home and Holland Monuments website)

Shyrell Lee (Cranor) Smith, 68, went home to be with the Lord suddenly Sunday, May 22, 2011 as she was traveling to work as a registered nurse (RN) at Freeman East, Joplin, MO. Shyrell's death, due to injuries sustained in the Joplin tornado, is a tragic loss for all family, friends, and associates who were touched by her. Shyrell lived in Pittsburg, Kansas for the past 13 years. Prior she resided in Altoona, Fredonia, and Coffeyville, Kansas.

She was born on January 13, 1943, to Forrest David & Nellie Mae (Foulke) Cranor. Shyrell was raised in Altoona, Kansas and graduated from Altoona Rural High School in 1961. She graduated from Phillips University, College of the Bible, Enid, Oklahoma, in 1965 with a Degree in Religion. In 1968, she received a Bachelor of Science Degree in Nursing from the University of Kansas. Shyrell received an advanced degree in Education Specialist and Human Resource Development in 2003 at Pittsburg State University.

Shyrell worked in the nursing field for over 45 years. She was the first county health nurse for Wilson County, and at the age of 68 was still working full time as an RN at Freeman East. She was an extraordinary nurse and loved her work.

Shyrell Lee Cranor married Arthur Eugene Smith on June 10, 1967 in Fredonia, Kansas, and they were later divorced. She was a member of the Westside Church of the Nazarene in Olathe, Walk Kansas, Pittsburg Family YMCA, American Red Cross Nurse, Phi Kappa Phi, and Weight Watchers.

She leaves her son, Eric Eugene Smith and his wife, April, of Olathe, Kansas; her daughter, Sharilyn LeeAnn Gardner, and her husband, Paul, of Pittsburg, Kansas; her brother, David Cranor, and sister-in-law, Lee Donna, of Georgetown, Texas; her sister, Pamela Sue Stanley, and brother-in-law, Gary, of Newtown, Pennsylvania; loving grandchildren, Riley, Benjamin, Troy, and Hannah Smith of Olathe, Kansas; and many nieces and nephews.

Shyrell dedicated her life to the medical profession, loving family, friends and helping others. She was preceded in death by her parents, maternal grandparents, and paternal grandparents.

LOIS SPARKS
(The following obituary is taken from the Mason-Woodard Mortuary website.)

Lois L. Sparks, age 92, Joplin, went to be with her Lord and Savior on Sunday May 22, 2011, from injuries sustained in the Joplin tornado.

Lois was born on June 8, 1918 in Wichita, Ks., the daughter of Mable and Will Schnoor in Wichita, Ks. She married Wallace Sparks April 26, 1936 in Wichita, they were married for seventy-one years. He preceded her in death on February 14, 2007. She was member of the Eastern Star and a devout member of the Baptist Church, attending both Harmony Heights Baptist Church and later Eastview Baptist Church, working many years in childhood evangelism.

She is survived by her son, Ralph Sparks and wife Charlene, Joplin; four grandchildren, Jerry and Nanda Sparks, Joplin, Travis and Cassie Sparks, Joplin, Jodi and Kevin Austin, Springfield, Missouri, and Ron Sparks, Tulsa, Okla.; and eight great-grandchildren.

STEVEN STEPHENS
(The following information is taken from the Parker Mortuary website.)

Steven J. Haack Stephens, age 28, passed away on Sunday, May 22, 2011 as a result of injuries sustained in the tornado.

Steven was born March 17, 1983 in Holdreg, Nebraska, son of Tracy Haack of Geneva, Nebraska and Tina Salsbury Davis of Savannah, Missouri. He was a construction worker and a Baptist.

He was preceded in death by a daughter, Aspen Haack Stephens, sister-in-law, Meranda Stephens, grandmothers, Linda Salbury and Shirley Clevenger.

Survivors include his wife, Tasha Stephens of Troy, Kansas; children, Dayton Stephens, Alexander Haack Stephens, Alaris Haack Stephens; father, Fred Piska of Wichita, Kansas; sister, Kali Haack of Savannah; grandfather, Mike Salsbury of Rockaway Beach, Missouri; mother-in-law, Terrie Stephens; father-in-law, Rusty Stephens; aunts, Nora Campbell, Robin Sisk; nephews, Juan DeDios, Zeke Soldanels, niece, Lyrik Stout; uncles, Steve Salsbury, Michael Salsbury; many other family members.

BETTY STOGSDILL

(The following obituary is taken from the Parker Mortuary website.)

Betty J. Stogsdill, age 83, Joplin, passed away on Wednesday, June 8, 2011 at Cox South Hospital in Springfield, Missouri as a result of injuries sustained in the Joplin tornado.

Betty was born April 10, 1928 in Joplin, daughter of the late George Toops and Gertrude Shelton Toops. She graduated from Carl Junction High School, and attended Joplin Junior College before receiving her Bachelor's Degree from DePaul University in Chicago. She also received a Master's Degree from Northwestern University, and a second Masters from University of Chicago. She was a high school teacher for many years in Chicago. She moved to Joplin in 1994 and was a substitute teacher for the Joplin School District for many years before retiring. She was a member of Forest Park Baptist Church, Joplin Woman's Club and was active in several Joplin Bridge Clubs. She also loved the arts and theater.

In addition to her parents, Betty was preceded in death by her husband, Ralph Stogsdill who died April 30, 2004; sisters, Cora Kope, Ruth Haliday, Alice Marley, and Leatha Tiberghien.

Survivors include a sister, Wanetta King and husband David of Joplin; several nieces and nephews.

RALPH STOVER
(The following information is taken from the Paul Thomas Funeral Home website.)

Ralph Gilbert Stover, 85, passed away on Friday, June 3, 2011 at the Miami Hospital after being in St. John's Hospital during the Joplin tornado.
Ralph was born July 16, 1925 to Louisa (Porter) and Chauncey Stover in Columbus, Kansas. Ralph married Betty Hudson on August 25, 1946 in Treece, Kansas. She survives of the home.

Ralph worked in the floor covering business since 1954. He started the Stover's Floor Covering in 1970 and retired in 2001. However, he continued to go to the store to "supervise" each morning.

He was a member of the First United Methodist Church. He loved wood working and gardening.

The family would like to give special thanks to Nurse Bekki Johnson at St John's Hospital and Nurse Kathy Hicks at the Miami Hospital for the special care they gave him. Also, to John Seay for his help carrying our dad to safety after the tornado.

Ralph is survived by his wife, Betty; one son and his wife, Rodney and Becky Stover of Miami; two daughters, Virginia Foster of Jenks and Belinda and husband Rod Pfeiffer of Pryor, Okla.; nine grandchildren, Lesley Whitewater, Greg Stover, Dusty Stover, Brian Foster, Rusty Stover, Levi Pfeiffer, Jason Scott, Kim Harmon and Ashlee Stover; and eight great-grandchildren and many nieces and nephews. He was preceded in death by his parents and four brothers.

J.T. STRICKLAND
(The following obituary was taken from the Simpson Funeral Home website.)

Mr. J.T. Strickland, age 85, of Joplin passed away Friday, July 8, 2011, at the Benchmark Health Care in Monett, from injuries sustained in the May 22nd Joplin tornado. Mr. Strickland was born on September 11, 1925 in Hoyt, OK.

Mr. Strickland served his country for 10 years in the U.S. Navy during World War II and the Korean War. He worked as a motel manager for many years. He was a member of the Peace Lutheran Church of Joplin.

He is survived by his wife Betty Strickland of the home, and a daughter Chrys Corcoran of Joplin, five Grandchildren and 10 Great Grand Children, and a sister Zula Dean Lake of Ocean Pines, Maryland.

GREGAN SWEET
(The following obituary was taken from the Parker Mortuary website.)

Gregan Douglas Sweet, age 59 of Joplin, passed away from injuries sustained in the tornado on May 22, 2011. Born January 6, 1952 in Joplin, he was the son the late Nathan and Evelyn Johnson Sweet. He was a member of Citywide Christian Fellowship in Joplin and worked as a carpenter in residential building for many years of his life. He also did prison ministry with the Bill Glass Team.

He married Vickie L. Fort on July 7, 1977 in Joplin; she survives. Other survivors include a daughter, Laramie Sweet of the home; a son, Paul Sweet of Tulsa, Okla.; one brother, Byran Sweet and his wife, Kuemok, of Gladstone, Mo.; one step brother, Terry Jackson of Dallas, Tex.; and three step sisters, Janet Fletcher of Neosho, Nancy Woodley of Neosho, and Cathy Jackson of Dallas.

Gregan is also survived by his special brother and sister in Christ, Brett Fowler and his sister, Laurie Fowler.

JEFF TAYLOR
(The following obituary is taken from the D. W. Newcomer's website.)

Jeff Taylor, 31, of Kansas City, Missouri, died Friday, June 3, 2011, as a result of injuries sustained while assisting in the rescue efforts in Joplin, Missouri.

Born March 7, 1980, in Cameron, Missouri, to Patricia (Steelman) Bestgen and Steve Taylor, Jeff graduated from Harrisonville High School in 1998 and attended Missouri Southern State University, receiving his POST Certificate in 2001. He began his law enforcement career in Webb City, and then served on Platte County Sheriff Department, before his current post with Riverside Department of Public Safety where he held the positions of Firefighter, SWAT, Master Patrol Officer, K9 Officer, and Field Training Officer.

Jeff was nominated and awarded Officer of the Year from Riverside DPS in 2008.

On Aug. 7, 1999, Jeff married his college sweetheart, Kelly Hawkins, in St. James, Missouri Jeff loved to golf, coached his sons soccer team, played softball with his friends from Riverside DPS, and always put his family first. Jeff was preceded in death by his sister, Jodi Lynn Gitthens; a niece, Trinity Faith Roberts; and a grandfather, Jefferson Steelman.

Survivors include his wife Kelly and sons, Caden and Cameron of Kansas City; parents, Steve and Rose Taylor of New Bloomfield, Missouri; mother, Patricia Bestgen of Osborn, Missouri; sister, Staci Roberts, of Overland Park, Kan.; two brothers, Zach and Nick Bestgen of Osborn; grandparents, Gerald and Phyllis Taylor of Cameron, Missouri, Ernest and Phyllis Denny of Maysville, Missouri, Betty Jean Jacobsen of Roeland Park, Kan.; as well as many aunts, uncles, nieces, nephews and cousins.

KAYLEIGH TEAL
(The following obituary was taken from the Paul Thomas Funeral Home website.)

Kayleigh Savannah Teal of Seneca, Missouri and Pittsburg, Kansas went to be with Jesus on May 22, 2011 in Joplin, Missouri. She was 16.

Kayleigh was born March 22, 1995 in Bamburg, Germany to Robert Eugene Teal and Karen Sue (Stanton) Long.

She attended Bluejacket and Welch Schools early and was attending Seneca High School where she loved mixed choir.

Kayleigh was employed as a waitress in the Joplin Pizza Hut and was of the Christian Faith.

She is survived by: Father: Robert and wife Karen Louise Teal of Pittsburg, KS, Mother: Karen Sue Long and step-father Shaun Higginbothan of Seneca, MO, three brothers: Rowdy Teal of Pittsburg, Trey Saltsman of Seneca, and Jordan Ray Bicknell of Pittsburg, 4 sisters: Shandra Renee Bicknell of Pittsburg, Brandi Sue Moore of Pittsburg, Tayler Higginbothan of Seneca, and Dakoata Higginbothan of Seneca. Paternal grandparents: William and Judy Fromm, Oklahoma City, OK, Richard Teal of Bluejacket, OK. Maternal grandmother: Betty Stanton (Davis) and paternal great grandmother Margarett Ann Teal of Chetopa, KS.

HEATHER TERRY
Heather Leigh Terry, 36, Joplin, died May 22, 2011 from injuries sustained in the May 22, 2011, tornado.

Heather was born Feb. 16, 1975 in Aurora, Mo., attended Aurora Schools and was a lifelong area resident. She currently worked at La Barge in Joplin. Heather married Michael Duane Terry on March 20, 2010, at Miami, Okla., and he survives. Additional survivors include her mother, Vicky Baum, Joplin; her father, Rex Baum, Carterville; her sister, Erin Baum-Smith, Joplin; two nieces, Bayleigh Smith and Ashleigh Smith and her maternal grandmother, Juanita Channel, Granby.

JOHN THOMAS
(The following obituary is taken from the Bath-Naylor Funeral Home website.)

John L. Thomas Jr. 40, of Joplin, Mo., died 5:30pm Sunday May 22, 2011 in the tragic tornado that hit Joplin, Missouri.

John was born April 27, 1971 in Wichita, Kan., the son of John L. Thomas Sr. and Kathie S. Campbell; he was a lifelong resident of the area and attended area schools.

On December 1, 1990 he married Lori Stevens in Frontenac, Kan.; they later divorced. On April 27, 2002, he married Carin Neely in Riverton, Kan.; they later divorced. John worked for Jasper products in Joplin, Mo.; he was of the Christian

Faith; enjoyed golfing, gambling, fishing, hunting, football, playing catch and was known to love work.

Survivors include his parents, children Caleb W. Thomas of Girard, Kan., Kevin W. Neely of Joplin, Mo., Adam L. Thomas of Girard, Kan., and Joel B. Thomas of Boston, Mass.; stepmother Chris Thomas; maternal grandmother Juanita Campbell of Pittsburg, Kan., and numerous aunts, uncles and cousins.

He was preceded in death by a brother Christopher D. Thomas, maternal grandfather Herman Campbell, paternal grandparents Lewin A. and Twilla I. Thomas.

SANDRA THOMAS
(The following obituary is taken from the Ulmer Funeral Home website.)

Sandra Thomas, 55, of Carthage passed away on Sunday, May 22, 2011.

Sandra was born on July 30, 1955 in Berryville, Ark. She was the daughter of Alvin and Betty Thomas.

Sandra was an employee of Justin Books for the past 20 years. She was a graduate of the Carthage High School in 1974. She was a member of the Joplin Full Gospel Church where she volunteered in the nursery. Sandra is survived by her parents and one sister, Latina Puebla.

ZACH TREADWELL
(The following obituary is taken from the Parker Mortuary website.)

Zachary Delbert Treadwell, age 9, Joplin, passed away on Sunday, May 22, 2011 as a result of injuries sustained in the tornado.

Zach was born August 10, 2001, in Joplin, and was currently a third grade student at Emerson Elementary School. He loved to be outdoors, playing soccer was a passion, and fishing. He was described as "all boy" with the dirt and scrapes that come with that description. He was a big fan of Pokemon, loved to sing, and had a mature sense of humor, always telling elaborate stories, or a joke.

Zach was preceded in death by grandparents, Manuel Berumen and Gerald Treadwell.

Survivors include his mother, Crystal Cogdill; brother, David Arreola'Berumen; sister, Whitley Treadwell; father, Jeffery Treadwell all of Joplin; grandparents, Rose Cast of Pittsburg, California, Glenda and Grady Carmical of Diamond, Missouri; great-grandparents, Lupe Berumen of Pittsburg, California; several uncles and aunts including Jessica Torres also of Pittsburg.

MARGARET TUTT
(The following obituary is taken from the Parker Mortuary website.)

Margaret Ann Tutt, age 92, passed away on May 22, 2011 at her home in Joplin, Missouri.

She was born Nov. 24, 1918, in Belvidere, Kan. Her husband, Jack H. Tutt, died on April 8, 1973. She is survived by her daughter, Mary Ann Christman and son-in-law, David Christman; two grandchildren Mary C. Sgroi and husband Fred of Prairie Village, Kan., Dr. Jim Christman and wife Debbie of Joplin; two great-grandchildren, Annie and Katie Sgroi; two great-step-grandchildren, James Brown and wife, Lauren, Sandy Brummitt and husband Justin; five great-great-step-grandchildren; one brother, Col. William T. Unger of Sunrise, Fla.

Margaret Ann was a volunteer worker with the Blind Association, Meals on Wheels, Crosslines and Friends of the Library.

MICHAEL TYNDALL

Michael Eugene Tyndall, age 33, of Joplin, was a victim of the recent storms.

Michael was born in Joplin, Missouri, on March 11, 1978, and was a graduate of Joplin High School Class of 1997. He was an equipment operator in construction.

Michael was preceded in death by his father, Dennis J. Tyndall Sr.; maternal grandparents, Victor and Mary DeCastro; paternal grandparents, Westin Fenton and Josephine Tyndall; and one sister, Victoria Lois. He is survived by three children, Kaylee and Carson Tyndall, Sarcoxie, and Arron Tyndall, Joplin; his mother and stepfather, Margie and Ronnie King, Duenweg; grandparents Ronald and Charlotte King, Duenweg; two brothers, Dennis Tyndall, Joplin, and Phillip King of Cassville; one sister, Amanda Sheehan, Neosho; and numerous aunts, uncles, nieces, and nephews.

DEE VANDERHOOFVEN

(The following obituary is taken from the Parker Mortuary website.)

Darian "Dee" Vanderhoofven, 44, left behind her mortal life on Sunday, May 22, 2011, in the rubble of her home caused by the tornado that evening.

Dee was born on June 28, 1966, to Gaylord "Charley" Weaver and Annette Denny Weaver in Dillon, Mont.

Darian moved to Joplin, Missouri, in 2004, and met her then-future husband, David A. Vanderhoofvan. Dee and David were married Feb. 11, 2010 at Jack and Nancy Dawson's log chapel in Webb City, Missouri. It was a wish come true for Dee.

Her second wish, to be a mom, was fulfilled on March 28, 2010, with the birth of her son, Joshua Dean Vanderhoofven, at Freeman Hospital in Joplin. Tragically, Joshua accompanied his mother in death on May 22, 2011. Darian's third wish was unable to be honored.

Dee was passionate about organ, eye and tissue donation and served as the Joplin Regional Manager for the Heartland Lion's Eye Bank. She strongly encouraged family and friends to become designated donors and she had also wished to donate. However the tragic circumstances of her death prevented that from occurring.

Darian was an accomplished cook and loved to entertain, host a party or bake a theme cake for someone special. Dee collected art glass media. She was an animal lover and took in strays.

Dee held a deep belief in her Lord and Savior, Jesus, and was a member of Wildwood Baptist Church in Joplin. She was an open, easygoing person who enjoyed making people laugh. Dee loved to visit, work in her garden or reminisce. Darian's path in life crossed so very many others, and she was loved by many. She will be greatly missed by all of us.

Aunt Dee was held in especially high regard by the children of her siblings, and she had favored status in all their lives. They have been extremely sorrowed by her loss. They are Braedon and Jesse Day, of Tucson, Ariz., Jason Weaver, of

Laramie, Wy., Kaili Holloway and Megan Weaver, of Casper, Wy., Kaden and Braylon Weaver, of Kingman, Ariz., and James Weaver, of Racine, Missouri.

Darian is also survived by her husband, David A. Vanderhoofven, and two stepchildren, Megan and Brian Vanderhoofven, of Joplin, Missouri; her father, Gaylord "Charley" Weaver and his wife, Linda, of Springdale, Arkansas; her father and mother-in-law, David S. and Marilynn Vanderhoofven, of Arvada, Colo.; her sister, Genelle Day and husband John, of Tucson; her brothers, Patrick Weaver and wife Amanda, of Kingman, Howard "Dean" Weaver, of Butte, Mont., and Dan Weaver and his wife, Cindy, of Racine; her stepbrother, Jeff Neal and his wife, Stephanie, and their children, Blake, Taylor and Tanner Neal, of Springdale, Arkansas; brother and sister-in-law Philip and Sue Vanderhoofven, of Kailuah, Ha.; John and Abby Vanderhoofven, of El Paso, Texas; and Nathan Vanderhoofven, of Arvada, Colo.; and sister-in-law Daneen Weaver, of Casper.

JOSH VANDERHOOFVEN
(The following obituary is taken from the Parker Mortuary website.)

Joshua Dean Vanderhoofven, 14 months, departed his worldly walk on Sunday, May 22, 2011, in the arms of his mother, as a result of that evening's tornado in Joplin, Missouri.

Joshua was born at Freeman Hospital in Joplin on March 28, 2010, to Darian Dee Vanderhoofven and David A. Vanderhoofven.

Joshua was a gift from God to both his parents. He was nearly always happy and smiling. He enjoyed watching Sponge Bob with his father and playing in his bounce swing. He had a voracious appetite. Joshua had just started to walk and liked to explore his home. He was the apple of his mother's eye and he will be missed by all of his family.

Joshua is survived by his father, David, of the home; and his grandparents, David S. and Marilynn Vanderhoofven, of Aurora, Colo.; Gaylord "Charley" Weaver and Linda Weaver, of Springdale, Arkansas. He was dearly loved by all of his mother Darian's survivors as well.

MIGUEL VASQUEZ-CASTILLO
(The following obituary is taken from the *Joplin Globe*)

Miguel Vasquez-Castillo, 29, of Joplin, was born in Mexico, where most of his family still lives. He was one of four children and described as the "life of the party" by Monica Lopez, who worked with him at the El Vaquero restaurant in Joplin. His girlfriend, Maria Alvarez-Torres, also died in the tornado.

DEAN WELLS
(The following obituary is taken from the Simpson Funeral Home website.)

M. "Dean" Wells, age 59 of Webb City, passed away Sunday, May 22, 2011 at the Home Depot as a result of the tornado. Dean was born August 31, 1951, at Ft. Carson, Co. to parents, Paul and Jean (Hall) Wells. He served his country in the U.S. Army.

Dean married Margaret Sue Simons May 23, 1969 in Boulder, Co., his death coming one day before their 42nd Anniversary. Sue survives of the home.

Dean was a member of the First Christian Church of Webb City where he sang with his church group every Tuesday at area nursing homes or with ill members of the church and community. He loved music and was very adept at whistling. He recorded records of his whistling and often sung and whistled for his church.

Dean was a department head at Home Depot. He saved several lives at Home Depot on May 22, 2011, and ultimately lost his life in the process. Anyone who knew him knew this was his style of living; helping others first.

Dean is also survived by his daughters, DeAnne Mancini and husband John of Tucson, Ariz., and Paulla Wells of Hot Springs, Ark., his mother, Jean Wells of Tucson, Ariz., 4 grandchildren, Ashley Gietz of Staten Island, New York, Anthony and Laura Larkin of Hot Springs and Dillon Gietz of Tucson; and a great grandson, Maximus Michael Jaslow.

TIERA WHITLEY

Tiera Nicole Whitley, age 20, of Fort Scott, Kansas, died Sunday May 22, 2011 as the result of the Joplin, Missouri tornado.

She was born September 20, 1990 in Overland Park, Kansas the daughter of Jerry and Mary Johnston Whitley. She attended Prescott, Kansas Elementary School and graduated from Jayhawk Linn High School in 2009.

Tiera was a talented artist and photographer and enjoyed fishing and wood working. She was currently employed as a shift manager at Taco Bell in Fort Scott. She was preceded in death by her maternal grandfather, Forrest "Bud" Johnston.

She is survived by mother and father, Mary and Jerry Whitley of Prescott, a sister Shelby Whitley, a brother Joseph Whitley both of Prescott, maternal grandmother Ladean Kempinger, husband Karl, paternal grandparents, Eldred and Carol Whitley, maternal great grandmother Virginia Dozier, and eternal friend, Ashley. Tiera was her entire family's pride and joy.

DOUGLAS WILLIAMS

(The following information is taken from White Funeral Home.)

Douglas Earl Williams, age 52, of Purdy, Missouri, passed away on Friday, June 3, 2011 at Cox South Hospital in Springfield, Missouri, from injuries sustained in the Joplin tornado.

Douglas, son of Dozier and Mattie (Ross) Williams, was born on October 28, 1958 in Nacogdoches, Texas. Douglas was raised in the Nacodgoches area and moved to Purdy, Missouri in 2005. He was united in marriage to Leah Nance on February 13, 2007 in Cassville, Missouri. Together they enjoyed raising horses, and Douglas loved spending time in his garden with his dog, Tuff.

Survivors include his wife, Leah Williams, of Purdy, Missouri; one daughter, Randi Williams and her companion, Jeff Freeman, both of Purdy, Missouri; four step-daughters, Marilyn, Katie, Jackie, and Kat Hughes, all of Purdy, Missouri; two brothers, Rex Williams, and his wife, Lisa, of Garrison, Texas, and Donald Ray Williams, and his wife, Bernadette, of Garrison, Texas; two sisters, Jeannie Williams, of Nacogdoches, Texas, and Bonita Finley, and her husband, David, of Hutchins, Texas; a mother-in-law, Leona Nance, of Berryville, Arkansas; two brothers-in-law, Monty Nance, of Eagle Rock, Missouri, and Mark Nance, Oak Grove, Arkansas; three sisters-in-law, Deborah Hammons, Newberry Park, California, Carla Dearing, of Gentry, Arkansas, and Samantha Minton, of Cassville, Missouri; and numerous nieces and nephews.

REGINA WILLIAMS
(The following obituary is taken from the Knell Mortuary website.)

Regina Mae Bloxham Williams, 55, Joplin, Mo., passed away Sunday, May 22, 2011 from injuries sustained in the Joplin tornado.

Regina Mae Kirkpatrick was born August 9, 1955 in Reno, Nevada, the daughter of George F. Kirkpatrick and Pauline (Porter) Kirkpatrick. She was a graduate of Hugg High School, Reno, Nev., and attended the University of Nevada for 3 years. She married Leslie Lynn Williams on October 2, 2009, he survives.

Regina worked for AT&T as a customer service representative. She moved from Nevada to Ozark, Mo., in 1992, then to Carthage and to Joplin in 2002. She was a member of the AT&T Pioneers. Survivors include her husband, Leslie Williams; three daughters, Jennifer (Chad) Bybee, Strafford, Mo., Catrina Bloxham, Joplin and Miranda Lynn Williams, Lebanon, Mo.; two sons, Kirk Bloxham, Joplin, Mo., and James Paul Williams, Springfield, Mo.; one sister, Candace Harrison, Las Vegas, Nev.; her mother, Pauline Kirkpatrick, Joplin, Mo.; two grandchildren and Edgar Allen Bloxham, Sacramento, Cali. She was preceded in death by her father, George Kirkpatrick.

ZACH WILLIAMS
(The obituary information below is taken from the Bradford Funeral Home website.)

Zachary Allen Williams was born June 19, 1998 at Fort Leonard Wood Memorial Community Hospital in Fort Leonard Wood, Missouri, to Franklin Eugene Williams and Tammy Renee Clark Niederhelman. He lost his life in the tornado at Joplin, Missouri, Sunday evening, May 22, 2011, making his age 12 years 11 months and 3 days.

Zach was a student at East Middle School in Joplin where he attended the 7th grade. He attended the Calvary Baptist Church in Joplin. Zach was a happy person who would strike up a conversation with anyone. He enjoyed hot wheel cars, legos, riding his bike, and spending time with his friends. He was looking forward to his summer vacation, so he could spend more time with family and read more of his favorite books.

He is preceded in death by his great grandpas, Howard Jackson and R.L. Clark, great-great grandfather Pearl Jaco, great-grandmother Maxine Clark, great-great grandmother Gladys Jaco.

Zach is survived by his mother Tammy Niederhelman and husband Tony of Joplin, Missouri; his father Frank Williams and wife Valerie of Mayesville, North Carolina, brother Andy Williams of Mayesville, North Carolina, grandparents Earnest and Kathy Clark of Summersville, Missouri; grandparents Jim and Kathleen Williams of Summersville, Missouri, Helen and Frank Jones of Terre Haute, Indiana; great grandmother Lillie Jackson of Summersville, Mo., uncle's and aunt's, Chad and Billie Clark and children, Austin and Brittani and future son-in-law Levi of Neosho, Mo., Jim Williams of Tulsa, Oklahoma, Warren Williams and wife Vicki of St. Louis,

Missouri, Cindy Heller Springfield, Missouri, several great uncles and aunts, cousins and friends.

CHARLES WRITER

Charles William Writer, age 74, of Purdy, Missouri, passed away Sunday, May 22, 2011, in the tornado in Joplin.

He was born October 29, 1936, in Barry County, Missouri, the son of Herbert and Georgia M. (Pryor) Writer. On February 20, 1954, he was united in marriage to Peggy Hyde (now Peggy Dalton), and to this union one son and one daughter were born. On December 1, 1978, in Miami, Oklahoma, he married Gerda (Ehrmann) Henderson, who survives.

Also surviving are four sons, Rick Writer and his wife, Peggy of Butterfield, Missouri, Jim Henderson and his wife, Linda of Monett, Missouri, John Henderson and his wife, Terri of Exeter, Missouri and Kenny Henderson and his wife, Misty of Collinsville, Oklahoma; four daughters, Rena Kennedy and her husband, Gary of Lampe, Missouri, Beverly Bacon and her husband, Joe of Cassville, Missouri, Debbie Henderson and Marty Wolf of Butterfield, Missouri and Brenda Fryman and her husband, Rob of Eureka, Missouri; one brother, Eugene Writer and his wife, Mava of Cassville, Missouri; two sisters, Yvonne Stumpff and her husband, Max of Cassville, Missouri and Linda

Mitchell and her husband, Richard of Washburn, Missouri; eighteen grandchildren and twenty-two great grandchildren.

Preceding him in death were his parents and a grandson, Chris Henderson.

Charles received his education at Sparks and Victory rural schools and Cassville and Southwest High Schools. From April 1, 1954, until December 18, 1964, he served in the United States Navy. After his discharge from the Navy he worked several years for Pryor Motor Company. He then owned and operated the DX Gas Station, High Point Trucking Company and a transport truck leasing company, retiring around ten years ago. Most of his life was spent cattle farming, which he loved. He also enjoyed his horses.

ABOUT THE AUTHORS

Randy Turner is an eighth grade English teacher at East Middle School in Joplin and spent more than two decades as a reporter an editor for southwest Missouri newspapers. He has written two novels and two non-fiction books.

John Hacker is the managing editor of *The Carthage Press* and has covered Missouri and Kansas news for two decades. A graduate of Missouri Southern State University, Hacker has won numerous awards for reporting and photography in Missouri and Kansas.

40103957R00129

Made in the USA
San Bernardino, CA
11 October 2016